PORT

MW01235716

DEBATE

Quincy, Illinois
November 7-10, 1950

Between
W. CURTIS PORTER
Monette, Arkansas

and

J. ERVIN WATERS
Lawrenceburg, Tennessee

Speeches Recorded and Manuscripts Prepared by
M. Lynnwood Smith

This debate was held November 7-10, 1950 in Quincy, Illinois. Four propositions involving two questions were discussed. 1) The number of cups (drinking vessels) to be used in distributing the fruit of the vine while observing the Lord's Supper. 2) When the church comes together to teach the Bible, may we divide into groups using women to teach some of the groups or classes?

ISBN 1-58427-075-6

Guardian of Truth Foundation
P.O. Box 9670
Bowling Green, Kentucky 42102

PREFACE

This debate occurred in Quincy, Illinois, on the evenings of November 7, 8, 9, and 10, 1950, in the Labor Temple, between J. Ervin Waters of Lawrenceburg, Tennessee, and W. Curtis Porter, of Monette, Arkansas. This was the second time these brethren had discussed these matters, having met previously in 1946 at Lawrenceburg, Tennessee.

It was agreed soon after plans were made for the discussion that I might publish this work. Great efforts have been put forth to get it into print. It was electrically recorded and transcribed. It appears in this book just as delivered with a few minor corrections made by the debaters. It is my belief that this debate will do much good since we have no such work in print of which I am aware. If some good accrues from this effort, then I shall be happy and repaid.

Good order prevailed throughout this discussion. The speakers conducted themselves in a dignified fashion. Of course they were in deep earnest, and the depth of their convictions led them to sometimes appear highly enthusiastic. They pressed their points with all the vigor they possessed. So let no one become alarmed at the earnestness with which they attack one another's positions. This only helps to enhance the importance of the debate.

Here at this point I feel it fitting to express my gratitude to some friends whose help made this book possible, and without whose help I would have been greatly delayed. First, I appreciate the fine cooperation of Brethren Waters and Porter. Next, I wish to thank C. Nelson and Johnny Elmore who rendered indispensable aid in the recording and arranging of this discussion. Then others, Dorothy Mathison, Brother and Sister Glen Bray, Harold King, and Geneva Whitiker. I am also indebted to the following homes where I was allowed to work on the transcribing: Joe Elmore, Tom Smith, W. M. McLemore, Ray Merideth, and Wood Morris. Perhaps others also.

We hope that this book will fall into the hands of someone who will learn the truth and be brought closer to the Lord and His way.

—M. Lynwood Smith
Wesson, Mississippi
May 5, 1951

PAUL TO TIMOTHY

"I charge thee therefore before God, and the Lord Jesus Christ, who shall judge the quick and the dead at his appearing and his kingdom; Preach the word; be instant in season, out of season; reprove, rebuke, exhort with all longsuffering and doctrine. For the time will come when they will not endure sound doctrine; but after their own lusts shall they heap to themselves teachers, having itching ears; And they shall turn away their ears from the truth, and shall be turned unto fables. But watch thou in all things, endure afflictions, do the work of an evangelist, make full proof of thy ministry."—2 Timothy 4:1-5.

INTRODUCTION

The Porter-Waters Debate will fill a definite need in our religious literature. For many years we have felt the need of some publication which would thoroughly discuss the issues involved and present both sides of the questions connected with the number of drinking vessels to be used on the communion table and the scriptural procedure for teaching God's word—that is, whether or not classes and women teachers may be used. This discussion presents the needed material.

Brethren W. Curtis Porter and J. Ervin Waters are humble and able men. I have known Brother Porter since I was a small child. He helped to teach my mother the truth. His father, Ben Porter, was an elder in my home congregation where I preached in my first meeting. Through the years W. Curtis Porter has defended the truth in many debates in all parts of the country. Those who love the truth love him. It is a joy to me to be able to assist in putting into permanent form this and other debates in which he has engaged. Brother M. Lynwood Smith and those associated with him consider Brother Waters an able and a representative man. The work of both men will speak for itself but I feel justified in saying I consider this an able presentation of both sides.

Brother M. Lynwood Smith recorded this debate and prepared the manuscripts. These manuscripts were read and corrected by Porter and Waters. Later both men read and corrected galley proofs and page proofs of this book. Brother Smith is due a special debt of gratitude for recording and preparing the book for the press. The book has been manufactured at the joint expense of Brother Smith and of DeHoff Publications. Brother Smith felt that in view of his efforts in preparing the debate that the book should be copyrighted in his name. The speeches of W. Curtis Porter are owned and controlled by Brother Porter and he has given his permission for Brother Smith to publish them.

It is always a good thing for brethren to come together to study God's word. Debating is an ancient and honorable method of arriving at the truth. Perhaps no other method of teaching reaches so many people with the truth. Jesus was the world's greatest debater. Paul was continually engaged in controversy. The church grows and prospers where open, full and free discussion is permitted.

George W. DeHoff

December 20, 1951

CONTENTS

ON THE NUMBER OF CONTAINERS ON THE COMMUNION TABLE

FIRST SESSION

SECOND SESSION

ON THE USE OF CLASSES AND WOMEN TEACHERS

THIRD SESSION

FOURTH SESSION

FIRST SESSION

Moderator Cook: Welcome one and all to this initial session of what is planned to be a four nights discussion. We trust you've come here for the purpose of hearing both sides of this question, as I'm sure you will before it is over. You know, we're interested in the truth or we wouldn't make the sacrifice that's necessary to hear a discussion of this kind. I see people here from several different states, from quite a distance. I'd hate to believe that you came for any purpose other than to learn the truth regardless of the source from which it may come. I do not believe that two men could have been chosen who would dig deeper and try harder to show you the truth than these men. Brother W. Curtis Porter is a representative man. I've heard him in discussion before and read a number of his debates. Of course the same is true of Brother J. Ervin Waters; he's a representative man and I've heard him a number of times. I recommend both to you as gentlemen. You know it would be a pathetic thing if we were to while away the days of our life and learn the truth too late. If truth can be learned, if it can be had, we want it now. One Chinese philosopher said, "We live in the present, we dream in the future, and we learn the truth in the past." I trust it will not be like that here. I hope we can learn the truth while we are here. If we learn it, why let us just accept it. That's all we can afford to do of course. We cannot all be right and differ so widely. So I believe that you are going to be benefited in this discussion.

Proposition No. 1 for discussion tonight reads as follows: "The Scriptures teach that an assembly of the church of Christ, for the communion, must use one cup (drinking vessel) in the distribution of the fruit of the vine." J. Ervin Waters affirms. W. Curtis Porter denies.

I might state also, before the speaker takes the stand, that with the consent of all concerned this discussion is being recorded for the purpose of publishing. And now the next speaker that you will hear will be the affirmative speaker tonight, Brother J. Ervin Waters.

First Session

J. Ervin Waters

FIRST AFFIRMATIVE

Brethren Moderators, Brother Porter, Brethren and Friends:

I count myself happy to stand before you tonight in affirmation of a proposition which I believe with all my heart to set forth the teaching of God's word. It is indeed a lamentable thing that we who are the Disciples of Jesus Christ are divided over such issues as this, but it is indeed commendable that in the midst of such division we are able to come together in the spirit of Christ to discuss these differences in the hope that we may be able to resolve them. I have much respect for my respondent, Brother Porter, in this discussion. I formerly had a discussion with him in 1946 at Lawrenceburg, Tenn. I will say that I have never met a man in discussion who conducted himself more like a Christian gentleman, and so it is with the confidence that I have in him that I opine that this discussion will be expedited with a minimum of ill will and objectionable features and that it will continue with a maximum of good will despite these differences. I hope that you will be able, without bias and prejudice, to consider every argument presented by either of us, every Scripture read, and every statement made. It is not to be thought that Brother Porter and I are disagreed on everything because we are disagreed on these things at issue in this debate for, in truth, we are agreed on far more things than we are disagreed on, and yet we must have these discussions because of the things about which we are disagreed.

SOME AGREEMENT

There are many things about which we would agree with reference to the communion question. We would both agree, I am sure, that we are to observe the communion on the first day of the week for all the evidence of antiquity concurs in evincing the fact that the early disciples met to break bread every first day of the week. I am sure, furthermore, that we would agree that in the communion service we should use unleavened bread. We both believe that we are to use the fruit of the vine, and yet there is a difference between us as pertains to the proper observance of the communion.

PROPOSITION DEFINED

The proposition reads as follows: "The Scriptures teach that an assembly of the church of Christ for the communion must use one cup (drinking vessel) in the distribution of the fruit of the vine." By Scriptures," I mean the word of God and a correct interpretation of the same. By "teach," I mean "to convey the thought or impart the instruction." By "an assembly," I mean "a congregation." By "Church of Christ," I refer, of course, to that universal body of which Jesus said in Matt. 16:18, "Upon this rock I will build my church." And by "an assembly of the church of Christ," I refer to a congregation of disciples locally of that universal body." "For the communion," I mean to observe the Lord's Supper. By "must", I just simply mean " it is obligatory," and by "use," I mean "utilize." By "one," I mean "one" (Waters smiles). By "cup," I mean "drinking vessel; that is the parenthetical definition in this proposition. By "distribution", I mean "apportionment or sharing". By "fruit of the vine", I mean the "juice of the grape". If that definition is not complete enough, and my respondent will call it to my attention, I will be glad to further elucidate concerning it. We now give our attention to the proof of this proposition.

HOW DO THE SCRIPTURES TEACH?

Since I am affirming "The Scriptures teach", I shall have recourse "to the law and testimony," Isaiah 8:20, that "truth which came by Christ Jesus " John 1:17, to see what it says concerning the matter at issue. Plainly resolved the question is this: How many drinking vessels or cups may a congregation or an assembly of the church of Christ for the communion use in the conveying of the fruit of the vine to the assembled disciples? I believe that an assembly must use one cup, not individual cups, in the distribution of the fruit of the vine to the assembled disciples. It is now our duty to find out what saith the Scriptures.

What does the word of God have to say about the matter? It is generally conceded by disciples that the Scriptures teach in several ways; that they teach *by example, by command, by statement, and by necessary inference.* If a thing be taught in the Scriptures by only one of these four ways, then the thing is taught by the word of God and is binding upon us, but tonight I think I shall prove to you that the use of one cup for an assembly is taught by not only one of these, *but by all of these.*

And if I am only able to prove that the Scriptures teach the use of one cup for an assembly by only one of these, then I have sustained the proposition at issue tonight.

CHART No. 1—On Communion

ONE CUP FOR AN ASSEMBLY IS TAUGHT BY:

    1. EXAMPLE — Matt. 26:27; Mark 14:23; Luke 22:20; 1 Cor. 11:25.

    2. COMMAND—Matt. 26:27; 1 Cor. 11:2, 23, 25; 1 Cor. 11:33, 28.

    3. STATEMENT—1 Cor. 10:16.

    4. INFERENCE—I Cor. 11:26, 27.

BY EXAMPLE

First, I shall prove that the Scriptures teach the use of *one cup by example,* and I call your attention to the chart. In Matt. 26:27, "And he took the cup", or as the Revised Version, or the American Standard Revised Version, renders it, "He took a cup, and gave thanks, and gave it to them." According to the example Jesus *took a cup.* It does not require much education, it does not require a stupendous intellect, to be able to understand the meaning of the language involved in the simple statement, "and he took the cup, and gave it to them." Is there a man present, is there a person present, who will deny that the Lord actually took one cup and that he gave it to them as Matt. 26:27 plainly says? Next we turn to Mark 14:23, "And he took the cup; and when had given thanks, he gave it to them: and they all drank of it." I Cor. 11:25, "After the same manner also, he took the cup, when he had supped, saying, This cup is the new testament in my blood; this do ye, as oft as ye drink it, in remembrance of me." These records of the Lord's Supper from Matthew, Mark and Paul all concur in teaching that when Jesus instituted the Communion He took "the cup," or He took "a cup," and Matthew and Mark plainly say that "He gave it to them." According to the example, what do we have? First, that Jesus took "one cup." Second, that He gave "one cup" to the assembled disciples. Third, that " they all drank of it" (Mark 14:23). Thus, *He took one, He gave one to them, they all drank of one.* That is the *example of the Holy Scriptures.*

BY COMMAND

Second, I shall prove that the Scriptures teach the use of *one cup by command.* In Matt. 26:27, "And he took the cup, and gave thanks, and gave it to them, saying, Drink ye all of it." ("ye all" is like our Southern "you all"; it means "all of you.") And so He said, *"Drink ye all, or all of you drink, of it."* Of what? Of that cup which He took and which He gave to them. Did they understand what He said? Mark 14:23 says, "and they all drank of it." They understood exactly what the Lord meant and they did what He said.

I next call to your attention 1 Cor. 11:2, "Now I praise you, brethren, that ye remember me in all things, and keep the ordinances, as I delivered them unto you." In this verse the Apostle Paul makes it mandatory that the disciples keep the ordinances and the traditions as delivered by him. But in verse 23 he said, "For I have received of the Lord that which also I delivered unto you, that the Lord Jesus the same night in which he was betrayed took bread." In verse 2, he said, "Keep the ordinances or traditions as I have delivered them unto you." In verse 23, he said, "that which I delivered unto you I have received of the Lord," and in verse 25, "after the same manner also *he took the cup."* Paul, in short, says, "What I have delivered unto you I want you to keep like I have delivered, because I have delivered to you what I have received of the Lord." And in verse 25, he tells of that which he had delivered, that which he had received of the Lord, *"that he took the cup."* Well the Apostle Paul delivered it like that. He said, "keep it like I have delivered it," and I submit tonight to you this fact, that there is not a man under the shining stars of heaven who has ever opened the pages of inspiration and learned how to convey the fruit of the vine to the disciples in an assembly in any other way. My honorable respondent has never opened his Bible and therein read where the apostle Paul ever delivered any other procedure. He has never opened the word of God and found there, by either command or example, any teaching or instruction concerning the distribution of the fruit of the vine to an assembly of disciples in individual cups. He has never found that in the word of God. The Apostle Paul did not receive it by inspiration, and he did not teach it in his Epistles.

But again we read in verse 33 of 1 Cor. 11, "Wherefore, my

brethren, when ye come together to eat, tarry one for another." That proves that the instructions given by the apostle Paul in 1 Cor. 11 obtained in an assembly of disciples for he said, "When ye come together to eat," talking about eating the communion. "When ye come together to eat," do what? In verse 28, he gives the command, "Let a man examine himself, and so let him eat of that bread, and *drink of that cup."* So the apostle Paul delivered the instructions to apply and obtain in an assembly of disciples according to 1 Cor. 11:33, and *he commands every one of that assembly to* "eat of that loaf and *drink of that cup,"* which, of course, is to be used therein. My respondent, in using a plurality of cups in the communion service, could not deliver the same instructions to an assembly of disciples present on the occasion and say, "let a man examine himself, and so let him eat of that bread, and drink of that cup," for he would have a plurality of cups. But *so the apostle Paul taught* and *so he instructed an assembly in 1 Cor. 11:28.*

BY STATEMENT

Third, I shall prove that the Scriptures also teach one cup *by statement.* In 1 Cor. 10:16, "The cup of blessing which we bless, is it not the communion of the blood of Christ?" It does not say 'the cups of blessing which we bless, are they not the communion of the blood of Christ."

BY INFERENCE

Fourth, I shall prove that the Scriptures also teach the use of *one cup by necessary inference,* and I am going to read to you several passages of Scripture in which I believe the use of one cup for an assembly is thus taught. The language necessarily involves the use of one cup. In 1 Cor. 11:26 "For as often as ye eat this bread, and drink this cup, ye do show the Lord's death till he come." When the Apostle gave instructions to obtain in an assembly, he said " as often as ye *drink this cup."* The expression, "drink this cup," of course is a figurative expression. It involves the use of a common figure of speech. That figure of speech is a Metonymy, and according to the figure of speech Metonymy, a cup may be named (it is a real and actual cup) to suggest it's real and actual contents. But according to that figure of speech we do not suggest the contents of any more cups than we name and where one cup is named the contents of only one is suggested. The apostle Paul said, " as often as ye drink this cup." He *named one cup* and he only *suggested the contents of one cup* when he said, "as often as ye *drink this cup.*" Who could comport with good usage of language and say to the assembly present, while handing to them a plurality of cups, "drink this cup." Why according to the same figure of speech Metonymy, if the idea of the contents of a plurality of cups were to be conveyed to the audience, you would have to say, "as often as you *drink these cups.*" You would have to say, "We thang Thee for *these cups,*" because you *cannot suggest the contents of a plurality of cups without naming a plurality of cups.*

We use that figure of speech commonly in our everyday language. Sometimes a housewife may say, "the kettle boils," or "the kettle is boiling." When she makes that statement, we all immediately know several things. We know, first, that there is an actual literal kettle. It is there. Second, we know that that actual literal kettle has contents. Third, we know that the contents of that actual literal kettle are boiling. But who would say, "the kettle is boiling," and by that statement grammatically connote the idea of the contents of a plurality of kettles? What woman would say, "the kettle is boiling," and mean to convey the idea that the contents of a plurality of kettles were boiling? *He has never heard it used that way, and I never have either.* And I predict that you will never hear it thus, unless it be in jest.

When a man says, "the radiator is boiling," no one gets the idea he is talking about the *contents of a plurality of radiators.* There never has been a person yet who understood the rudiments of language to any degree who thus understood. It is strange to me that when we, in our everyday language, use that same figure of speech, everyone understands what we mean, and they understand that when we say, "the kettle is boiling", there is a literal kettle and there is but one there involved in the statement made, and they understand that that literal kettle has contents which are boiling; and there is not a one of us who would be so ignorant to say, "Why, lady, if you say, 'the kettle is boiling,' and you actually have a literal kettle necessarily involved in the statement, then that literal kettle is boiling." Yet we all understand that the literal kettle is there. There is but one mentioned and understood by that statement. We all understand.

And so the Scriptures teach the use of one cup by necessary

inference because *one cup is necessarily involved in such language.*
1 Cor. 11:27, "Wherefore whosoever shall eat this bread, and
drink this cup of the Lord, unworthily, shall be guilty of the
body and blood of the Lord." There again we have the same
metonymical usage necessarily involving the use of one literal cup
because that one literal cup; which is use'd in the communion, is
named to suggest its contents in 1 Cor. 11:26, 27.

PROPOSITION PROVED

I have proved my proposition—the use of one cup for an,
assembly—by scriptural example, by scriptural command, by
scriptural statement, and by scriptural inference. The Bible, as
far as I know, is not able to, or does not, teach anything in any
other way and I just wonder, you can't keep me from wondering,
I wonder if every one of these Scripture's which I have read said
*"cups" where "cup" is, would my Brother Porter believe it meant
a plurality of cups.* I wonder if it would *mean "cups" if it said*
"cups." But he is going to deny that it means "cup" when it
says "cup". I venture the assertion that if everywhere that "a
cup" is found in these Scriptures, "cups" were found instead, my
brother, if called in question concerning his practice, would read
every one of those verses to sustain "cups." If these' Scriptures
do not teach the use of one cup in an assembly, may I question
how the Scriptures could teach anything? *What would the Scriptures have to say if the Lord wanted us to use one?*

CHART No. 2—On Communion

ONE CUP

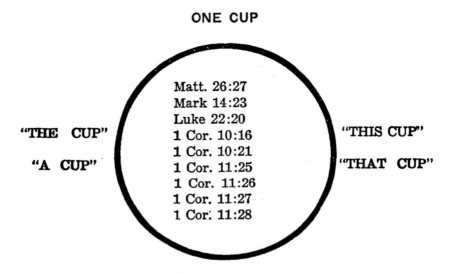

"THE CUP"

"A CUP"

Matt. 26:27
Mark 14:23
Luke 22:20
1 Cor. 10:16
1 Cor. 10:21
1 Cor. 11:25
1 Cor. 11:26
1 Cor. 11:27
1 Cor. 11:28

"THIS CUP"

"THAT CUP"

INDIVIDUAL CUPS

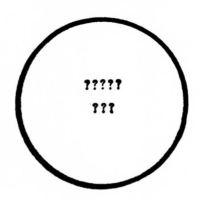

?????
???

Where Are They

I have, furthermore, on this chart two circles. I have over the first circle the word "cup" and in it I have every reference in the New Testament where the word "cup" is used with reference to the communion service. It is in the singular every time. *"The* cup." *"That* cup." *"This* cup." .."A cup." I have another circle with the word "cups" over it, and you will note that in it there are only question marks. I only put question marks in there because I didn't have any Scriptures to put in there. And if my respondent is able to put the Scriptures in there which say anything about *"these* cups" or *"those* cups" in the communion service, let him do it, and rapidly this discussion will draw to a close.

MORE ARGUMENTS

I want to submit to you several arguments:

1. Christ took "one cup." Matt. 26:27, Mark 14:23, Luke 22:20, 1 Cor. 11:25.

2. Christ gave only "one cup" to his disciples. Matt. 26:27, Mk. 14:23.

3. He commanded his disciples to drink of "one cup." Matt. 26:27.

4. His disciples obeyed and drank of "one cup." Mark 14:23.

5. He called the contents of "one cup" his blood. Matt. 26:28, Mark 14:24.

6. Paul delivered "one cup" for an assembly. 1 Cor. 11:2, 23, 33, 25 and 28.

7. "Only one " is a tradition received of the Apostles. 2 Thess. 3:6, "Withdraw yourselves from every brother that walketh disorderly, and not after the tradition which he received of us;" but we received the tradition of using "one cup" for an assembly from the apostles.

8. We can use but "one cup" and walk by the same rule. Phil. 3:16-17, "Nevertheless, whereto we have already attained, let us walk by the same rule, let us mind the same thing;" but that one rule by which we are to walk says nothing about a plurality of cups in the

distribution of the fruit of the vine. To the contrary, every reference uses the word "cup" in the singular.

9. We can use "one cup" and speak as the oracles of God. 1 Pet. 4:11, "If any man speak, let him speak as the oracles of God." The oracles of God say "cup," but they say nothing whatsoever about the use of individual cups.

10. "One cup" is a plant of God. Matt. 15:13, "Every plant, which my heavenly Father hath not planted, shall be rooted up." The heavenly Father in His word planted the use of "one cup" in the conveyance of the fruit of the vine to an assembly, but He has not therein planted the use of a plurality, and consequently we cannot jeopardize the salvation of our souls by using them.

11. "One cup" is a good work, or the use of "one cup" in the distribution of the fruit of the vine is a good work. 2 Tim. 3:16-17, "All scripture is given by inspiration of God, and is profitable for doctrine, for reproof, for correction, for instruction in righteousness: That the man of God may be perfect, throughly furnished unto all good works." The Scriptures furnish us the use of "one cup" in an assembly of disciples for the communion, but nowhere do they furnish us the use of a plurality.

12. The use of "one cup" is of faith. Rom. 10:17, "Faith cometh by hearing, and hearing by the word of God." The word of God conveys us the use of "one cup" in an assembly. Nowhere does it convey to us the use of a plurality.

13. "One cup" in such an assembly can be used and its users endeavor "to keep the unity of the Spirit in the bond of peace." Eph. 4:3.

14. Only the use of "one cup" in an assembly "pertains to life and godliness." 2 Pet. 1:3, "According as his divine power hath given unto us all things that pertain unto life and godliness."

15. We can use "one cup" and have unity because division is condemned (1 Cor. 1:10), but the advocates of "cups" cannot find their use in the word of God.

16. We can use "one cup" and be safe.

17. We can use "one cup" and worship God in truth. John 4:23, "for God seeketh such to worship Him." That truth "which came by Christ Jesus" (John 1:17), and which is God's word (John 17:17), teaches the use of "one cup" but says nothing about a plurality.

18. "One cup" is taught by the Spirit. Jesus said, "The Spirit will guide you into all truth" and "he shall teach you all things, and bring all things to your remembrance." (John 16:13, 14:26) "As many as are led by the Spirit of God, they are the sons of God." (Rom. 8:14) But the Spirit of God through the word teaches us the use of "one." It nowhere teaches us the use of a plurality.

19. "One cup" for an assembly is found in the truth. John 1:17, 16:23, 17:17.

20. "One cup" for an assembly is found in the counsel of God. Paul said in Acts 20:27, "I have not shunned to declare unto you all the counsel of God."

And I thank you.

FIRST SESSION

W. Curtis Porter

FIRST NEGATIVE

Moderator Sterl A. Watson:

Ladies and Gentlemen: We are happy to present unto you now Brother W. Curtis Porter who will now answer the speech to which you just listened. Brother W. Curtis Porter—

Brethren Moderators, Brother Waters, Ladies and Gentlemen:

I could not say unreservedly that I am glad to be here to-night, because the condition that makes this debate necessary is deplorable, lamentable; and that was, of course, mentioned in part by Brother Waters who preceded me. And we regret that conditions are such that a debate of this kind is necessary, because it takes away some of the gladness that might otherwise exist. I appreciate the ability of Brother Waters. He mentioned that we met four years ago in a debate at Lawrenceburg, Tennessee. He is one of the ablest debaters who stand with him relative to this position, and I could well wish that his ability and intelligence might be used in the proclamation of those things that would further the church of Jesus Christ rather than some hobby that would hinder its progress and development in the Lord's work. I regard him as an intelligent man, and I believe his intelligence is great enough, and that he ought to be able, to see that the things which he condemns in this debate are altogether parallel with many things that he accepts and uses without question; and if he can ever come to that place where he can see that they are parallel, I believe his sincerity will lead him to renounce his present position, and take the position which I occupy upon this occasion.

Now, I shall pay my attention to the speech to which you have just listened. I want to get to everything that Brother Waters said, if I possibly can, and don't intend to skip anything, but shall notice all the arguments presented.

We agree, he says, on many things, and certainly that's true. But we differ upon this proposition tonight and the one to follow, to be discussed following this question, but on many things we *do agree* regarding the work and worship of the church, even with respect to the Communion Service as already has been mentioned by him.

The definition of this proposition is acceptable so far as I think just now. The proposition is very simply written. It isn't hard to understand, and we know what the issue is upon this occasion. Summing up that issue, he said it is simply this: "How many drinking vessels may be used in the Lord's Supper for the distribution of the fruit of the vine?" He is affirming, of course, that only one can be used, and that "one cup" (and that word "cup" in his proposition is defined in parenthesis to mean "drinking vessel"—one drinking vessel) *must be used* in the distribution of the fruit of the vine. He said he meant by the word "must" that it is "obligatory." Certainly, that's the significance of the term, and Brother Waters means, of course, that *this must be done or you'll stand condemned before God at last.* So if you use more than one drinking vessel for the fruit of the vine, or in the distribution of the fruit of the vine, then the condemnation of God will rest upon you, and you will be lost because you have done that. So he is affirming that it *must* be that way. Now, we'll want to keep that in mind as we go along during this discussion of this proposition.

He tells us that the Scriptures teach by different ways: by

example, by command, by statement, by necessary inference. And he elaborated upon each of these as he went along, endeavoring to show that one drinking vessel for the Communion Service, *and one only, must be used* in the Lord's Supper.

Some Questions

But before I reply to that series of arguments given along that line, and those which followed, I have about a half dozen questions I want to submit to Brother Waters. Now, some of these questions I asked Brother Waters in our former debate in Tennessee, but he refused to answer on the ground that he was not in the affirmative on this question. He affirmed on another question. So he refused to answer the questions because he was *not in the affirmative*. It so happens this time that he *is in the affirmative*, and we shall expect an answer.

1. As the bread pictures the body of Christ, and the fruit of the vine pictures His blood, what is pictured by the drinking vessel?

2. If, while serving the congregation the communion, the loaf should be accidentally broken into other pieces besides that which each communicant breaks for himself, could the unserved portion of the congregation Scripturally partake of it? Now, this question is based on the fact that Brother Waters reasons there must be just "one" piece of bread that must not be broken just as there must be "one" cup. He makes them parallel.

3. While passing the fruit of the vine to the assembly, if the cup should be accidentally dropped and broken and its contents spilled, how would you Scripturally serve the remainder of the assembly?

4. When individual cups are used on the table, does it constitute the Lord's table or the table of devils?

5. When Paul, in 1 Cor. 10:16, said that Christians at both Ephesus and Corinth blessed "the cup," would not the expression, "the cup," have to refer to a least two drinking vessels—one at Ephesus and one at Corinth?

6. And when he said, in that same connection, that we are all partakers of that "one bread," did he not refer to at least two pieces of bread—one at Ephesus and one at Corinth?

FOUR WAYS OF TEACHING

Now, with those questions before you, I will return to the arguments presented. In presenting this idea that things may be taught by example, by command, by statement, and by necessary inference, Brother Waters said that if a thing is taught in only one way, then it must be bound upon us. But he said "the cup" is taught in all four ways, and so it must be binding that we use only one cup in the Communion Service.

CHART No. 1—On Communion

ONE CUP FOR AN ASSEMBLY IS TAUGHT BY:

1. EXAMPLE — Matt. 26:27; Mark 14:23; Luke 22:20; 1 Cor. 11:25.

2.. COMMAND—Matt. 26:27; 1 Cor. 11:2, 23, 25; 1 Cor. 11:33, 28.

3. STATEMENT—1 Cor. 10:16.

4. INFERENCE—1 Cor. 11:26, 27.

By EXAMPLE

He gave Matt. 26:27 as the example that Christ took "the cup," or as the Revised Version says, "a cup." And Mark 14:23, He took "the cup" and said "drink of it." And the same in Luke 22:20 and also in I Cor. 11:25. All of these speak of "the cup" and drink "of it." He insists that this means they all drank *from one drinking vessel;* that is the drinking vessel had to be passed around and every man had to *put his lips to it* and *sip from the same container.* That is his idea. Now, certainly liquids require containers. There's no question about containers being necessary for liquids. There's no debate about that, but the question is: What significance does the container have? It does not picture the blood of Jesus Christ, because the blood of Jesus Christ is pictured by the fruit of the vine. It does not picture the body of Jesus Christ, because the body is pictured by the bread. So the question involves: What is the significance of the drinking vessel? *What does it picture?* We want him to tell us something about that.

THE UPPER ROOM

Now if we follow his rule of reasoning about this, and the method which he followed in trying to bind "one cup," or drinking vessel, upon a congregation, by *the same process* we could bind the upper room, for when the Lord instituted His supper in Mark 14:14-16, 22-25, we have the fact mentioned that it was done in an *upper room*. The *upper room is mentioned.* There is the example of Jesus when He instituted the supper; He instituted it in an upper room. And if such a thing is mentioned, even by way of example, my opponent says it is bound on us. And for that reason, in order to partake of the Lord's Supper Scripturally, *it must be done in an upper room,* according to his arguments. Also in Acts 20:7-9 (the example we have of the apostles in the New Testament), we have the fact mentioned also that they were *in the upper chamber,* and even *in the third story.* Consequently, according to his rule, and according to his interpretation and argument upon this, since *these things are mentioned* by way of example, then the Lord's Supper *must be observed* in an upper room, on the third floor. Brethren, you're unscriptural here (referring to the Labor Temple) because you're *on the second floor.* You better get up here. (Debate was on third floor) You brethren who are contending for that better move up to the third loft—the third floor. You're on the second floor; you're at the wrong place. You ought to come up another story in order to be Scriptural. As long as you stay on that second floor, you are unscriptural, according to Brother Waters' argument.

BY COMMAND

And then he came to the command. But in connection with that, however, he emphasized that here is "one cup." The "one cup" was given. They all drank "of it." They drank of "one cup." And he assumes to drink of one cup, they must all drink out of the same vessel; that is, it passed from lip to lip. The same container passed from lip to lip because they all "drank of it."

HOW ABOUT JACOB'S WELL?

Well, I happened to read over in John, the 4th chapter and verse 12, the statement made regarding Jacob's well. Now, the Lord was sitting there at Jacob's well discussing some matters with the Samaritan woman, and He told her if she would ask, He would give her living water. She said, "You have nothing to draw with, and the well is deep: from whence then hast thou that living water?" She said, "Art thou greater than our father Jacob, which gave us this well, and drank thereof himself, his cattle, and his sons?", or as some translations give it, "drank *from it*." All right, then, here are Jacob, his sons, and his cattle, who all *drank from the same well*. Does that mean that all put their lips to the well? They all drank from the same well? According to his reasoning, their lips must have been put to the well, and everyone drank from it in that way, because they drank all "from it"—the very same expression that you have with regard to drinking from the cup. Matt. 26:27 and Mark 14:23. And in I Cor. 11.2, 23-25—the command—"drink of it." Here he tells us that this is the communion assembly that Paul speaks of here. So be careful about that. You might get into trouble further down the road.

BY STATEMENT

And then not only that, but with respect to this example and command and the statement made, we note also the fact that there is the mention of a table. When the Lord instituted His supper, there was a "table" present, and it is even referred to as such in Luke 22. "That ye may eat and drink at my table in my kingdom." And Paul, in the Corinthian letter, referred to the matter of eating at the "Lord's table." Well, is the table as literal as the cup? And must the table be just as literal as the cup? And must it be just "one table" like the cup must be "one cup?" Well, is the table "one table" like the cup must be "one cup?" Would the Lord's Supper on this pulpit stand be Scriptural? Or would you have to have a table with four legs or six legs or something of that kind to make it so? The table is mentioned just as definitely as the cup, but he said there was no plurality of cups delivered. But since he came to that a little later, I'll get to it in the next place.

I Cor. 11:33. "They came together to eat." And this was eating the bread of the Lord's Supper, verse 28, and no dispute about that. But he said Paul said "drink of that cup" and "let a man examine himself and eat of that bread and drink of that cup." You could not say drink of "that cup" if there were a plurality of them. Well, we'll see more about that when he elaborates upon that a little later. Then by statement, 1 Cor. 10:16, "the cup of blessing which we bless." We'll wait further to reply to that till I get an answer to my questions.

BY NECESSARY INFERENCE

I Cor. 11:26. "As oft as ye drink this cup you do show the Lord's death till He comes." Now, he's made his argument along here about "the cup," "this cup," and "that cup" and insists, because of that, there cannot be but one drinking vessel in the Communion Service. Just "one'—that's all. But I remember one time the Lord said in Mark 9:41 to His disciples, "If any man shall give to you a cup of water in My name, because you belong to Me, he shall not lose his reward." Now, of course, if he gave him two cups of water, he would lose his reward—if it means just "one," you see. So, if he gives him a cup of water in the name of Christ, because he belonged to Christ, he'll not lose his reward. "A cup." Just "one cup." Not "cups," but "one cup." And if he gives him two cups or three cups or a dozen cups of water, he loses his reward, because Jesus said "a cup.' "A cup." But when Paul said, "As oft as ye drink this cup," he said: "Now, that's a figurative expression there." He would have to say that. Then "cup" doesn't always mean container, does it? Now, the word "cup" doesn't always mean container. Here he says it doesn't, and, of course, the reason he said that was because Paul talked about drinking "this cup." He knew if he said that was a container, I would want to know how they could *drink the cup*. The cup's the container, of course—that's the idea of it, in the congregation, if they all drank one cup. And so he had to say "the cup" in this case is not the container, but he refers to the contents of it, by the figure of speech that is called Metonymy. But he said there was a *literal cup* and *literal contents,* and when one cup is named that means the contents of only one. He elaborated upon that quite extensively, but it means the contents of only one cup if it says "the cup." It means the contents of only one. He admits that "cup" sometimes refers to its contents, but you have the contents of as many cups as you name. If you name only one, it is the contents of only one. And, consequently, if only one cup is named in connection with the communion, then there must be the contents of only one cup. He went on to reason that no kind of language, that is at all acceptable, would convey any such idea as the contents of more than one vessel if only one vessel were named. And he rather waxed confident about that matter, I presume, and it's too bad to have to explode it, but I'm going to do it.

ONE VESSEL NAMED MAY MEAN CONTENTS OF MORE THAN ONE

Brother Waters, suppose you and I are visiting some man, and we walk down to his basement, and we see a dozen jugs of liquor sitting there. Brother Waters says, "My, this man loves his jug, doesn't he?" I say, "Brother Waters, what jug are you talking about?" "Brother Waters, which jug do you mean?" You said, "The man loves his jug. Here are a dozen of them. The contents of which jug are you referring to, Brother Waters?" Why, there's an occasion in which the term is used, referring to the matter *in the singular number* but meaning *the contents of a number of them,* although naming only one. And in the same connection, we sometimes talk about a man who drinks a lot. We say, "The man has been hitting the bottle." Does that mean he's using just one bottle? We refer to the contents of the bottle. We *name only one;* therefore, it's the contents of only one? All right, another case. I hear a woman speaking regarding her children. There's a half a dozen of them, ranging in age, perhaps, from 10 to 30. And the woman says, "I raised all my babies on the bottle." Of course, she refers to the contents of the bottle. But Brother Waters, I want you to tell me just which bottle it was, and were all the babies raised on the same bottle? Or does that refer to the contents of more than one bottle? "I raised all my babies on the bottle." She named but *one bottle,* suggesting *the contents of many bottles.* This old argument that you can't name or suggest the contents of more than one container when you name one container goes with the wind. It blows up. It can't stand. There are many examples in which it is used that way.

He illustrated by saying "the kettle boils" and "the radiator boils." And when he says "the kettle boils," that indicates that there is a literal kettle. Second place, that it has contents. And in the third place, the contents are boiling. And the same thing about the radiator—"the radiator is boiling." He said that means it was one radiator—to say "the radiator is boiling." Well, I walk into a garage, and I say to the man, "There's something wrong with my radiator." He looks at it and says, "Yes, the thing's frozen up." And he starts thawing it out and gets it to boiling, and I say, "I didn't know that's the way you boil the radiator." He says, "We all boil the radiator this way." "We all *boil the radiator* this way." "We" who? Why the garages all over town. Yes, "we all boil the radiator." Just one—just that one? Why, no.

In that case he refers to *the radiator,* suggesting *many of them,* although he *mentions only one.* So his argument doesn't stand.

THAT CUP — THAT CITY — THAT MAN

I Cor. 11:27. "This cup of the Lord unworthily." He emphasized "this cup" and "that cup." "The cup" means only one container can be used. Well, I happen to notice in Matt. 10:14-15 that Jesus sent out His apostles under the limited commission and said if you go into a city and they refuse you or reject you and don't receive My word, "shake off the dust off your feet," as a testimony against them. The Lord said, "I say unto you, It shall be more tolerable for the land of Sodom and Gomorrah in the day of judgment, than for *that city.*" "That city." That means just one city? Just one involved, because He said "that city?" And in James 3:5-7, James told a man to pray in faith, and if he didn't pray in faith, he wouldn't receive anything. And he said "Let not *that man* think that he shall receive anything of the Lord." "That man." That means only *one* man, of course. Can't apply to but one because it said "that man." It didn't say "those men," but "that man." And Paul, in 2 Cor. 11, declared on one occasion, regarding his perils, that he was in perils "in the city.' "The city.' That was just one city? Let Brother Waters tell us what city it was that Paul referred to. He was in perils "in the city." So you have "the city" and "that city" and "that man" and expressions like that, just as you have "the cup," "this cup" and "that cup.' And if in one case it means only one is possible, it means the same in the other.

He comes then to his circles on the board. I wonder if I might have a litle piece of crayon up here. (Porter looks around **for crayon.)**

CHART No. 2—On Communion

ONE CUP

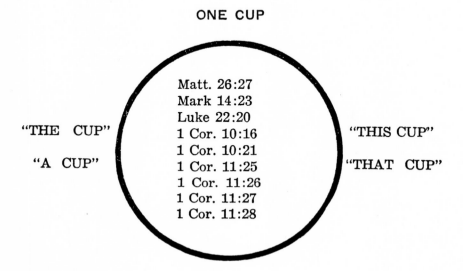

"THE CUP"

"A CUP"

Matt. 26:27
Mark 14:23
Luke 22:20
1 Cor. 10:16
1 Cor. 10:21
1 Cor. 11:25
1 Cor. 11:26
1 Cor. 11:27
1 Cor. 11:28

"THIS CUP"

"THAT CUP"

INDIVIDUAL CUPS

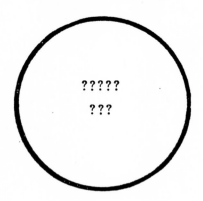

?????
???

(By Waters)

He has his circles on the board here and references in here that mention 'the cup.'" Over here, he has "cups." (Waters hands Porter crayon.) He put some question marks there and wants me to put Scriptures there for "cups." All right, Brother Waters, I'm going to put something else here. Over on this side, in the Scriptures, we have "no plate" (refers to circle on the board, indicating "cup"), but Brother Waters, and brethren who stand with him, use the plate in the Communion Service to pass the bread around to the congregation. Now, Brother Waters, I'll tell you what I'll do. (Porter writes word "plate" in Waters' circle where "cups" are mentioned). The very minute you put in the Scripture that says "the plate" for the bread, I'll put in the passage that says "500 cups." What do you say? What do you think of it, Brother Waters? *Will you do it?* Will you put the Scripture that says "the plate"? You use it, don't you? I don't know if they do here in Quincy or not, but they do down in the section where I came from. I have an idea they have a plate up here. Where did you get your authority for it? You put the passage in here that says "the plate" and I'll put the passage in that says "500 cups," because in the Bible there is no plate mentioned in connection with it. If you use the plate, where do you get your authority for it? I noticed in the opening of the service tonight, that we used song books. And I'll tell you what I'll do, Brother Waters. If you'll put the Scripture in here that mentions the song books which you brethren used tonight in singing, I'll put the passage in there that mentions "a thousand cups." *Will you do it?* I mentioned a while ago that Brother Waters ought to have intelligence enough, and I believe that he does, that some day he'll be able to see that the things which he is condemning in this debate are parallel with the things which he accepts and uses without question. He uses song books and he uses the plate without any Scripture mentioned about them whatsoever. He has no qualms of conscience about it; and yet, neither the plate nor the song book is mentioned in the Scriptures. Let him produce them, and we shall see what we shall see.

SEVERAL ARGUMENTS

All right, he rather summed up the matter then that Christ took "one cup." And second, that He gave "only one." Third, He commanded them to drink "of one," and he gave the Scripture which I have already given. Third, they obeyed and used "one." And fifth, that the contents of "one" was His blood. And sixth, Paul delivered "one." And seventh, "only one" in the tradition of the apostles, and on down through the line. Eighth, we can use "only one" and walk by the same rule. And he gave about twenty of them. Well, we'll get them now carefully as we go along.

1. Notice, he says now, Christ took "one cup." Therefore we cannot take two. If we do, we'll be lost. All right, Brother Waters, Christ took "no plate." You cannot take one, or you'll stand in the same position. Christ took "no plate." Brother Waters takes one. Where does he get his authority for it?

2. Christ gave only "one cup." All right, Brother Waters, Christ gave "no plate." Therefore you have no right to use one.

3. He commanded them to drink "of one." He commanded them to eat of "no plate." It isn't even mentioned.

4. They obeyed and drank "of it." And you didn't say where they used "one plate."

5. The contents of one was His blood. All right then, you didn't find where "the plate" was His body.

6. Paul delivered "one." I Cor. 11—"keep the ordinances as I delivered them to you." He mentioned that before. Paul delivered but "one." He says we can use only "one." If we use more than that, we are unscriptural and will be lost. And so, Brother Waters, tell us how many plates Paul delivered so we'll know how many we can use of that. Don't forget it now.

7. Only "one" in the tradition of the apostles (2 Thess. 3). All right, tell us now how many plates are in the tradition of the apostles?

8. Can use only "one" and walk by the same rule (Phil. 3:15-17). All right, how many plates can you use and walk by the same rule?

Now these things stand or fall together. The container is not the significant thing. The fruit of the vine pictures the blood of the Lord, and the bread pictures His body, but "the plate" and "the cup" have no significance with respect to it. They are mere incidentals in the matter. But, of course, you must have a container of some kind to pass the liquid in, and ordinarily we have a container of some kind to pass the bread in. Though the Lord didn't mention the container—He didn't mention the plate—Brother Waters uses one. According to his line of argument, he does so without divine authority and so stands condemned.

9. We can use only "one cup," he says, and speak as the oracles of God. Peter said in I Peter 4:11, "If any man speak, let him speak as the oracles of God." All right, Brother Waters, tell us now how many plates a man can use for the bread and speak as the oracles of God. And where do the oracles of God say anything about the plate?

10. Only "one cup" is planted of God. Matt. 13:15. "Every plant which my heavenly Father hath not planted shall be rooted up." The Lord planted no plate and we can't use one. Don't you see? Brother Waters, who planted the plate? The Lord didn't. There's no mention made of it. You use it. *Where did you get it?*

11. Only "one cup" is a good work. 2 Tim. 3:16-17 said the Scriptures furnish "the man of God unto all good works." It doesn't furnish him with the use of individual cups; therefore they're not a good work. Well, try it on him. The Scriptures thoroughly furnish the man unto all good works, but it doesn't furnish the man a plate for the bread; and, therefore, using the plate for the bread is not a good work.

12. You must use "one cup" in order to walk by faith. Rom. 10:17. "Faith comes by hearing the word of God." You can't use more than one. All right, "faith comes by hearing the word of God," but the word of God says nothing about a plate for the bread. Therefore you can't use a plate for the bread and walk by faith, according to his line of argument.

13. You must use "one cup" if you're going to keep the unity of the faith. Yes, and some of these times the plate is going to become a division, a wedge of division, if somebody makes a law that you can't use it. And I'm just certain of that fact. My opponent, Brother Waters, will not take the position

during this debate that he'd give up a thing of that kind for the sake of unity. You watch and see if he does. I challenge him to do it.

14. Must use "one cup" or rather "one cup" is according to life and godliness. 2 Peter 1:3. "He has given us all things that pertain to life and godliness." He gave us no individual cups; therefore, they have no reference to life and godliness. All right, now, since He gave us no plate for the bread, then the plate does not pertain to life and godliness on the other side of the thing.

15. And No. 15 was the wedge of division which I have already mentioned.

16. Use "one cup" and be safe. Well, I just wonder if he's going to stand by that principle. Wait and see.

17. We can worship God in truth if we use "one cup." Because John 4:24 and John 1:17 reveals: "We should worship God in truth." But the truth reveals no individual cups. We can't do it and worship God in truth. The truth doesn't reveal a plate for the bread, and we can't use the plate and worship God in truth, according to Brother Waters' argument.

18. Only "one cup" was taught by the Spirit (John 16:13; John 14:26). All right, and parallel with that, no plate was taught by the Spirit. Therefore we can't follow the Spirit and use a plate for the bread.

19. We can use just "one cup" and be in the truth. John 17:17. "Thy word is truth," and it doesn't mention individual cups. It doesn't mention one plate for the bread, and we stand or fall together, Brother Waters.

20. Part of the counsel of God. Acts 20:27. Paul says, "I have delivered unto you all the counsel of God." I have preached the counsel of God unto you. I have delivered all of God's counsel, and "one cup" is a part of that counsel—individual cups are not. From the same standpoint, the counsel of God says nothing about a plate for the bread and, therefore, is not of the counsel of God.

Thank you.

First Session

Waters' Second Affirmative

Cup Question

Brethren Moderators, Brother Porter, Brethren and Friends:

May I present Brother Porter with a cup of cold water? (Waters hands Porter a cup of cold water.)

Porter speaks from seat: "Wouldn't give me two, would you?"

Waters: How many did I give you?

Porter: "If you give me another, would you be condemned?"

Waters: I just wonder how many I gave him.

Porter: "If you gave me another, would you stand condemned?"

The Digressive Dodge

There's some of us who have been here during the past few minutes who would have thought we were discussing tonight the *use of a plate* in the communion service rather than the *use of a cup,* because he spent quite a bit of his speech speaking of a *plate.* You know, I just wondered why Brother Porter was spending so much time on the *plate,* unless it was that he learned that argument from the *Instrumental Music Brethren.* Practically every instrumental music man whom you meet in discussion will, in defense of instrumental music, present almost every kind of an *incidental* and *expedient* in the discussion in an attempt to prove his instrumental music; and every time that he tries to do that—brethren who may defend the use of cups but oppose instrumental music will, in that discussion, tell him that he is rambling off the issue and that they are *not* debating about song books, about plates, about chairs, about upper rooms and Jacob's well and a thousand other things, but that they are debating *instrumental music.* But the instrumental music man will come right back in the next speech and will talk about song books and chairs and upper rooms and plates; . . . he will do it every time. Brother Porter knows that. Of course, he's been in the field of polemics for quite a few years and he's learned that *old digressive dodge.* He's learned how to make that old digressive argument, and he knows that there never has been a digressive who ever lifted his head who has not used precisely the same line of reasoning by which to prove his own digression. *Every one of them does it.*

Foy E. Wallace says, "Quit It"

I want to call your attention to what Foy E. Wallace, a very able man among Brother Porter's brethren, has to say in Vol. I, No. 3, the September, 1950 issue, of his paper "The Torch." Listen, *"It is palpably weak to offer to affirm that something is as scriptural as something else."*

What has Brother Porter done? Has he actually tried to prove that cups are scriptural by going to the word of God and reading about them? *He has not.* He has been just as silent as the grave could ever be as far as reading from the word of God—the Scriptures that teach a plurality of cups. But what has he done? Why he said, "they are just as scriptural as a plate." Brother Wallace said," It is palpably weak to offer to affirm that something is as scriptural as something else." Wallace further writes, *"Nothing is scriptural unless it is."* In other words, cups are not scriptural unless they are. It is not a matter of whether the use of a plate is scriptural or not. That doesn't make any difference at all as far as the discussion tonight is concerned. Cups are either scriptural or they are not. There is no "as" about it. Now you be a man, Brother Porter. Don't get up here and say, "Well, they are 'as' scriptural as something else." You get up here and be a man, turn to the word of God and prove it. You do that. Listen to Wallace again, *"That is mighty poor logic and men who are always doing it are afraid of their ground."* There's one of your old buddies, Brother Porter. He says, "Men who are always doing that are afraid of their ground."

Now when you are debating the instrumental music, the Instrumental Music Man wants to debate the plate and the song books. When you are debating the cups, the cups man wants to debate the plate, and so on it goes. Now it's that way every time and if you brethren don't believe it, I invite you to go to Cedar Rapids, Iowa, where a discussion is going to begin Monday night between G. K. Wallace, one of his brethren, and an Instrumental Music Man, Burton Barber, and see if you don't hear Barber talk about song books and plates. I challenge you to go up there next week. I intend to go. I invite you brethren to go along with me and hear Barber talk about song books and plates. Then you'll know how to use it the next time when you're debating the cups. You ought to do that. Brother Foy E. Wallace further said, *"It's time to quit talking about who said this or did that, and start giving scriptural precedent for the practices that are being promoted."* It's time to come to the word of God and see what it says about the thing at issue and not try to wander about all over creation talking about something else. You've been a long time learning that, haven't you, Brother Porter?—Wallace says, "It's time to quit careering around all over creation and cite the Scriptures that prove the practice."

What Are We Debating

What are we debating tonight? We're debating the number of cups to be used. We don't have time to discuss multitudinous other matters about which there may be agreement or disagreement. We have, tonight, only enough time to discuss the issue that we have in the proposition tonight. These brethren will do it every time. I have never seen it fail. They follow the line of every other digressive. *What did he do with the twenty scriptural arguments I presented in proof of one cup?* He took almost every one of them and *instead of just proving they teach the use of a plurality of cups,* or *that they do not teach the use of one,* he just tried to substitute a plate for cups in every one of the arguments.

Where I Learned These Arguments

But I want you to know where I learned to make the kind of arguments that I introduced tonight. On page 112 of that famous little *C. R. Nichol's Pocket Bible Encyclopedia,* we have argument after argument given that I gave you against the use of cups and for the use of one, but he made these arguments against instrumental music, page after page of the same arguments.

I refer you to another little book that has been printed by the tens of thousands . . . *"Bible Briefs and Sermon Outlines."* . . . *by Showalter & Davis,* put out by his brethren. Beginning with page 100, just Scripture after Scripture and argument after argument is given against instrumental music which I used against the cups. The same principle that applies to cups applies to instrumental music in these arguments. Brother Nichol and Brother Showalter used these arguments against the Instrumental Music Man. You know what the Instrumental Music Man will do? He'll get up and in every place he'll substitute plate where they put instrumental music. *Do you ever solve anything by doing that?* Brother Porter, I candidly ask you, *is that debating?* Is that stepping up and just actually considering the thing at issue? Is it? I believe, Brother Porter, that you want to be a fair man. I want to ask you frankly . . . *is that real debating?* If so, do you admit that all those instrumental music men who substitute the same thing which you substituted in the arguments are doing some real debating? I'd like to know how you feel about that. I'm going to be listening for it.

Oh, yes, but we have here Brother Gus Nichols in his *"Sermons,"* Vol. 1, beginning with page 130, "Objections to Instrumental Music." Now almost every objection he gave to instrumental music, I gave to cups. Tonight, Brother Porter just brushes the arguments aside and puts plate there in every argument where cups are found. The Instrumental Music Man, likewise, takes every one of the Gus Nichols' arguments and just substitutes song books and plates. *Do you get anywhere debating like that? Do you solve anything?* I wonder, Brother Porter, if you didn't learn that same type of debating from the digressive who stepped further along the line than you. Let's see about that.

Watch The Digressives

Here is the *Hunt-Inman Debate on Instrumental Music* between *Julian O. Hunt* and *Roger C. Inman* . . . Hunt, the Instrumental Music Man, and Inman, the Anti-Instrumental Music Man. I want to call your attention on Page 10 to what Julian O. Hunt offers in favor of instrumental music . . . "My argument is this: If earphones, glasses, radios, false teeth, hammers and gloves, crutches and canes, shoes, seats, etc., will not prevent the body from being presented wholly and acceptable unto God, then the piano, or any music instrument that aids the individual to sing, will not." There you are . . . He just went Brother Porter one better . . . *He got a whole lot more in there than Brother Porter did.* All right, let's notice again on page 31 . . . "I call upon him," Brother Hunt says, "to show that any individual has no authority to present in the worship service any musical aid unless that aid is mentioned in the New Testament. Then I ask by what authority does he bring in the song books, tuning fork, etc? . . . And he failed to give a sufficient reply." Let us notice again, on Page 28, "The argument was made in my first speech which showed that before he could prove that instrumental music was not an acceptable aid when used in the service of God, you have to prove that the individual has no authority to bring in any aid unless that aid is mentioned in the New Testament. Then, by what authority does he bring in the song book, the tuning fork, the pulpit, the radio, the collection plate?"

Don't you notice that the Instrumental Music Man just makes Brother Porter's line of argument in attempting to prove Instrumental Music? If you meet an Instrumental Music Man, that's all he's going to do. *Is that debating?* Is that the way to prove the instrument of music scriptural? Is that the way for you, Brother Porter, to prove that cups are scriptural?

Porter's Questions

I will now notice the questions which he submitted to me.

(1) As the bread pictures the body of Christ and the fruit of the vine pictures His blood, what is pictured by the drinking vessel?

Answer: The debate is *not* over whether the vessel represents anything or not; it is over the *number of cups* or vessels to be used. And now he wants to get off the *number* to be used and just argue about what do you think the cup *represents*. Now, if I should not think it *represents anything,* would that have anything to do with what the word of God teaches about the *number to be used?* It does not have a thing in the world to do with it, but since you want it, Brother Porter, and so you can talk about it if you want to, because you will anyway: The cup represents the New Testament. Get the Scriptures that I give, too . . . Luke 22:20; 1 Cor. 11:25.

(2) If, while serving the congregation the Communion, the loaf should be accidentally broken into other pieces besides that which each communicant breaks for himself, could the unserved portion of the congregation scripturally partake of it?

Answer: *I think so, but one may accidentally do what he may not intentionally do as a part of worship.* In other words, you may accidentally stumble and you may drop the cup. But, Brother, if you *intentionally* throw that cup down, you'll do wrong. If you intentionally do to the loaf that for which you have no authority as a part of worship, you are doing wrong. *He knows that.*

(3) While passing the fruit of the vine to the assembly, if the cup should be accidentally broken and its contents spilled, how would you scripturally serve the remainder of the assembly?

Answer: *Now I know how the word of God teaches us to commune in an assembly, but the word of God is not a big enough book to contemplate every accidental eventuality which may arise.* It is not big enough to do that. It gives us the pattern to follow and that pattern to follow is the *use of one cup for an assembly.* It is not big enough to tell us what to do in detail about every accident that may happen. But, hypothetically, it is possible for the cup to be dropped and for it to be broken and for its contents to be spilled, and he says if that happened, "What would you do?" Well, he wants to talk about something other than the individual cups he uses to convey the fruit of the vine to the assembly; he wants to do that and he's going to do that anyway.

The answer: *I would get a cup of the fruit of the vine and serve the entire congregation.*

(4) When individual cups are used on the table, does it constitute the Lord's Table or the Table of Devils?

Answer: *Neither, as set forth in 1 Cor. 10:21. However, this table with the individual cups on it would be of the devil.*

(5) When Paul in 1 Cor. 10:16, said the Christians at both Ephesus and Corinth blessed the cup, did not the expression, "the cup" have to refer to at least two drinking vessels, one at Ephesus and one at Corinth?

Answer: Since these instructions all obtain in an assembly (1 Cor. 11:33), "When ye come together to eat," *one cup in each assembly is taught* just as one speaker to speak at the time in one assembly was taught in 1 Cor. 14:31, "You may all prophecy one by one," and just as, "You may all prophecy one by one," was given to the *church universally* to obtain in each *individual assembly.* In the assembly at Corinth, and in the assembly at Ephesus, if they met simultaneously and in each assembly you had one speaking at the time, would you not have two speaking simultaneously? Considering both places? And yet Paul said, "Prophecy one by one." This takes not into consideration any controversy we may have about when 1 Cor. 14 applies or doesn't apply. But whenever it applies according to your understanding, the instructions say, "You may all prophecy one by one," and it applies to all assemblies,—one by one in each assembly.

(6) When he said, in the same connection, that we are all partakers of that one bread, did he not refer to at least two pieces of bread?

Answer: Loaves of bread, in other words. I suppose he means one loaf at Ephesus and one loaf at Corinth, etc., the same principle obtaining as given in answer to question No. 5.

CHART No. 1—On Communion

ONE CUP FOR AN ASSEMBLY IS TAUGHT BY:

1. EXAMPLE — Matt. 26:27; Mark 14:23; Luke 22:20; 1 Cor. 11:25.

2.. COMMAND—Matt. 26:27; 1 Cor. 11:2, 23, 25; 1 Cor. 11:33, 28.

3. STATEMENT—1 Cor. 10:16.

4. INFERENCE—1 Cor. 11:26, 27.

Now then, you will notice in defining my proposition and in my chart I mentioned that the Scriptures teach by example, by command, by statement, and by inference, and I proved that the Scriptures teach *one cup by command,* by statement, by example and by inference. Consider the example, "And he took 'a cup' or 'the cup' and he gave it to them." (Matt. 26:27).

Porter Admits Christ Took Literal Cup

Does Brother Porter believe that the Lord actually took one literal cup at the institution of the Communion? Does he believe that? Here are my notes in my own handwriting as I took them down when I formerly debated him in Tennessee on the question. Here's what he said, *"We will have no dispute about whether the word 'cup' is used literally in Matt. 26:27."* What does it say? *"He took a cup."* Brother Porter says he'll not dispute about whether or not that was *literal.* Then he admits that the Lord

took a literal cup, and according to the language, "one." That's
the example. He gave it to them and he said, *"Drink all of you
(or ye all) of it."* Brother Porter admits the Lord took a literal
cup and that he gave it to them. Now Jesus said, "Drink all of
you of it." *Is that hard to understand?* If you were not trying
to prove something not mentioned in the Bible, I wonder if you
could not understand that language. If you were trying to understand just exactly what it says, would you be able to understand
that a plurality was involved? But he says a liquid requires a
container; that's right. But if Jesus had a container for the liquid,
what was it? The Bible says it was "a cup." Brother Porter says
we'll not dispute as to whether it was literal in Matt. 26:27. So
he admits that the Lord had a literal cup containing the fruit of
the vine in Matt. 26:27. That's just what I believe. And according to the Scripture, "He gave it to them and they all drank
of it." (Mark 14:23)

Porter Tormented Before The Time

He says, "Brother Waters, when you talk about the command
(in I Cor. 11:2) 'I praise you, brethren, that ye remember me in
all things, and keep the ordinances, as I delivered them to you,' . . .
watch out! You might get into trouble on the next proposition
about women prophesying, because instructions about prophecying
are given in 1 Cor. 11." Well, I don't wonder, Brother Porter, that
you're tormented before the time in trying to bring in the women
teaching and prophesying before we get to the issue. But don't
you think for one moment I won't take care of that when the
time comes.

Metonymy

But of 1 Cor. 11:26, "As often as ye eat this bread, and
drink this cup, ye do show the Lord's death till he come," he
said, "Certainly, that's the figure of speech Metonymy." Certainly, it's Metonymy. We say it is. Brother Porter says that it
is. But by the figure of speech Metonymy we *name a literal vessel*
to suggest its contents, and there the apostle Paul named a literal
vessel, "a cup," and suggested "its contents." When you brethren
pass a plurality of cups to an assembly and the contents of that
plurality are drunk, can it be said that "they drank the cup?"

A Number of Jugs!

Well, he supposes that he and I visit a man and the man
takes us to his cellar and there are *a number of jugs there.* What's

that? *A number of jugs!* Plural! You notice that he had to say *"jugs"* so we would understand that there were *"jugs"* there. Isn't that right? *How do we know that there were jugs there?* Because Brother Porter said *"jugs."* He stepped in it then, didn't he? How do we know there were jugs there? Brother Porter said so. But what if he had said·he and I went with a man to his cellar and *"a jug" was there?* I wonder where we would get the idea there was a *plurality of jugs* there? The only reason we knew there was a *plurality of jugs* was that Porter said there were *jugs.* Don't you see? You have to construct a parallel. Suppose it were said, "We went to the cellar and the man took a jug and drank of it." You get a parallel. I want to know if that were said who would get the idea that there was a plurality of jugs involved in that. You construct an actual parallel. Certainly you may have a singular noun sometimes used in the sense of numerical value of species, but whenever you say that *"he took a jug,"* that means *one,* doesn't it? And when Brother Porter says, "there was a *number of jugs* there," that means *a plurality,* doesn't it?

The Bottle

Oh! But he says about a man that "he is hitting the bottle." Well, I never saw a man drink out of two at one time in my life. But, listen! Suppose that you narrowed that down to a specific instance, just like Matthew and Mark narrows this down where he took "a cup" and gave "it" to them, . . . and said concerning that man: "I saw him take a bottle. I saw him drink of it. I saw him give it to his companions and I saw *all of them drink of it."* Do you get the idea there was a *plurality of bottles* involved now? We narrow that down, as Matthew and Mark did, to a specific consideration and not something that's general. When you do that, what do you have?

Oh! But the woman says, I raised all of my babies on the bottle." But narrow it down to a parallel, a parallel with Matthew's and a parallel with Mark's record, and deal with a specific instance, "The mother gave *the baby the bottle,* and *the baby drank the bottle."* Now you narrow that down to a *specific* consideration and who gets the idea that a *plurality of bottles* was involved? Who would? You see? You get that down to a parallel with Matthew and Mark . . . Don't get away from the language as used by them. Everybody knows that if it were said that the mother gave the bottle to the baby and the baby drank it, or drank of it, that just one bottle is involved.

The Radiator

Brother Porter says we go into a garage and "the radiator" is frozen. *How many* radiators were frozen when he made that statement? The idea of how many frozen radiators are connoted? Then he says, "This is the way we all boil the radiator." But, now then, get it down to a parallel with Matthew and Mark and have it said concerning the mechanic that, "He boiled the radiator." A specific mechanic and a specific radiator. *"He boiled the radiator."* How many radiators are involved now? Get your parallel, Brother Porter. I'll stay with you every time.

But he mentions Matt. 10:13-15 where Jesus said, "It would be more tolerable for Sodom and Gomorrha than for that city" . . . Narrow it down to a parallel with Matthew and Mark, and make a specific statement in regard to a specific city. Matthew and Mark said, "He took a cup." You do that, will you?

Jacob's Well

But he can talk about plates, upper rooms, song books and Jacob's well. We don't want to miss that. In John, the 4th chapter and 12th verse, he says "that they all drank thereof." But you know that Jacob's well proves too much for Brother Porter. You know why? *Because there's just one literal well involved.* There's not but one literal well involved. Who understood when it said "Jacob's well" that there was more than one well involved? There was just one well involved; no plurality of wells. And when it was said they "drank thereof," was it understood that they were drinking from the source of a *plurality of wells?* Now, remember, you brethren have a plurality of cups and you do not start out even with one cup and its contents and pour from that one into the plurality you use. You'll have to find where, when they "drank of Jacob's well," they picked up Jacob's well, poured the contents of it into a plurality of little wells, all drank out of the little wells, and it was said that "they drank out of Jacob's well." Jacob's well is too much for you because it is a literal well. There's not but one involved, and that doesn't suit you because you do not want just one literal cup to be involved in the Communion Service. You don't want that.

CHART No. 2—On Communion

ONE CUP

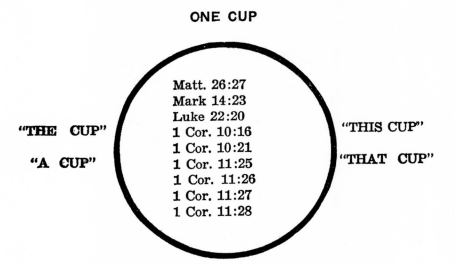

"THE CUP"

"A CUP"

Matt. 26:27
Mark 14:23
Luke 22:20
1 Cor. 10:16
1 Cor. 10:21
1 Cor. 11:25
1 Cor. 11:26
1 Cor. 11:27
1 Cor. 11:28

"THIS CUP"

"THAT CUP"

INDIVIDUAL CUPS

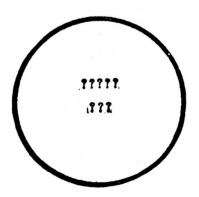

But what did he do with the circle over there. He just entered "the plate." The circle is still there, the question marks are still in it, and we're waiting for "cups." And if he talks about the plate from now on, it will not solve the problem of how many cups are to be used in the communion service. It won't solve it because that's dodging the issue.

One Cup Is Bound

"One cup" is bound in heaven. (Matt. 16:19). Jesus gives
the instructions, "Whatsoever thou shalt bind on earth shall be
bound in heaven," and the use of one was bound by the apostle
Paul in 1. Cor. 11, and by those who recorded the institution of
the communion service.

Would "Cups" Mean "Cups"

I have proved the use of "one cup" for an assembly by example, by command, by statement, and by inference. If he could
find as many verses as I have over here for one cup, that mention
"cups," I wonder if he wouldn't quote those verses in an attempt
to prove "cups," and *if they said "cups," I wonder if they would
mean "cups."* Because when the Bible says "cup," Brother Porter
doesn't want that; he has to try some way or other to slip through
that statement the use of a plurality of cups.

I thank you.

First Session
Porter's Second Negative
Cup Question

Brethren Moderators, Brother Waters, Ladies and Gentlemen:
I am glad to pay my respects to the speech, to which you
have just listened, by my worthy opponent in his effort to sustain his proposition that only one drinking vessel can be used in
the distribution of the fruit of the vine. Brother Waters, at the
beginning, handed me a cup of cold water. It wasn't very cold,
but it was wet anyway, and that was the way he had of replying
to my argument based upon Mark 9:41. There the Lor said,
"Whosoever shall give unto you a cup of water in My Name, because ye belong to Me, he shall not lose his reward." I called attention to the fact that Jesus said "a cup." "A cup." And that is
just as literal as any cup that he has found, with its contents
just as literal as any he has found anywhere. Jesus said, "If he
shall give to you *a cup* of water in My Name. he shall not lose
his reward." I asked Brother Waters to tell me, if he should give
two cups, or three cups, would he lose his reward? What did he
say about it? Nothing. Why? Couldn't afford to, because the
case is parallel with his argument. If, because the record says
"a cup"—Jesus "took a cup"—does that mean that I will stand
condemned if I take two cups? Then from the same standpoint,

Jesus said if a man "gives you *a cup* of water, he will not lose his reward." But if he gives two cups of water, he goes to hell, according to Brother Waters' argument. Why didn't you notice that, Ervin? What did you skip that for? You just brushed over the argument; you just brushed around the thing. You didn't even mention what I was talking about at all. You just referred to it and missed the thing completely.

We Drank From The Bottle

By the way, Ervin, when you gave me this cup of water, I wonder if we both drank *from this bottle* (pointing to bottle the water was poured from). (Porter turns to Waters) Did we? *Come on now!* Did we *both drink from this bottle?* You drank out of this cup awhile ago, and I drank of it. Did we both drink *from this bottle?* Come on now! We did, didn't we, Ervin? We both drank *from this bottle.* Yet the lips of Waters and the lips of Porter did not touch the bottle. But we both drank *from this bottle.* Let's shake hands on that. We agree on some things. We will agree on that, won't we? (Audience laughs). Won't you agree with me that we both drank from that bottle? Come on now, Ervin, won't you do it? *Did we both drink from this bottle,* Ervin? Come on now and tell us. This audience has a right to know. What do you say about it? Did we both drink from this bottle? Too bad, but you got yourself into it by giving me a drink from that bottle.

Now, then, we see what his illustration did for him. He would better have kept this cold water—he's just about lost his reward.

Is Instrumental Music Parallel?

Now, he says, "Brother Porter talks about plates, song books and this, that, and the other." He said, "We don't have time to discuss all of those things. We are not discussing song books and plates. That's not the issue, but how many cups to be used in the Lord's Supper. So I don't have time to deal with those things. I don't have time to deal with song books and things of that kind." Then he took about fifteen minutes reading from Brother Foy Wallace, and Brother Showalter, and Brother Gus Nichols, and the Hunt-Inman Debate. He put in about half of his speech reading from them. *He had time for that.* What's the matter, Ervin? You had time for all of that, but didn't have time to discuss plates. No, sir, the issue is something else, and he didn't have time to fool with that, but he had time to fool with these things, you see, and based his argument upon what they said about it. But he didn't have time to deal with the plates. Well, we're not through with that.

Now, he said that the arguments made by Brother Porter are the same as those made by the *other digressives*. And that's what another group of hobby riders would say about him. "Some other digressives." They would talk about him the same way that he talks about me, and that these others depend upon the same kind of argument to defend their instruments of music. When you discuss the matter with them, about the Scriptural ground for it, they will say, "Well, what about the song books, the plates, the radios, the pulpits and the pews, and the electric lights and the tuning forks, etc." Well, we'll get to that, but I want you to bear in mind this fact. We will take the song book, and the plate, and the cup, and the instrumental music. Now, then, the Lord said, regarding the bread, to "eat of it." Yes, He gave to them to eat, and said "eat of it." All right, there's the command *to eat*. *We eat the bread.* There's the command to eat. All right, regarding the fruit of the vine, He gave the commandment "to drink;" and regarding our praise to God, He gave us the command to "sing." Now I want to know, Brother Waters, since the Lord said "eat of the bread," if I use the plate while I eat the bread, am I doing anything besides eating? If I eat the bread out of one plate or out of no plate, am I still eating? Just what the Lord said to do, isn't it? All right, the Lord said, "Drink the fruit of the vine," and if I drink it out of one cup, or a dozen cups, I am still doing what the Lord said—I am drinking. But when the man plays on the instrument, is he doing what the Lord said, when He said "sing?" Now you know better than that kind of logic, Ervin. You know that the *command to eat* the bread could *involve the plate,* and the *command to drink* the fruit of the vine could *involve the container;* but the *command to sing never involves the instrument of music*. They don't stand parallel at all, and Ervin Waters knows they don't. Don't you Ervin? You know that, don't you? You know the command to sing doesn't involve the instrument, does it? When a man plays the instrument, he does something besides sing, doesen't he? When a man eats out of a plate, he is doing nothing but eat, is he? He is not doing something besides eat. If he drinks out of

cups, he is doing nothing but drink, is he? But when he plays
the instrument, he is doing something besides sing, isn't he?
And so *your cases are not parallel at all.* That's why the instrumental music man is in the same predicament that you are in; he
can't defend his practice because he makes parallels where there
are not parallels. And the cases do not stand on the same basis
at all.

Cups And Plates Are Parallel

Well, Brother Foy Wallace said in "The Torch" that "it is
weak to affirm that something is as Scriptural as something
else," and "nothing is Scriptural unless it is," and "men who do
so are afraid of their ground, etc." Well, I *am not affirming* that
one thing is *as Scriptural* as something else. I am trying to show
you, Ervin, and those who stand with you, that if your intelligence is broad enough to see that you can use a plate (although
the Bible says nothing about it), that the *command to eat* would
involve the container upon which it was placed. Then you ought
to see the same thing regarding the other. I believe that *they
both are in harmony with Scripture.* Would you affirm, or would
you deny, that the use of the plate is Scriptural? Which would
you do? Suppose I affirm the use of the plate is Scriptural.
Would you deny it? You use it; you couldn't afford to deny it.
And so he believes the plate is Scriptural. I am trying to show
him that cups are parallel with plates; and, therefore, if the plate
is Scriptural (and he and I both believe that it is—that it can
be done without any violation of Scripture), then the two stand
together. And I am trying to show him that, to be consistent, he
must give up his agitation of this matter and take his stand with
me on the cups, and other things relative thereto. I am not trying to prove one thing is as Scriptural as something else. But
the "instrumental music man," when you bring the matter up
with him, "wants to debate on the song book and the plate."
And that's something that shouldn't be done, and that's no way
at all to do proper debating. But I happen to remember in our
former debate, Ervin, that when I was affirming on the teaching question, you brought up the Missionary Society and tried
to make that parallel. *I wonder if that was good debating.* It's
all right when Ervin does it, but it's all wrong when Porter
does it. You see? And before he gets through with the teaching
question you will doubtless find him doing the same thing. They
all do. They bring up the Missionary Society, and they will bring

up the instrumental music on the other issue, and try to make the class teaching parallel with the Missionary Societies and instrumental music. But he says, "That's not good debating." Do you believe it is, Ervin? That's the way you did the other time. Have you learned since then? (Audience laughs). You did it that way, didn't you? Yes, that's the way he did it before, but now he says that's not good debating. He will probably change his mind again, by the next time we meet. We will likely have another debate sometime in the future.

Well, he said, "What about the twenty arguments that I introduced?" "Well," he said, "He just substituted plates." That's all right—they're parallel. One is the container for the bread, the other one for the fruit of the vine. And they stand parallel. And, consequently, if one is Scriptural, the other is, and I believe both of them are. I believe there is no violation of Scripture in either of them, because the container has no significance.

The Lord's Table

I asked him about *the table,* "the Lord's table," and he has said nothing about that. I believe he thought it would not be "good debating" to mention it. Maybe. So he skipped the matter of "the table." I want to know if it *must be a literal table* and *how literal it must be.* And must the Lord's Supper be placed on a *literal table* in order for it to be Scriptural ■ Why didn't you tell us about it, Ervin?

A Poor Student On Instrumental Music

He came to Nichol's Encyclopedia, page 112, the arguments against instrumental music; and Showalter's Sermon Outlines, page 100, against instruments of music; and Gus Nichols' book, on page 130, regarding the same matter. And here he read all these arguments against instrumental music and said, "Here's where I learned it." Well, you were a poor student, Ervin, for the simple fact that they were dealing with *a thing not involved in the command to sing.* The Bible said "to sing," but the Bible nowhere said "to play" the instrument. And when they play the instrument, they are doing something besides sing; but when we drink out of one cup or two cups or forty cups, we are *doing nothing but drinking.* So you substituted something that was entirely "unparallel;" it isn't parallel with it at all.

The Hunt-Inman Debate, page 10, the radio, the seats; and

page 21, the song books, the tuning forks; and page 28, the song books, the tuning forks, the pulpits, and the radio, etc. He is trying to show that I occupy the same stand the digressives occupy regarding instrumental music. Well, if the command *to sing* ever involves the instrument, I'll agree that that's right. But until Ervin says the command to sing involves the playing of an instrument, his parallel breaks down. Will you say it, Ervin? That the comand to sing involves the instrument? If it does, then they are parallel, because the command to drink involves the container, and the command to eat involves the container. You can have it on a plate, or you can have it without a plate, of course, but in any case, the plate is not excluded by the command to eat. You eat with one plate or you eat without it, and you are still eating. You drink with one cup or you drink out of two, and you are still drinking. But you play an instrument, and you are not still singing; you are making a coordinate element with an instrument of music. You have *added something* else to it. So the cases are not parallel at all. Now then to the questions:

His Answers To My Questions

First. "As the bread pictures the body of Christ, and the fruit of the vine pictures His blood, what is pictured by the drinking vessel?" He said, "Well, we are not on what the drinking vessel pictures; doesn't matter about that. We are discussing how many." Well, I know, but I had a purpose in asking that question. I have already given "how many" an investigation. Well, the bread pictures the body, and the fruit of the vine pictures the blood. So *what is pictured by the drinking vessel?*

Cup Pictures New Testament

He said, "But I'll tell you what it pictures. It pictures the New Testament (Luke 22:20, 1 Cor. 11:25)" "This cup is the New Testament in My blood." And so he says now, "This cup pictures the New Testament." All right—*one drinking vessel* and *one Testament* to an assembly. See? If you have two copies of it, you are going to hell, because there must be one drinking vessel, Brother Waters, and one New Testament. You can't have two copies of it; you can't have three copies of it; you can't have four copies of it because of this. "The New Testament"—just one. Oh, he might say, one is a reproduction of the other. All right; so is the cup. That doesn't help him any. One cup is ex-

actly a reproduction of the other. And I have seen Testaments
of different shapes and sizes—numbers of them. And, consequently, he stands upon that ground now with respect to the New
Testament. Just one cup to an assembly is all he can have, according to his argument.

Now, then, I want to get some other things in that connection. He says now that the drinking vessel refers to the New
Testament; it pictures the New Testament. Now if that is so,
then the "cup of blessing" in 1 Cor. 10:16, is not the drinking
vessel. For Paul says, "The cup of blesing which we bless, is
it not the communion of the blood of Christ?" All right, *the cup*
referred to there *is the communion of the blood,* not the New
Testament. So *the cup of blessing is not the drinking vessel,* because Paul said the cup of blessing is "the communion of the
blood." Brother Waters says the drinking vesesl is the New
Testament. So "the cup of blessing" is not the New Testament,
according to his argument. In his little tract on the communion,
he argues that it is. If he denies it, I'll prove it. And, furthermore, "the cup of the Lord," in the same connection, is the same
as "the cup of blessing," but it's not the vessel, according to that.
I Cor. 11:25 shows that it is the cup of the Lord and speaks of
the cup which "is the New Testament in My blood.' I Cor. 11:25-
27 speaks of the man who drinks "of *this cup* unworthily." What
does "this cup" refer to? The drinking vessel? That's what he
argues in his little tract. "The cup of the Lord," he says, "is a
literal drinking vessel." And by the way, he has the doctrine of
transubstantiation in connection with it. You know the Catho-
lics teach the doctrine of transubstantiation. The doctrine of
transubstantiaion means when the bread and fruit of the vine
are blessed by the Priest they are changed into the actual body and
blood of Christ. Now Brother Waters says that *literal drinking
vessel,* when you give thanks for it, *is changed* into the cup of
the Lord; that *"after thanks, it becomes the cup of the Lord."*
Page 30. The literal drinking vesel does. But Paul, referring to
this, says, "Whosoever drinks this cup,'' that is, this cup of the
Lord, "unworthily," is *"guilty of the blood."* Didn't say he was
guilty of the New Testament. Furthermore, in verse 29, "He that
eateth and drinketh unworthily, eateth and drinketh damnation
unto himself, not discerning the Lords body." Which cup? "The
cup of the Lord." "Not discerning the Lord's body." He didn't
say "not discerning the New Testament." So that's *not the vessel.*

And in I Cor. 11:26, he shows "the Lord's death till he comes"—
when he drinks this cup. But it doesn't show the New Testament
till he comes. So in this case, "the cup" doesn't refer to "the
drinking vessel"—it refers to the fruit of the vine. And so all
the arguments he has made about "this cup' and "the cup of
the Lord" being a literal container goes down in his answer to
this question—that it's the New Testament.

Bread Broken Accidentally

Second. "If, while serving the congregation the communion,
the loaf should be accidentally broken into other pieces besides
that which each communicant breaks for himself, could the unserved portion of the congregation Scripturally partake of it?"
He says, "I think so, because if it's broken accidentally, and not
on purpose, then they could go ahead and it would be Scriptural."
But if they did it on purpose, then of course, they would go to
hell for it. In his little tract on communion, he argues about the
unity of the body, and tries to prove that there must be no breaking of the loaf except that which a man breaks to eat. If there is
any other breaking of it, it becomes divided, and the body of
Christ is divided. It's wrong. But now he says you can *divide the
body of Christ accidentally,* and it will be all right. But if you do
it on purpose, it's wrong. But, of course, now if you break the
loaf accidentally, and thus you divide the body of Christ accidentally, that's all right. If you didn't do it on purpose, and
didn't do it intentionally, it would be all right. But you turn
around and *intentionally eat* that which has already been broken,
you intentionally eat that part of it. Now, then, he does that on
purpose. What about that? And then another question.

Waters Would Use Two Cups

Third. "While passing the fruit of the vine to the assembly,
if the cup should be accidentally dropped and broken and its contents spilled, how would you Scripturally serve the remainder of
the assembly?" He said the word of God is not big enough to tell
us about all the accidents that might occur. But he says this is
possible. Yes, I know it is. I know of places where it happened. It
might happen anytime. But he said, "I'll tell you what I would do.
I would get a cup and serve the whole congregation." *Again,* Brother Waters? After half of them had already taken it? "I would get
another cup and I would serve the whole congregation." All
right, the congregation, then, which had already been served, you

serve out of two cups. You have part of that assembly drinking out of two cups (Porter and audience laughs) because you said you would serve *the whole congregation again.* And you have two cups for part of them, and the rest of them one cup—An entirely different cup from what the others used before it was broken. Thus you use two cups, Brother Waters—two drinking vessels—for the same assembly, and you have said good-bye to your proposition. You have said good-bye to your proposition for it said, "That in an assembly of the Church of Christ, for the communion, the Scriptures teach that we *must use one cup (one drinking vessel)* in the distribution of the fruit of the vine." *We must do it.* He didn't say we must do it except when some accident occurs. He says we must do it. *We must use one drinking vessel* in the distribution of the fruit of the vine. Waters says, "I would get another cup, another drinking vessel, and serve the whole congregation again." So you would have two drinking vessels in that assembly, Brother Waters. (Looks at Waters). Do you want to take it back. Do you want to take it back, Ervin? Brother Waters thought I was discussing something besides the number of cups, but I think now he sees that the number was involved. Yes, the *number of cups* was involved, and Brother Waters has agreed with me that there are circumstances under which more than one drinking vessel can be used to serve the assembly of the saints. Absolutely so. Let's shake hands on that, Brother Waters. (Offers to shake with Waters). We have agreed on it that far—that there are circumstances under which *two cups* can be used. There are. You said so, Ervin. Come on— let's shake hands on it. Won't you do it, Ervin? *Let's shake hands on it.* There are circumstances under which two cups can be used for an assembly. You have agreed, haven't you? Because you said you would get another cup. Well, another cup would be two, wouldn't it? If you had one cup and break it, and then get another one, how many does that make, Brother Waters? One broken cup and one unbroken cup would make two cups, wouldn't it? And part of the congregation drinks out of both of them. I never do that—I never drink out of but one. But you have some of the members of the congregation drinking out of two. Well, that's further than I have ever gone, Brother Waters. You are further digressive than I ever have any idea of going. Why, the very idea, Ervin. You have a number of the members of the church drinking out of two cups; part of them get only one; but a part of them have two. And so you have *two cups* to *one assembly.* (Porter looks at Waters) Can you add? One broken cup, and one unbroken cup, make how many cups, Ervin? And you say you can use them in one assembly, and that one man can drink out of both of them—that a number of them can drink out of both of them. Did you say it? Do you want to take it back? Will you deny that you said it? Now, then, Brother Waters is gone world without end; he'll never recover himself from that. He has cut himself loose from his proposition, for it says "there must be one," and he said by the word "must" I mean "obligatory.' No way around it. But now he says there is a way around it. There *is a way around it*—"I would get another cup.' "I would get the second cup and serve the whole congregation." And so he has a part of the congregation drinking from two drinking vessels, when his proposition says there must be only one for an assembly. Good-bye, Brother Waters. Well, we are not through.

The Devil's Table

Fourth. "When individual cups are used on the table, does it constitute the Lord's table or the table of devils?" He said it was neither of those in I Cor. 10, but it would be of the devil. So if it's of the devil, then it's the table of devils. And you would have a number of drinking vessels on the table of devils. Yet in your little tract you say the table of devils has only *one cup* on it just as the table of the Lord has.

"The Cup" Can Mean Two

Fifth. "When Paul, in I Cor. 10:16, said that Christians in both Ephesus and Corinth blessed 'the cup,' would not the expression, 'the cup,' have to refer to at least two drinking vessels —one at Ephesus and one at Corinth?" He said it had reference to one cup in each assembly. Well, there's a place, Brother Waters, where one cup means two. You wanted me to give proof of any place where any such expression was ever used to mean more than one. Paul said, *"The cup* which we bless"—we in Ephesus and you in Corinth. *"The cup* which *we bless."* It didn't say 'the cups which we bless," but it said "the cup which we bless." Singular number, Ervin. You say that means one in Ephesus and one in Corinth. So it means two, doesn't it? You have admitted that there's an expression in the Bible that says "the cup" which means two cups, at least. And if they should happen to break one of them in each assembly, there would be four of them, because they could still have two. They could get another one and still serve the whole congregation. You would have four cups then, according to his own argument. Thank you, Ervin. Thank you very much. Now, then, hurriedly, to some other matters.

One Container—Plural Contents

Now, then, regarding the jug. He said, "The man loves his jug." He said, "We see a number of jugs there—in the plural. Well, how do we know there were *jugs* there? Well, Porter said there were." Well, the point is, Brother Waters, you said, "There is no sense in which we can name one container and refer to the contents of more than one." *That's what you said.* "We cannot name one container and refer to the contents of more than one." Well, I said, "Ervin says the man loves his *jug.*" Why didn't you notice that? That's what the argument is based on. Why did you dodge that and talk about the other things? Why certainly I said there were jugs there, but in the illustration Ervin says the man "loves his jug." Well, he mentions one. Does that mean one, or more than one? *Put it down and tell us about.* You will have a chance tomorrow night to tell us about that. Tell us! Does "the jug" in that case mean more than one jug? And the same thing about "hitting the bottle." Well, he says, "I never saw a man drink out of two at once." Well, maybe not, but I have seen men drink out of more than one. Not at the same time. But he never saw men drink out of two at once. Brother Waters, in the communion service, you never saw men drink out of two cups at once. Did you ever see any brother who stands with me on this issue drink out of two cups at once? Why certainly not.

And then regarding the baby. The woman says she "raised all of her babies on the bottle." He says, "Narrow that down." "Narrow that down." Yes, but the thing is, when you get it that way it ruins what you said about it. Your argument was: "You cannot refer to one container and mean the contents of more than one." That's what I'm talking about. And the woman says, "I raised all my babies on the bottle." Only one container is mentioned. Does that mean the contents of more than one? Why didn't you answer? *You didn't answer.* You said, "Narrow it down to one bottle, one baby, etc." Give the bottle to the baby, or something of that kind. *Narrow it down.* Well, I'm wanting to know: Does "the bottle," when the woman says, "I raised all my babies on the bottle," mean only one? How many containers does she mention, Ervin? "The bottle" mentions one, doesn't it?

Just one. Mentions only one container. I want to know if that meant the contents of only one container, Ervin? *That's the point.* Why, you didn't touch it at all. Won't you tell us about it tomorrow night? Did the woman raise all her babies on the contents of the same bottle? That's the point. He wants to narrow it down and get one baby and one bottle. Well, that's all right. When you do that we just have one communicant and one cup. You haven't changed the matter at all on that.

But then to the radiator—"boiling the radiator." He said, "How many radiators?" Well, when the man says, "This is the way we all boil the radiator," he mentioned only one. How many did he mean? There is a case in which "the radiator," one container being referred to, means more than one radiator—just as with these other things given already.

That Cup—That City—That Man

Then in Matt. 10:14-15, regarding "that city"—"Shake off the dust of your feet against them, because it shall be more tolerable for the land of Sodom and Gomorrah, in the day of judgment, than for *that city.*" "Yes, but Matthew and Mark say 'a cup,' but that didn't say 'a city'." Well, but Paul said "that cup." You made an argument on that. "Let a man examine himself, and so let him eat of that bread and drink of that cup." "That cup," and "this cup," and "that bread,' and "this bread.' And you said "that cup" means only one. Well, then, here we have 'that city,' just exactly as you gave "that cup." So that means *only one city.* I gave "that man" and "the city"—Paul was in perils in "the city.' I asked Brother Waters to tell us what city it was. "The city," according to his argument, means only one city. I want to know what city it was.

Jacob's Well Again

Then Jacob's well—I must get to that. About how much time do I have, about two or three minutes? All right.

Jacob's well. His argument was that "they drank of it," and since *they all drank of it,* that they all *put their lips to the same container* and *sipped out of the same vessel,* for they "drank of it." He said, "Porter will not deny that there was a literal container, because in the other debate he said there is no dispute about there being a literal container." I have never disputed about a container, but I am affirming that the container has no significance. The liquid must be confined in a container—certainly so—but it's the liquid, the fruit of the vine, that pictures the blood of Jesus Christ. And so regarding Jacob's well. But here's Jacob, and his sons, and his cattle, *all drinking of it.* But he said there was just one well, and there were not many other little wells. There was just one well. But, Brother Waters, there had to be some *other containers,* didn't there? That's what I'm getting at. There had to be some other containers, didn't there? There's one well, but these people and this stock all had different containers. They all *drank of the well,* but they drank from other containers just like we drank out of *this container* awhile ago (referring to glass) when we drank *from this bottle,* didn't we? Did we? Now, then, we both drank *from that* (referring to bottle of water on Waters' table) didn't we? Come on now! I drank *from this* and you drank *from this* (referring to cup out of which they drank) and *we both drank from that* (referring to bottle) didn't we? Come on. To drink from a cup, must we put our lips to the cup, Ervin? Didn't we drink from this, Ervin (referring to bottle)? Come on! *Did we drink from this?* You admit that Jacob and his sons and their cattle *drank from the well.* But they didn't put their lips to the well, and the well didn't have to be upset and poured out, but the contents of the well was put into other containers. And there were other containers besides the well from which they drank. But in *drinking from the other containers,* they were *drinking from the well.* And so I suppose if we were to put it all into a big container and then pour it out into little containers, it will be all right because it is then parallel with Jacob's well. Is the time up?

Thank you, Ladies and Gentlemen.

Moderators At End Of The First Session

Moderator Clovis T. Cook:

Well, I am sure that all will agree that the speakers have been gentlemen tonight. I am sure you have been well paid for whatever trouble you have gone to in being with us. I invite you back again tomorrow night. I predict that this sort of conduct will contribute more to the quietness of this debate, than perhaps anything else, and we want you to be present every night. (He reads the proposition for the second session). Is there anything to be said now before we are dismissed?

Moderator Sterl Watson:

Brother Cook, I would like to make a few statements. I could see that while these men were delivering their speeches the audience was completely relaxed. Now you have enjoyed this tonight, haven't you? It's educational, and all of us enjoyed it. I met Brother Waters sometime ago. He is a pleasant lovable sort of fellow, and he is certainly recommended as one of the best representatives, if not the best, on his side of the issue. I have known Brother Porter, I don't know how many years. I have never known a man in whom I had more confidence nor loved more dearly than W. Curtis Porter. And should we fail in these discussions, we wouldn't have anybody else to turn to. Now, that's the kind of representative men that you have before you discussing these issues, over which the body of Christ has been troubled so much, and that has caused so much regret in the hearts of God's people. Let us study these things every night just as prayerfully as we have thus far. I hope you can attend every night. I think I shall have to miss tomorrow night, but by the providence of God, I hope to be back the next two nights. And I hope all of you can come every night.

Moderator Cook:

Thank you Brother Watson. I agree with you one hundred percent, that if these two men can't dig up the Truth on it, why it might be a long time before we can bring two more to the front that would try as hard and at the same time show a spirit that would be conducive to as much tranquility and peace as the spirits of these two men. If there is nothing more, we shall stand to our feet and be dismissed.

(Brother Billy Orten, of Lawrenceburg, Tennessee, dismissed the audience.)

Second Session

Prayer was led by Brother G. K. Wallace.
Brother L. H. Newell moderated the second night in the place of Brother Watson.

Brother Newell:

Brother Sterl Watson couldn't be with us tonight; so I am taking his place as moderator for Brother Porter. We are happy to have you here, and we do hope that you have come for no other purpose than to investigate the word of the Lord. So as these two men stand before you and speak the word of God, each of us should consider carefully and seriously, the things they say. These brethren conducted themselves as brethren last evening, and all of you who were here are impressed with that, I am sure, and, furthermore, you are edified in the study of the word of the Lord. I am sure that will be true this evening, in this service, and I am sure it will be true likewise in the remaining services of this discussion.

Come, if you possibly can, to every service and bring someone with you, that we might learn the will of the Lord. Come with an open mind and a receptive heart for those things that are presented as we learn that they are according to a "thus saith the Lord." And let's practice them. If, perchance, we might be doing those things that are not pleasing to the Lord, then let's give them up. That's the way to be honest with ourselves, with our own souls before God, and before our fellowman. This evening, the proposition that is under discussion reads like this: "In an assembly of the Church of Christ, for the communion, it is Scriptural to use individual cups (drinking vessels) in the distribution of the fruit of the vine." Brother W. Curtis Porter affirms this; Brother J. Ervin Waters denies. So at this time I present to you Brother W. Curtis Porter.

Second Session
Porter's First Affirmative
Cup Question

Brethren Moderators, Brother Waters, Ladies and Gentlemen: I am happy to be in your presence to affirm the proposition to which you just listened; and this proposition is, of course, the reverse of the one we discussed last night. We have the same question under consideration as to the number of cups that may be permissible, or that may be used, in the distribution of the fruit of the vine. Brother Waters affirmed last night, as you remember, that there must be one drinking vessel, and he made the word "must" mean "obligatory." I'm affirming that the use of more than one, or individual cups, is Scriptural in that service. Perhaps it's unnecessary to give much definition to the terms of the proposition, but by "an assembly" I mean a group of people gathered together, or a congregation. By "the Church of Christ" we mean the institution for which the Lord died, and said He would build upon the rock, that is sometimes called the kingdom of Christ. And by the word "communion" reference is made to the Lord's Supper comprising the fruit of the vine and the bread. By "individual cups" I mean, as the parentheses of the proposition show, "drinking vessels." And "the distribution of the fruit of the vine"—we mean simply the matter of serving the congregation or giving the fruit of the vine to the congregation, to those who partake. And by "the fruit of the vine" we mean, of course, the juice of the grape. And that this "is Scriptural"—that is, it does not violate Scriptural principles or Scriptural teaching. So with that idea before you, I proceed to a study of some things I wish to bring before you tonight.

Waters' Admission Renders Further Discussion Unnecessary

The first thing I want to call to your attention is the fact that it's totally unnecessary even to discuss this proposition tonight in view of the admission made by Brother Waters in his second speech last night. You remember I asked him some questions at that time. One of the questions was this: Question No. 2: "If, while serving the congregation the communion, the loaf should be accidentally broken into other pieces besides that which each communicant breaks for himself, could the unserved portion of the congregation Scripturally partake of it?" And he said, "Yes, he thought so, if they didn't do it on purpose." Then, Question No. 3: "While passing the fruit of the vine to the assembly, if the cup should be accidentally dropped and broken and its contents spilled, how would you Scripturally serve the remainder of the assembly?" Brother Waters said, "I'd get another cup and serve the whole congregation." Now, I called attention to the fact last night that in giving that answer to that question, he admitted that *under some circumsances* an assembly *could use two drinking vessels* for the distribution of the fruit of the vine. A part of the assembly in the case given is already served the contents of the cup, but in some way during the service the container is dropped and the contents are spilled, and Brother Waters says in order to serve the remainder of the congregation, "I'd just get me another cup and serve the whole congregation again." Whenever he gets another cup, that makes *two drinking vessels* he has for that particular assembly. And, of course, if he can have two drinking vessels for one assembly, there's no reason why he couldn't have two hundred. If that second cup should be dropped and its contents spilled, then he'd have to get a third one and go over the whole routine again. And if that should be dropped, the same thing would occur. He would have to get a fourth one, and on and on, and thus he surrendered the whole contention that he made on that proposition last night—that in the distribution of the fruit of the vine *only one drinking vessel must be used*. Now he says that at least two can be used under some circumstances; and if under some circumstances two can be used, then it's not true that *one must be used*. Now, that being true, then it's wholly unnecessary to discuss this proposition tonight, because Brother Waters has agreed with me that more than one drinking vessel *can be used* in an assembly of the church for the distribution of the fruit of the vine *under some circumstances*. And, if so, it is Scriptural to do so under some circumstances. I shall await his attention to that and see what he's going to say about it in trying to fix up that predicament he got himself into.

Then, in the second place, I want to call your attention briefly to the chart that he has hanging on the wall. He hasn't said anything about this chart, but he has it hanging there where you can see it. Now, I want to help you look at it just a little bit at this particular time.

CHART No· 3—On Communion

(By Waters)

MATTHEW 26:27

"He Took The Cup, And Gave Thanks, And Gave It To Them, Saying, Drink Ye All Of It—(R.V.—A.S.V.—R.S.V., "A Cup")

MARK 14:23

"He Took The Cup, And When He Had Given Thanks, He Gave It To Them: And They All Drank Of It"—(R.V.,—A.S.V.—R.S.V., "A Cup")

"A drinking vessel, a cup" ....Robinson P-611
"A cup, a drinking vessel" ....Thayer P-533
"The vessel out of which one drinks"...................Thayer P-510
"The thing out of which one drinks" ....Thayer P-189

LUKE 22:17

"He Took The Cup, And Gave Thanks, And Said, Take This And Divide It Among Yourselves"   (R.V.—A.S.V.—R.S.V., "A Cup")
"A drinking vessel, a cup" ....Robinson P-611
"A cup, a drinking vessel" ....Thayer P.533

LUKE 22:20

"Likewise Also The Cup After Supper, Saying, This Cup Is The New Testament In My Blood, Which Is Shed For You"

1 COR. 11:25

"After The Same Manner Also He Took The Cup, When He Had Supped, Saying, This Cup Is The New Testament In My Blood"

"A drinking vessel, a cup" ....Robinson P-611
"A cup, a drinking vessel" .... Thayer P-533
"Cup containing wine"..Thayer P-15
By Metonymy of the container for the contained Thayer P-533
"Metonymy, a cup for the contents of a cup, cup-full, E. G.,
a cup of wine; So of the wine drank at the Eucharist" —)
.... Robinson P-611

1 Cor. 11:26

"As Often As Ye Eat This Break, And Drink This Cup, Ye Do Shew The Lord's Death Till He Come"

"Metonymy, a cup for the contents . . . E. G., A cup of wine".. Robinson P-611

1 Cor. 11:27

"Whosoever Shall Eat This Bread And Drink This Cup Of The Lord Unworthily, Shall Be Guilty of the Body and Blood of the Lord"

"What is in the cup"..Thayer P-510

"Metonymy, a cup for the contents . . .E. G., A cup of wine"—
....Robinson P-611

1 Cor. 11:28

"But Let a Man Examine Himself, And So Let Him Eat of That Bread, and Drink of That Cup"

"The thing out of which one drinks" ....Thayer P-189
"The vessel out of which one drinks" ....Thayer P-510

"A cup of wine; So of wine drank at the Eucharist"
.... Robinson P-611

1 COR. 10:21

"Ye Cannot Drink The Cup of the Lord, and the Cup of Devils"
What is in the cup"..Thayer P-510

"Metonymy, a cup for the contents, E. G., A cup of wine—
.... Robinson P-611

"The Cup Of Blessing Which We Bless, Is It Not The Communion of the Blood of Christ?"

1 COR. 10:16

"A cup of wine; So of the wine drank at the Eucharist —
.... Robinson P-611

(Bible Dictionary by "American Tract Society—based on Dictionary of Holy Bible by Edward Robinson"); "The master of the feast took a cup of unfermented wine, and having tasted it, passed it around .... 1 Cor. 10:16"

You'll note there a number of references from the New Testament containing the expression "the cup," and similar expressions. Under each Scripture, or each group of Scriptures, he has the definitions given, or the meaning of "the cup," in that particular passage or those particular passages.

In the first two, Matt. 26:27, Mark 14:23, he has the definition written there in the red leters that mean a "drinking vessel" or a "cup" in that sense. And he follows that plan on down through the chart.

He comes to Luke 22:17 which is the second group. "He took the cup, and gave thanks, and said, 'Take this, and divide it among yourselves.' " He defines the word there to mean a "drinking vessel, a cup." Or "a cup, a drinking vessel." So he makes the Scripture in that particular passage emphasize the drinking vessel, the container, and has the Lord saying, "Take this container and divide it among yourselves." Since there were at least twelve of them present, that means, of course, that they would have to break the container into twelve pieces in order that it might be divided among themselves, and each man would have to swallow his piece. But I'm wondering what would become of the contents when they broke it into twelve pieces according to his definition of this particular passage.

And we drop on down a little further on this chart and we find that he gives I Cor. 11:27 "Whosoever shall eat this bread, and drink this cup of the Lord, unworthily, shall be guilty of the body and blood of the Lord." He defines the word "cup" in that passage to mean "what is in it . . . in the cup." Or "metonymy, a cup for the contents," giving both Thayer and Robinson.

Then down just a little later, 1 Cor. 10:21: "Cannot drink the cup of the Lord, and the cup of devils." Here again, he defines cup to be "what is in the cup," or the contents, instead of the container. Now note that that's his application of I Cor. 11:27 and I Cor. 10:21. Here he says that "the cup of the Lord" referred to is the "contents of the cup" or "what is in the cup." Not the drinking vessel, now. In some of these others, we have the drinking vessel; but here he says it's "the contents, the thing that's in the cup." So "the cup of the Lord" is what's in the cup; it's the contents and not the vessel. I have a little tract here written by Brother Ervin Waters on the communion, and on page 30 of this tract, he says, "Some ask, 'What is the cup of the Lord' ?"

Now that's the same thing he's giving there (pointing to chart). What is "the cup of the Lord"? "Well, because in Metonymy we *name one thing* to suggest *something else,* 'the cup of the Lord' is the *name of a cup* and *not the name of the thing suggested."* Page 30. Now note that in the tract Brother Waters says, "The cup of the Lord is *the name of a cup* and *not the name of the thing suggested"*—that "the cup of the Lord" refers to the container and not the contents. But on this chart on the wall, he reverses himself and says that "the cup of the Lord" *is the contents* and *not the container.* I would like to see Brother Waters fix up this contradiction between himself.

Literal Cup Becomes Cup Of The Lord

He says, "Therefore there must be a literal cup named 'the cup of the Lord'. What cup? 'The cup of blessing which we bless, is it not the communion of the blood of Christ?' (I Cor. 10:16). *The literal cup,* containing the fruit of the vine, in an assembly of the church for the communion *becomes, after thanks, the cup of the Lord."* Page 30. Now notice that he says *the container* is "*the cup of the Lord."* On his chart he says "*the cup of the Lord"* is *the contents* and *not the container,* but in the tract, he says "*the cup of the Lord"* is *the container* and *not the contents.* And that this literal cup of the Lord, or this literal container, *becomes the cup of the Lord, after thanks.* I mentioned last night that's getting dangerously close to the Catholic doctrine of transubstantiation. "After thanks," the literal drinking vessel "becomes the cup of the Lord." But, of course, when the service is over, it changes back into something else. And next Sunday, they have to give thanks again and change it all over again into the cup of the Lord. If he uses the same drinking vessel next Sunday he used the Sunday before, and he changed it into the cup of the Lord by giving thanks for it last Sunday, why isn't it still the cup of the Lord next Sunday without giving thanks? And does it go back into something else when the services are over, and then he has to convert the thing into the cup of the Lord again when he comes to worship again the next Sunday? According to Brother Waters, that's what we have to have.

Law And Expediency

In the third place, I want to call your attention to an argument that I want to base upon what I shall call "law and expediency;" and I wish that I had an extra blackboard that I might put a diagram on it, but we haven't. So I shall try to get this over to you anyway so that you can understand. In the Bible there are a number of things that are commanded—some items given—and with those items there are certain incidentals or expedients that are involved or included in the command to do the particular thing mentioned.

On Baptism

For example, we have the item of baptism revealed to us in the New Testament. With respect to that, there is something definite commanded to be done. In Romans 6:3-4, we are told by the apostle Paul that it's by a burial and resurrection. So the thing commanded is what we call immersion, a burial and a resurrection, according to the language of the apostle Paul; but there are some incidentals, which surround that, that certainly can be done Scripturally, although they are not specifically mentioned in the Scriptures. And that, in the first place, would be *the manner* of that said immersion. That is, whether a man baptizes somebody left-handed or right-handed, face forward or backward, or whatever the case may be, in order to accomplish the burial, are mere incidents. But those things do not violate Scripture. They are according to Scriptural principles. And furthermore, *the place* in which the baptizing may be done. Some people have opposed the use of a baptistry upon the same ground that Brother Waters opposes these things that we are discussing tonight. But the command to baptize involves a place in which the baptizing must be done. There must be something to contain the water in which the immersion must be accomplished. Whether it's within the banks of a river, or whether it's within the walls of a baptistry, or wherever it may be, are but incidental matters, but those things fall within the realm of Scriptural principles. Baptizing involves the place in which baptizing must be done.

On Singing

And so with respect to the matter of singing. The Lord commanded us to sing. In Eph. 5:19 we are told what He commands. He comands that we sing "psalms and hymns and spiritual songs." So here's the thing commanded—the Lord commanded us *to sing* spiritual songs, psalms and hymns. But that involves a number of incidentals or expedients; as, what *voice parts* shall we sing? Shall we sing bass or tenor, soprano, alto, or what? Well, the Bible doesn't say. There's nothing said about singing soprano. There's nothing said about singing alto, bass or tenor. Somebody might jump up and say, "I demand the Scripture for it, and if you can't produce the Scripture where anybody ever sang soprano, where anybody ever sang bass or alto or tenor, in the New Testament, then I'm going to split the church over the proposition. And you must introduce the passage that says 'sing bass' or we'll not have it." Well, that would be parallel to the position followed by my opponent and the brethren who stand with him. Furthermore, there are the *song books*. And the Bible says nothing about them. But I believe we can use song books Scripturally, because when we sing, whether we use song books or not, we still sing.

On The Contribution

And the same thing with respect to the contribution. I Cor. 16:1-2. The Lord commanded us to "lay by in store" or to give as we have been prospered. There's the thing commanded, but there are incidentals surrounding that, as to whether the collection or the contribution should be placed in a hat, a box, or a basket. Although the Bible says nothing about a hat or a box or a basket in that connection, I'm certain that those things can be used Scripturally, because they violate no principle of Scripture.

On The Communion

And just so with the communion service. We have the Lord giving two commands regarding that: one is *to eat the bread* and the other *to drink the fruit of the vine.* That's the command, and there are a number of incidentals involved in it—*the place of assembly,* for example, and furthermore, *the table* upon which it is placed. I've been asking Brother Waters to tell me. Must there be a literal table with the same significance that he attaches to the literal drinking vessel? So far, he hasn't told me a thing about it.

And then the use of the plate for the bread, which is practiced by Brother Waters and his brethren. Nothing at all is found in God's Book about it. I believe that a plate can be used Scripturally, because if they use a plate in distributing the bread, they're not doing a thing but eating. If they eat the bread with the plate or without it, they're still eating. That's all there is to it. And these all stand upon the same conditions; they are parallel with one another.

But instrumental music, which he introduced, is not parallel with those ideas, for the simple fact that when the Lord said to immerse or bury, whether you bury or baptize a man in a baptistry, in a lake, in a pond, or wherever you may be, you are doing nothing but baptize. And whenever you lay by in store of your means, if you put it in a hat, a box, or a basket, you do nothing but give, and that's what the Lord says. And whenever you eat the bread, whether it's in the plate or out of the plate, you do nothing but eat. And whenever you drink, whether it's out of one container or a dozen containers, you're doing nothing but drink. Whenever you sing, whether you sing bass or tenor, whether you sing with a song book or without a song book, you're doing nothing but sing. When you play an instrument, you're *doing something else* that the Lord didn't say do. You're *adding a co-ordinate element of music,* and the cases are not parallel at all. That will stand untouched and unscathed by my opponent while this debate goes on.

One Bread And One Cup

And in the fourth place, I call your attention to an argument concerning the one bread and the one cup. In I Cor. 16:8 we read that the apostle wrote to the church at Corinth from the city of Ephesus. All right, in writing to the church at Corinth from the city of Ephesus, Paul said in I Cor. 10:17 that "we are all partakers of that one bread," and in I Cor. 10:16, "The bread which we break, is it not the communion of the body of Christ?" Now in both these passages, the word "bread" comes from that word that may be translated "loaf," which Brother Waters, in his little tract on the communion, insists must be in one piece—just as the fruit of the vine must be in one drinking vessel. That there must be just one loaf—it must not be broken into any other pieces besides that which each communicant breaks for himself. And so there must be one loaf, he says, but Paul writing to Corinth from Ephesus says that "we are all"—Christians in Ephesus and Christians in Corinth—"we are all partakers of that one bread, of that one loaf." I want to know if the church in Corinth, the brethren over in Corinth, ate from the same piece of bread that the brethren in Ephesus did. And if they did, I want to know how they got it over there after Ephesus had finished with it on Sunday morning or whatever the hour may have been. How did they get it to Corinth in time for them to eat out of the same loaf? And then in the same connection (I Cor. 10:16), Paul said,

"The cup of blessing which we bless, is it not the communion of the blood of Christ?" "The cup which *we* bless." We who? "We," in Corinth, and "we,' in Ephesus, including those to whom he was writing and including those with him at Ephesus. Christians in Corinth and Christians in Ephesus were blessing "the cup.' And if that means just one drinking vessel, then the same drinking vessel used at Ephesus had to be used at Corinth. When they got through with it at Ephesus, they had to get it to Corinth in some way in order for them to have it in time to observe the Lord's Supper on that particular day. For there must be *one drinking vessel.* That's the condition into which my opponent's position forces him with respect to this matter. But upon these questions which I gave him, he admitted that wasn't true, for he said, when I asked him this question concerning these matters, that there were at least two involved. But Paul, in I Cor. 10:16, said the Christians both in Ephesus and Corinth blesed "the cup." Would not the expression "the cup" have to refer to at least two drinking vessels, one at Ephesus and one at Corinth? And he said there would be one cup in each assembly. So Brother Waters has admitted in answering that question that "the cup" sometimes means more than one cup, that it sometimes means more than one drinking vessel. For here, he says, the expression means one in Ephesus and one at Corinth; it can mean a plurality. All that he has said about a plurality falls flat.

Metonymy—The Container For The Contents

And then passing on from that, I notice again, in the fifth place, some figurative language—the figure of speech called Metonymy that we spoke about last night, in which the container is mentioned to refer to the contents. And we gave some illustrations of that, such as the bottle and the jug, you remember. And I'm still asking Brother Waters to tell us, when we say that a man loves his jug, just which jug it is. He hasn't told us yet. He said you can't refer to one jug or one container and mean the contents of more than one. If you refer to one container, it must be the contents of one container. It can't be more than that. Then when we say the man loves his jug, which jug is it? And when the woman says, "I raised all my babies on the bottle," and she has about a half dozen of them, ranging in age from 10 years to 30 perhaps, I want to know if the reference is made to the contents of more than one container. He hasn't told us a word about that yet. I'm still waiting for him to tell us something about it.

And, incidentally, we drank water out of that bottle last night. He gave me a drink, you know, out of the cup. Handed it over to me and I drank. And so I came back and asked Brother Waters, "Did we both drink from that bottle?" Until now, he's not told us a word about it. He's insisting that to drink from the cup, we both must sip from it. We both must put our lips to the cup to drink from it. I want to know: Did we drink from that bottle last night? As yet, he hasn't told me. So we shall expect him to answer tonight.

Well, in fact that figure of speech, Metonymy, in which we refer to the contents by naming the container, we have some statements in the Book of God along that line. In I Cor. 10:16, Paul said, "The cup of blessing which we bless, is it not the communion of the blood of Christ?" "The cup of blessing which we bless, is it not the communion of the blood of Christ?" He puts it down here (pointing to chart), "A drinking vessel." And he makes the cup of blessing a drinking vessel, but the cup of the Lord the contents of it, in the other passage—and a drinking vessel in his tract. So I don't know which he wants. We'll wait and see just which one he prefers in the matter. But Paul said, "The cup of blessing which we bless, is it not the communion of the blood of Christ?" Now "the cup" referred to here is *the communion of the blood.* Brother Waters said last night the drinking vessel did not picture the blood—it pictured the New Testament. All right then, the word "cup" in this case is used by the figure of speech Metonymy. We refer to the contents and not the drinking vessel, and it is called "the cup." And he says that could be at least two, one at Corinth and one at Ephesus.

"The Cup" May Mean Two Cups

All right, if "the cup" can be in two drinking vessels, one at Ephesus and one at Corinth, why can't it be in two hundred and still be "the cup?" I demand that he answer tonight.

Drinking The Cup

And furthermore, in I Cor. 10:21, Paul said "Ye cannot drink the cup of the Lord and the cup of Devils." In I Cor. 11:26, "As oft as ye drink this cup." And I Cor. 11:27, "Whosoever shall drink this cup of the Lord unworthily." So we find them *drinking* "the cup." Well, he makes one of those literal vessels here. The *cup of the Lord,* he says, is *the literal vessel,* in his tract here—that it refers to the literal container. The cup of the Lord is the literal container. And Paul says, "We drink the cup of the Lord." Therefore, we swallow the container. I want to know, when the first man swallows it, how the rest of them are going to get it. I'm still demanding that he answer.

Plurality By Species

Then I pass on to the sixth argument based upon the idea of species. He made the statement last night, in reference to the jug, that the word "jug," the singular number, sometimes means plurality by species. I want you to remember that. That's almost the exact words he used. So "jug," singular number, sometimes means plurality by species. That is, you say "the jug," you mean any jug, by way of species. All right, now, just grant him that the word "cup" is literal in all these passages. It's not. But just grant for the sake of argument that it is and see the consequences of it. So we have "individual" and "species." Now then, we say, "The man picked up the ant." Well, of course, that's an individual. It means one ant. When Solomon said, "Go to the ant, thou sluggard' (Proverbs 6:6), he used the same expression, "the ant," but he used species in order to refer to a plurality. Just any ant.

And then again, in the second place, "The man cut down the vine." That would be one vine—just one. But in species, we might speak of "the fruit of the vine." Now, when the Lord said "the fruit of the vine," He didn't mean that the fruit must come from any particular vine, that it just had to be one vine—it couldn't be any other vine. But he used it by way of species to mean the fruit of any vine.

Now if the word "cup" is used literally in all of these passages (except the few exceptions he gives—there are very few of them that he does give), the same thing is true regarding his statement concerning species. We might say that the man "broke the cup." Well, that's the cup, you know, that we illustrated last night, with which we were serving the congregation. He gets it about half way around, and he drops it and spills it. All the contents are poured out. He "broke the cup." Well, that means the drinking vessel—there's just one. Brother Waters goes and gets another, of course, and has the second cup for the same assembly and serves them out of the second cup. Some of them drink twice, once from the first and once from the second. So they drink twice, and each communicant in that case uses two cups. In our service no communicant ever uses more than one; but in his, why, he can use two cups and still be Scriptural. All right, he "broke the cup." That's one cup. That's the individual idea of it. Now, from the standpoint of species, Paul says, "The cup which we bless." Waters makes that mean a *literal drinking vessel* here in his tract, though he changes it on his chart. But he makes it mean a literal drinking vessel here. The container is "the cup of blessing which we bless." Well then, if that's so, you have species, one at Corinth and one at Ephesus. It can't be one drinking vessel there. It's used in the sense of species, if it means a literal cup, and therefore denotes *plurality*. And so his own argument, given last night, in the statement he made regarding the fact "the jug", singular, may sometimes mean plurality by way of species, certainly holds good in this tonight and overthrows the contention that Brother Waters is making regarding these matters.

Some Unities

Then, in the seventh place, I want to call your attention to some unities. In the first place, I note the fact that there is one baptism (Eph. 4:5). The apostle said, "There is one Lord, one faith and one baptism." Now there's the unity taught in the book of God; there's one baptism. I showed you awhile ago that there are many incidentals that might surround it; the place where the baptizing might occur, the container in which the liquid is held, and various other things may be involved, and they may be done Scripturally, although the Bible doesn't specifically mention them. But we have *one baptism*. And I want to know, does that mean that every person in the same community has to be immersed in the same pond? Or in the same body of water, in the same container? If it's a baptistry, if it's a pond, if it's a bathing pool, or whatever it may be, does that mean that each person in that community must be baptized in that particular body of water— in that particular pond, in that particular baptistry, in order to have the one baptism? There's just one. Must it all be, and must the water all be, confined to one container in order for there to be one baptism?

Well, in the second place, there is one New Testament. In Matt. 26:28, Jesus, when he instituted the supper, regarding the fruit of the vine, the cup which He gave them, said that "this is the blood of the New Testament"—"this is My blood of the New

Testament which is shed for many for the remission of sins."
Now note the fact that he says, "This is the blood of the New
Testament." "My blood of the New Testament." That's one. All
right, then in I Cor. 11:25 (Brother Waters introduced it last
night along with the statement also in Luke, the 22nd chapter),
that "the cup is the New Testament in My blood which is shed
for you." All right, here we have "the cup is the New
Testament in My blood." Here we have *the New Testament* mentioned in all three of the passages. There is *one
New Testament*—"the New Testament." Now, I want to know,
does that mean that in the assembly of the saints there can be
only one copy of the New Testament? If you have more than one
copy of the New Testament, then you're unscriptural. You are
going to hell because the Bible says "the New Testament," and
that means only one. "The New Testament" means one. Not a
plurality. And, therefore, if Brother Waters uses in the assembly
of the saints where he labors more than one copy of the New
Testament, then he stands condemned, because he has a plurality
where the Bible says one. Oh, he may say (I mentioned that last
night, but he hasn't said yet—perhaps he will tonight), that each
New Testament is a reproduction of the other—that each volume
is a reproduction of the other. So you just have one. Each cup is
a reproduction of the other. So that wouldn't help any, because
each drinking vesel is a reproduction of the other drinking vessel.
And if there is a difference in the shape and size of the cups,
does that mean that it's unscriptural? Then, you'd have to have
all your New Testament volumes the same shape and size. If
you had another edition that is not the same shape and size, then
you'd have the same problem facing you regarding that.

Paul said, "The cup of blessing which we bless, is it not the
communion of the blood of Christ? Now, we have *one baptism*.
We have *one New Testament*. We have "the New Testament."
We have *"the cup."* I'm insisting that one baptism is one baptism
whether it's performed in one container or a hundred different
containers. I'm insisting that one New Testament is still one,
whether it's in one volume or in a thousand volumes—whether
the assembly has one volume or two thousand in its meeting place.
I'm insisting that "the cup" is one cup, whether it's in one container or in a hundred containers, or a thousand. For the simple
fact that Paul says, "The cup of blessing which we bless, is it
not the communion of the blood of Christ? Therefore, Paul said

the cup is the blood. The cup is the communion of the blood of Christ, not the New Testament. The cup is the blood. The thing referred to here called "the cup" is the blood, and the fruit of the vine pictures the blood. Brother Waters has agreed.

And I thank you, Ladies and Gentlemen.

Second Session

Waters' First Negative

Cups Question

Brethren Moderators, Brother Porter, Brethren and Friends:

I count myself happy to stand before you tonight in denial of the proposition affirmed by Brother Porter, which I disbelieve with all my heart. That proposition reads as follows: "In an assembly of the Church of Christ for the communion, it is Scriptural to use individual cups (drinking vessels) in the distribution of the fruit of the vine."

Where Is His Proof?

To the penetrating analysis and the scrutinizing perusal of the unbiased and unprejudiced student, what evidence would this speech yield as far as the Bible is concerned? His speech will be found to be' as fruitless and as barren as a desert waste. Has he given us one passage of Scripture which, by example, teaches the use of individual cups? Has he given us the Scripture which states that the Lord used them at the' institution of the communion? Has he provided the Scripture which states, as a result of apostolic record, that any congregation or assembly of disciples ever so used individual cups? Has he produced in the Word of God any command which essentially involves the use of individual cups? He has not. And he has not even brought in individual cups under what might be called necessary inference. They are not necessarily inferred. Has he given us in the word of God a statement, Biblical and apostolic, inspired and divine, which necessarily connotes the idea of individual cups? He has not. *And so he has failed,* either by statement, necessary inference, command or example, to produce any passage of Scripture whatsoever that necessarily conveys the idea of the use of a plurality of cups, or individual cups as his proposition calls for.

Why would a man, as intelligent and as able as Brother

Porter, stand before an audience for thirty minutes in defense of a proposition, which he says is a Scriptural proposition setting forth Scriptural practices, and during those thirty minutes fail to produce one command that mentions individual cups, one example that mentions individual cups, one statement that mentions individual cups, and one necessary inference, or one way by which we may necessarily infer from any statement or implication in the word of God, that individual cups may be used? He just hasn't found it. Brother Porter, why have you stood before us for thirty minutes with a speech which has been so unfruitful and infertile insofar as the production of actual proof is concerned? Why have you thus dealt with us, Brother Porter? *We have a right to expect better of you.* We have a right to expect a man, who so affirms a proposition and a practice to be Scriptural, to produce for us the law, the testimony, the principle, the statement, the command, the example, the necessary inference, which involves and points out to us that practice. Why has he not done it? ....echo answers, "Why??" But we have some questions for Brother Porter tonight.

Questions For Porter

1st. In Christ's statement, "This cup is the New Testament" (Luke 22:20; I Cor. 11:25), does the word "cup" refer to the literal cup or to the fruit of the vine?

2nd. If while passing the individual communion set to the assembly, the set is dropped and broken and the contents spilled, and another communion set is supplied, would you give thanks for the second set before passing to the remainder of the assembly, or pass it to them without giving thanks? He was dealing with accidental eventualities, you know, in his questions last evening.

3rd. While attempting to baptize a candidate if, because of your slipping or his struggles, you only half immerse him, would you now attempt again, and completely immerse him? Or would you only immerse the half of him that was not immersed the first time? (Audience laughs) *This is going to be interesting.*

4th. Aside from other considerations, may an assembly of the church of Christ use one cup (drinking vessel) in the distribution of the fruit of the vine, and be Scriptural in such practice?

5th. Is there a Scripture in the New Testament mentioning

individual cups in the communion? *It will just take one to convert us.* You couldn't expect me to receive or accept any less than that. I'm not being too hard on the man, am I? When I just simply call for one? I don't need two or a dozen. But I do need one because, when I stand before God in the day of judgment, I can't stand on any less than one.

6th. In the metonymy of the "container for the contained" is there an actual container named which sustains a relationship to the thing suggested?

Metonymy

Remember now, in dealing with the figure of speech "Metonymy," we are not dealing with jangling nonsense. When you deal with that figure of speech you actually name a vessel, an actual literal vessel, and, by naming that actual literal vessel, you suggest its actual literal contents.

I have before me "Composition and Rhetoric" by Williams, and we have on Page 21 this statement: "In metonymy, an object is suggested by mentioning some prominent property, quality, or characteristic." Again now, in considering Metonymy and Metaphor, "Each of these figures presents an object to the mind by *naming something else.*" Is the "cup of the Lord" the name of the object presented to the mind, the fruit of the vine, or the *name of something else?* You say it's Metonymy. "Composition and Rhetoric" says that this figure presents an object to the mind by naming *"something else."* The "cup of the Lord" never was *the name of a liquid,* and never will be, according to "Composition and Rhetoric." Metaphor *implies* a comparison between what is said and what is meant, just an implied comparison. But Metonymy does not; it's not an implied comparison. "In *metonymy* one mentions *something* that is *so related* as readily to *suggest* the idea intended." In other words, there is a *relationship* existing between the thing you *name* and the thing you *suggest.* Now then, according to that definition of Metonymy, in 1. Cor 11:27., where the "cup of the Lord" is used in the expression, "Whosoever shall drink this cup of the Lord," the "cup of the Lord" is *not* the name of the *thing suggested; it is the name of something else.* The "something else" is named, however, to suggest the other, but does the thing named exist? And according to "Composition and Rhetoric," is there a *relationship* existing between that thing *named* and that thing *suggested?* Why according to the grammar there is a *relation*. Listen! "Kinds of Metonymy," page 220, "Composition and Rhetoric," by Williams: "Owing to varied *relations* by which things may be connected, there are many kinds of this figure. The most common relations that give rise to Metonymy are—. No. 3, *"Container and the thing contained."* Not an imaginary container and the thing *not* contained in it. But the "container and the thing contained." I have a few more remarks that I want to make with reference to Metonymy.

"Metonymy is a figure of speech in which an object is presented to the mind, *not by naming it,* but by *naming something else* that readily suggests it" (Williams' "Composition and Rhetoric," page 220). In giving the "Kinds of Metonymy," he says: No. 3. "The container and the thing contained.' He gives as an example, "The kettle boils (meaning, of course, the liquid in the kettle).

Tanner, in his "Composition and Rhetoric," page 324, says, "Metonymy is a figure of speech in which the *name of one object* is used for that of *another* which it clearly suggests." He gives the same example, "The kettle boils (that is, the water in the kettle boils.)"

J. C. Nesfield, in his "Idiom, Grammar, And Synthesis," page 396, gives under Metonymy: "(c) *The container for the thing contained: He drank the cup—the contents of the cup."* There was an actual cup there and he drank the cup; and when he did that, he drank its contents. He didn't swallow the vessel when he did it either. But he "drank the cup" by drinking the "contents of the cup." Now the audience never did "drink the cup" by drinking the "contents of a plurality of cups." They never did do it. If we intended to convey the idea of the contents of a *plurality of cups,* metonymically, we would have to say, *"The audience drank the cups."* You would have to say *"cups"* if you meant to metonymically refer to the *contents of cups.*

From the above definitions of Metonymy we learn several facts about this figure of speech:

1. The object named is *not the thing suggested.*
2. There is a *real object,* not an imaginary one, named.
3. Both the *thing named* and the *thing suggested* must exist.
4. In the Metonymy of the "container for the contained," the *container named must contain the thing suggested.*

5. One can only suggest the contents of *as many cups* as he names.

These facts are evident even to the superficial student, so do not let the big word "Metonymy" frighten you. It simply means that two things are suggested to the mind by the mention of one of them which readily suggests the other. Thus the cup and its contents are suggested to the mind by the mention of the cup which readily suggests its contents.

Paul used this figure of speech, "For as often as ye eat this bread, and drink this cup, ye do show the Lord's death till he come. Wherefore whosoever shall eat this bread, and drink this cup of the Lord, unworthily, shall be guilty of the body and blood of the Lord." (1 Cor. 11:26,27).

From what we have learned of Metonymy we must grammatically conclude from this Scripture:

(1) Paul named "this cup," or "this cup of the Lord," to suggest its contents, the fruit of the vine.

(2) Since the *object named* is not the *thing suggested,* "this cup" is *not* the fruit of the vine.

(3) There is a *real cup named.*

(4) Both the cup, which is named, and the contents, which are suggested, must exist.

(5) The cup, which is named, *must contain the thing which is suggested,* the fruit of the vine.

(6) Since one cup was named, the *contents of only one* are suggested.

This is the inescapable conclusion. One may appeal to both prejudice and ignorance by ignoring the above rules of language and say the cup does not have to exist, but when he stands before the eternal Judge and is shorn of his sophistry, what then?

Some ask, "What is the cup of the Lord"? Because in Metonymy, we *name one thing* to suggest *something else,* "the cup of the Lord" is the *name of a cup* and *not* the name of the thing suggested. Therefore, *there must be a literal cup named "the cup of the Lord"* in an assembly of disciples for the communion. What cup? "The cup of blessing which we bless, is it not the communion of the blood of Christ?" (1 Cor. 10:16). The word "communion" means "joint-participation". You brethren try to have the joint-participation without the joint. The literal cup, containing the fruit of the vine, in an assembly of the church for the communion becomes, after thanks, "the cup of the Lord". It is not an empty cup because it contains the fruit of the vine, the blood of Christ. But one questions with a triumphant air, "then how will you drink the cup of the Lord? You cannot swallow the literal cup." To this I reply that we never have taught anyone to swallow the literal cup. Here is where the understanding and the interpretation of language comes in. To ignore language is to ignore the Truth because the Truth was couched by the Holy Spirit in language. "This cup of the Lord" is mentioned by Paul to suggest its contents. That is the use of a common figure of speech. How do we drink the cup of the Lord? By drinking "what is in the cup" (Thayer, lexicon, Page 510). He referred to that on the chart. Thayer so defines it, *"by drinking what is in the cup,"* not what *is in the cups*. Does this get away from a literal cup? Of course not. The cup of the Lord contains the blood of Christ. Will the "cups" fraternity produce the evidence that one can refer to the fruit of the vine in a plurality of cups in an assembly by saying "the cup?" The Holy Spirit did not use jangling nonsense in the Bible.

CHART No. 3—On Communion

(By Waters)

MATTHEW 26:27

"He Took The Cup, And Gave Thanks, And Gave It To Them, Saying, Drink Ye All Of It—(R.V.—A.S.V.—R.S.V., "A Cup")

MARK 14:23

"He Took The Cup, And When He Had Given Thanks, He Gave It To Them: And They All Drank Of It"—(R.V.—A.S.V.—R.S.V., "A Cup")

"A drinking vessel, a cup"..................................Robinson P-611
"A cup, a drinking vessel"....................................Thayer P-533
"The vessel out of which one drinks"...................Thayer P-510
"The thing out of which one drinks"...................Thayer P-189

LUKE 22:17

"He Took The Cup, And Gave Thanks, And Said, Take This And Divide It Among Yourselves"   (R..—A.S.V.—R.S.V., "A Cup")
"A drinking vessel, a cup"..............................Robinson P-611
"A cup, a drinking vessel"....................................Thayer P-533

LUKE 22:20

"Likewise Also The Cup After Supper, Saying, This Cup Is The New Testament In My Blood, Which Is Shed For You"

1 COR. 11:25

"After The Same Manner Also He Took The Cup, When He Had Supped, Saying, This Cup Is The New Testament In My Blood"

"A drinking vessel, a cup"..................................Robinson P-611
"A cup, a drinking vessel"....................................Thayer P-533
"Cup containing wine"..Thayer P-15
By Metonymy of the container for the contained Thayer P-533
"Metonymy, a cup for the contents of a cup, cup-full, E. G., a cup of wine; So of the wine drank at the Eucharist"—
.... Robinson P-611

1 Cor. 11:26

"As Often As Ye Eat This Break, And Drink This Cup, Ye Do Shew The Lord's Death Till He Come"

> *"Metonymy, a cup for the contents . . . E. G., A cup of wine"*... Robinson P-611

1 Cor. 11:27

"Whosoever Shall Eat This Bread And Drink This Cup Of The Lord Unworthily, Shall Be Guilty of the Body and Blood of the Lord"

> *"What is in the cup"*..Thayer P-510
> *"Metonymy, a cup for the contents . . .E. G., A cup of wine"*—
> ....Robinson P-611

1 Cor. 11:28

"But Let a Man Examine Himself, And So Let Him Eat of That Bread, and Drink of That Cup"

> *"The thing out of which one drinks"* ....Thayer P-189
> *"The vessel out of which one drinks"* ....Thayer P-510

> *"A cup of wine; So of wine drank at the Eucharist"*
> .... Robinson P-611

1 COR. 10:21

"Ye Cannot Drink The Cup of the Lord, and the Cup of Devils"
> *What is in the cup"*..Thayer P-510

> *"Metonymy, a cup for the contents, E. G., A cup of wine*—
> .... Robinson P-611

"The Cup Of Blessing Which We Bless, Is It Not The Communion of the Blood of Christ?"

1 COR. 10:16

> *"A cup of wine; So of the wine drank at the Eucharist* —
> .... Robinson P-611

(Bible Dictionary by "American Tract Society—based on Dictionary of Holy Bible by Edward Robinson"); "The master of the feast took a cup of unfermented wine, and having tasted it, passed it around .... 1 Cor. 10:16"

I want you to notice the chart on the board, which has been there last night and tonight. I have on that chart the Scriptures in which the word "cup" is used. And I have under them the definition and use of the word as used in those Scriptures, by Thayer and Robinson in their excellent lexicons. *Those definitions by these Greek scholars are absolutely in harmony with the position which I hold with reference to this subject.* But they are not in harmony with the position held by my respondent. They are entirely out of harmony with his position; he is entirely out of harmony with the meaning of the language involved in every verse.

G. C. Brewer Introduced Them

From whence came individual cups? My brother has not produced the Scripture which mentions them. From whence came they? Let's see where they came from in the church of Christ. On page twelve of the Preface to "Forty Years on the Firing Line" by G. C. Brewer, one of Porter's brethren, G. C. Brewer said, "I think I was the first preacher to advocate the use of the individual communion cup and the first church in the State of Tennessee that adopted it was the church for which I was preaching, the Central Church of Christ at Chattanooga, Tennessee, then meeting in the Masonic Temple. My next work was with the church at Columbia, Tennessee, and, after a long struggle, I got the individual communion service into that congregation . About this time, Bro. G. Dallas Smith began to advocate the individual communion service and he introduced it at Fayetteville, Tennessee; then later at Murfreesboro. Of course, I was fought both privately and publicly and several brethren took me to task in the religious papers and called me digressive. Bro. Smith came to my rescue and, in the year 1915, Bro. David Lipscomb wrote a short paragraph (in his old age just before his death, *Waters*) in the Gospel advocate saying that he had changed his view in reference to the communion cup and that he did not believe it was any digression or in any way a corruption of the service to use as many cups as might be demanded by the occasion. This brought that controversy to an end and, from then on, the churches began using the individual communion cup everywhere." You can appeal to no higher authority for the use of individual cups, my brother, than G. C. Brewer in the church of Christ.

I want you to remember that last evening he spent at least thirty minutes out of his sixty minutes talking about a plate and such irrelevant matters. He didn't have quite as much to say about the plate tonight as he did last night. I guess he got tired talking about it, but he did have a lot to say about a lot of other incidentals which he considered to be expedient. Do you know where Brother Porter makes his mistake? It's that he fails to differentiate between an expedient—an incidental—and a precedent. He fails to differentiate between that which is incidental and that which is a precedent. And that's why he's confused, no doubt, on the cups question.

Well, let's see about this. He has asked me to show the difference in the use of a plate and the use of cups. Last evening, you will remember, that I put all these Scriptures in this circle with "cup" over it.

CHART No. 2—On Communion

ONE CUP

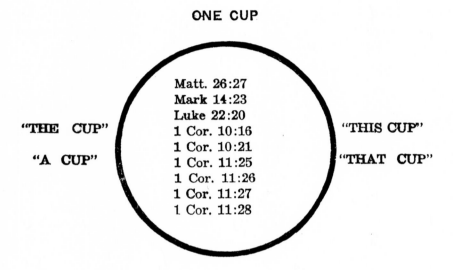

"THE CUP"

"A CUP"

Matt. 26:27
Mark 14:23
Luke 22:20
1 Cor. 10:16
1 Cor. 10:21
1 Cor. 11:25
1 Cor. 11:26
1 Cor. 11:27
1 Cor. 11:28

"THIS CUP"

"THAT CUP"

INDIVIDUAL CUPS

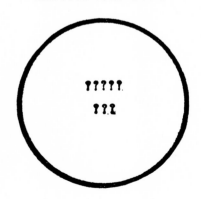

And I, in this circle over which I placed "cups," put question marks. I asked him to put the Scripture in that circle which authorized individual cups and which taught individual cups. Has he put one in there yet? Has he found a Scripture which mentions individual cups and teaches individual cups? I have the ones in this circle which teach the use of one cup. What did he do? He just came back and said, "Well, you put one in there that mentions the plate." As if we were debating about the plate last night and tonight. And over here, where I had Scriptures mentioning the cup, what did he do? He just said, "no plate." Why, brother, I could add maybe a thousand things that I didn't have Scriptural mention of over there in that circle. But we are dealing with the cups question.

(Porter speaks from seat: "Would they be scriptural?"

Waters: They might be, some of them. But what does he do? Why, he says, "What about the plate? What about the song books? What about the baptistry? What about the chairs? What about the bass? What about the alto? What about this, and what about that?" I never heard a digressive yet but what would do that.

Difference Between A Plate And Individual Cups

But now I'm going to show you that I'm willing to come right up and meet you on it. As pertains to the bread, let's see. "And Jesus took bread,—— and gave it to the disciples, and said, Take, eat" (Matt. 26:26).

Chart on Parallels

1. Bread—Eat	(Plate does not violate
	(Beef steak does violate
2. Cup—Drink of it	("Cups" violate "cup"
3. Sing—Make melody	(Song books do not violate
in heart	(Instrumental music does violate

The plate, the use of a plate, does not in any way involve a violation of "bread" or the "eating of bread". Neither the thing nor the thing commanded to be done with it are violated. A beefsteak would involve a violation. You could "eat" it, but it wouldn't be "bread".

Notice the difference. "He took a cup,—and gave it to them, saying, Drink all of you of it" (Matt. 26:27). Cups violate *"a cup."* When a brother takes the individual cups, he violates *"a cup.* Can you see the difference, Brother Porter? Cups violate, set aside and substitute for *"a cup."* Furthermore, the audience cannot obey the command *"drink of it"* when they *"drink of them."* So with individual cups they not only violate "a cup" but force a violation of the command involved likewise. Can you now see the difference in a precedent and an incident?

Instrumental Music on Par With Individual Cups

He said that instrumental music was not on par with individual cups. Let's see. He said that the Bible said "sing" and when you play, you are not singing. Now, just a moment, let's get all of that. It says "sing and make melody" (Eph. 5:19). "Making melody in your heart to the Lord." Get this. "Making melody in your heart." Now there are two ways of making melody. He talks about coordinate elements. That's right; there are two ways of "making melody". You can make melody on the strings of a musical instrument, or you can make melody in your heart. Then, as far as "making melody" is concerned, instrumental music doesn't violate that. You could make melody on the strings of an instrument, but the Bible doesn't stop there. It says "in your heart." It names the instrument, and when you use a mechanical instrument of music, you violate the command, "Making melody in your heart." Individual cups violate "a cup" and when you drink of individual cups, that violates the command, "drink all of you of it," just as much so as instrumental music involves a violation of "making melody in your heart."

He says that instrumental music is a coordinate element, but cups aren't. Let us see. When it comes to drinking the fruit of the vine in the communion service, there are two ways that you can do it: *either the audience can drink the fruit of the vine out of one cup or they can drink the fruit of the vine out of a plurality of cups.* And you tell me they are not coordinate elements, brother? Here are two ways of doing a thing and there are two ways of "making melody." Making melody on the strings of an instrument of music, being a coordinate element, is another way of making melody, different from making melody in your heart. Isn't it?

What about drinking from cups? Isn't that another way? An

unscriptural way of doing it? Yes, I can meet you on that ground, my brother. But I just said, Why not debate the issue? If you brethren want to hear about song books, plates, chairs, church houses, and all of those things; if you want to hear the dodges that every digressive has made, go to Cedar Rapids with me to hear G. K. Wallace debate Burton Barber beginning next Monday night,—if you want to hear about those things. The instrumental music man will make the same arguments in favor of instrumental music that my Brother Porter attempts to make in favor of individual cups. If you don't believe it, I challenge you to go up there; I invite you to go because I would like for you to get a little bit sicker of that plate deal. (Audience laughs) And see how you like it. Don't you forget that Burton Barber will use those things on you brethren.

Foy E. Wallace Says "It is Weak"

Brother Foy Wallace, in the September issue of "The Torch," says, "It is palpably weak to offer to affirm that something is as Scriptural as something else." What have you done? Why, instead of getting up here like a man and just debating the cups, and staying with that, you are affirming that cups are "as Scriptural as something else." And you spend your speeches now trying to prove that cups are "as Scriptural" as a plate, or "as Scriptural" as song books, or "as Scriptural" as a baptistry, "or as Scriptural as something else." "It is palpably weak,' your old buddy says, to do that. (Reads from "The Torch" again) Again he said, "Nothing is Scriptural unless it is. And there is no 'as' about it. That is mighty poor logic, and men who are always doing it are afraid of their ground. It is time to stop talking about who did this, or said that, and start giving Scriptural precedents for the practices that are being promoted. It is time to stop careering around all over creation and cite the Scriptures to prove practices."

Debate The Issue

Brother Porter said, "Brother Waters, you mentioned instrumental music and the Missionary Society at Lawrenceburg, Tennessee, when we were debating the class question."

(Porter: "May I see that, Brother Waters?" Referring to "The Torch")

You may. Look at it good. (Audience laughs) You said, "You mentioned the Missionary Society at Lawrenceburg when we debated the class question in our former discussion." Brother Porter, if I did, it was after you had already brought in all these extraneous matters from the beginning of the debate, from the very first night, and my notes show it. And I'll tell you what,—it's too late now in this discussion, Brother Porter, I'll tell you what I'm willing to do. Insofar as my affirmative is concerned, I'm willing, on the class question, to not affirm that the classes or the Sunday School are as "unscriptural as anything else." I'll not have a thing to say about anything else. I will just deal with the issue. I never have spent most of my time in a debate dealing with things "as unscriptural" or "as scriptural" as something else. *Deal with the issue.*

Remember now, I have proved time after time that the instrumental music brethren do just precisely what I said they did. I read now from Julian O. Hunt in the Hunt-Inman Debate, Page 45, where he says, "I contend that the same authority that we have or my respondent has for using a song book, tuning fork, radio, church house, collection basket, chart, communion set, blackboard, note book, reference book, lights, seats, earphones, shoes, crutches, canes, false teeth, automobiles, trains, ships, airplanes, and all aids that we use in carrying out the commandments of God we have for the instrument." You brethren say that's not the way for them to debate; but when you do that, that's the way to debate. Is it, Brother Porter? He says if we have authority for one, we have authority for all. They all stand or fall together.

Old Debating Maneuver

It is an old debating maneuver, in affirming that something is scriptural, to try to associate the thing in question in that debate with something, or some things, that most people consider to be scriptural, and by association to try to prejudice. Or in affirming something is unscriptural, to try to associate that thing, which the debater considers to be unscriptural, with some things that the audience considers to be unscriptural, and by that association the minds of the people will be prejudiced. That is just exactly what my brother has tried to do during this discussion.

Did Christ Use One Cup?

But remember, Brother Porter said, "We will have no dispute about whether the word 'cup' was used literally in Matt. 26:27." He said, "We will have no dispute about that." We just will not call that in question at all. We will have no dispute about that at all.

And in my remaining few seconds, I would like to quote the answers of one of Porter's brethren, who is present, to two questions. Brother Monroe E. Hawley, in the September, 1950, issue of the "Gospel Broadcast,"

> (1) Did Christ use a vessel containing the fruit of the vine in instituting the Lord's Supper called a cup? Did he actually use a cup? Answer: "Yes."
>
> (2) Did He use more than one afterwards? Answer: *"We are not told that He did."*

I wonder if you agree, Brother Porter.

We Want The Truth

In the thirty minutes speech of my respondent, remember this, He did not produce the Bible command that mentions "individual cups". He did not produce the Bible example that mentions "individual cups". And he did not produce the Bible statement that mentions "individual cups". And he has not produced the implication in the word of God from which we may necessarily infer the use of individual cups. Yet he's affirming that they are Scriptural. We want him to get up here and produce the law and the testimony which so teaches. He cannot expect us to have enough confidence in him to accept his mere ipse dixit, to believe that merely because *he said it. We want the truth.* We want what the Bible says about it and not what Brother Porter may think about it.

And I thank you.

SECOND SESSION

Porter's Second Affirmative

CUP QUESTION

Brethren Moderators, Brother Waters, Ladies and Gentlemen:

I am delighted to pay my attention to the speech, to which you have just listened, by my worthy opponent, in his efforts to set aside the arguments that I made in the opening speech of this service. However, you will note that he said very little about any argument that I made. Although I enumerated them from one to seven, he paid very little attention to any of them and talked about everything else that he could think of and read from various books and things of that kind, in an effort to make you forget what I had said about it. But I don't think you are that easy to forget, and I am going to emphasize some of them again so I am sure you will not, and show you the utter failure that Brother Waters made in replying to the speech that I made. But first, I want to get to his questions. He said this is going to be rich, and it is.

Brother Waters' Questions

"1st. In Christ's statement, "This cup is the New Testament" (Luke 22:20; I Cor. 11:25), does the word 'cup' refer to the literal cup or to the fruit of the vine?" The container is named to refer to the fruit of the vine, Brother Waters.

"2nd. If while passing the individual communion set to the assembly the set is dropped and broken and the contents spilled, and another communion set is supplied, would you give thanks for this second set before passing it to the remainder of the assembly, or pass it to them without giving thanks?" Well, I think I would give thanks for it, if no thanks had been offered for it. They had no part in that for which thanks had been given.

"3rd. While attempting to baptize a candidate, if because of your slipping or his struggles, you only half immerse him, would you now attempt again and completely immerse him or would you only immerse the half of him unimmersed the first time?" I would immerse the whole fellow, Brother Waters. If I failed the first time, I would try it the second time; and if I failed then, I would try it over until I got him immersed. But Brother Waters, if I had immersed the fellow right in front of him, I would not grab him and put him under, too. (Audience laughs) And yet that's the thing you do with respect to the cup. You have half the congregation already finished drinking the fruit of the vine, and then you make them drink it again. That *is* rich, Ervin. It surely is, old boy. (Porter laughs and pats Waters on the leg). I would not immerse any man that I had already immersed, because I had failed on this man. But he makes the person who had already drunk the fruit of the vine drink it again because some of them hadn't had it yet. Yes, that's rich.

The "Order Of Worship" Brethren

"4th. Aside from other considerations may an assembly of the Church of Christ use one cup in the distribution of the fruit of the vine and be Scriptural in such practice?" Yes, I'm not saying that one cup could not be Scriptural. I am not saying that a person or congregation couldn't Scripturally drink from one drinking vessel. But what's the purpose of that question? Brother Waters is driving at this: That if I admit that his practice is Scriptural—that one cup may be used—then I should surrender my practice, my position, for his, since he denies that mine is. That's the purpose of it, isn't it, Ervin? I'm sure that's the purpose of it. Excuse me just a minute. (Walks to his hand bag and gets a paper). There's another group of non-class or anti-class brethren, led in particular by Brother J. D. Phillips of Austin, Texas, who don't only oppose the cups or individual cups and the classes, but insist that there must also be a certain order of worship. Acts 2:42. "They continued steadfastly in the apostles' doctrine, and fellowship, in breaking of bread, and in prayers." Now, J. D. Phillips says that in the service you must first have the "apostles' doctrine," then you must have the "fellowship" or the contribution, and then you must have the "breaking of bread," or the Lord's Supper, and then the "prayers" last. That you must follow that order. That's the divine order of worship, he says, because it's mentioned that way in Acts 2:42. Brother Waters says, "No, we don't do it that way." Brother Waters and the brethren who stand with him, perhaps, have singing first, and then the apostles' doctrine, or teaching, and do some praying between them. Singing, then prayers, and then the teaching, then the Lord's Supper, and then the contribution and then maybe prayers and singing again. So he is not following the same order that Brother J. D. Phillips is following. And there is division in their ranks over the matter. They are divided over that particular thing, and Brother Waters, will you admit that a man could follow the plan followed by Brother Phillips in Acts 2:42 and be Scriptural? Come on now! Come on now! Let's shake hands on that. He could do that and be Scriptural? I'll agree with him. Won't you? That that order could be followed, and it would be Scriptural? I'll agree with him—won't you? Come on, Ervin. You've already done it in preaching. Just as well do it now. You've already done it, Ervin; just as well do it now. Come on You will agree that he can do that and be Scriptural, won't you? Then why don't you give up your order and take his? I'll show you that I know what I'm talking about.

I have an article here in the "Old Paths Advocate," June,

1950, written by Brother Waters on the Order of Worship, and he is discussing this matter relative to Brother Phillips and his position. And he says, "I told the publisher of 'The Truth'" (and that's J. D. Phillips) "that the strongest argument that I knew of his having made was when he posed the question to us, 'Brethren, if it makes no difference, what difference does it make?' He meant if, as we say" (that's Brother Waters and his brethren now). He meant that "if, as we say, that one order is as good as another, then why have anything to say when they try to press that order on the brethren? We can quickly reply that hundreds of churches will not submit to an order not bound by apostolic authority as a matter of faith." Now, Brother Waters admits that the order of worship followed by Brother J. D. Phillips is all right. It makes no difference. He can do it and be Scriptural. But he says, "I won't let you put it on me because you're making a law and say I must do it." I will say the same thing to him that he said to Phillips. The very same thing, Brother Waters. They stand or fall together. All right.

"5th. Is there a Scripture in the New Testament mentioning individual cups in the communion?" I'm not claiming that individual cups are specifically mentioned, any more than the plate, or the song books, or a thousand other things that you said could be put in there that the Scriptures didn't say anything about and yet would be Scriptural. All right.

"6th. In the metonymy of the 'container for the contained' is there an actual container named which sustains a relationship to the thing suggested?" Why, I told you time and time and time again that a liquid had to be contained in some kind of container. That if you are going to drink a liquid, it has to be confined to some kind of container. Certainly a container is suggested, because you can't confine a liquid without a container. The same is true with water with respect to baptism and a lot of other things along that line.

Contents Of How Many Bottles?

Now, then, I didn't intend to ask him any questions, but I'm going to ask him one, because he can't remember. I have asked it over and over and over and he just can't think to say a word about it; and since he either can't write it down or can't read his writing after he writes it down, then I'm going to give him this in my writing. I can barely read it after I have written it

down, but at least he will have something before him. If he
gets to wondering what it is, when he comes to make his next
speech, if he will just turn to me and ask me what this is, I will
read it for him. And the question is: "When the woman says, 'I
raised all my babies on the bottle,' does she refer to the contents
of more than one bottle?" Now, can you remember to reply to
that question? I won't have any chance to reply to it, Ervin, but
I would like to see you answer it. I would just like to see that go
into the book. I would just like to see your answer to that in the
next debate we have. I won't have any chance now, but I would
just like to see you answer. "When the woman says, 'I raised all
my babies on the bottle,' does she refer to the contents of more
than one bottle?" He said you can't say one container and mean
the contents of more than one; that's the whole gist of his argument. If you say one container, you mean the contents of only
one container, and it can't be any other way. Well, the woman
has six children she has raised, ranging in age from ten to thirty
years, and she says, "I raised them all on the bottle." She just
mentioned one. Now, I want to know if that was the contents of
one bottle. And if not, then down goes your whole argument on
it because you must admit that the contents of more than one
container can be referred to by naming one container.

Items That Are Parallel

Well, he said, "What evidence did Brother Porter give? Not
one passage where Christ commanded the individual cups to be
used. Not one passage where Christ used them by way of example, and not one passage where the disciples ever used them."
And, therefore, it must go down because not one passage was giv-
en. I haven't tried to give a passage where they are specifically
mentioned. I have showed you that they are parallel with a number
of things that my opponent accepts and uses without question.
As, for example, the song books and the plate. I wrote up there
on the circle "no plate" and "the plate."

CHART No. 2—On Communion

ONE CUP

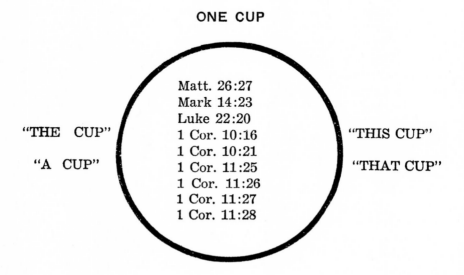

"THE CUP"

"A CUP"

Matt. 26:27
Mark 14:23
Luke 22:20
1 Cor. 10:16
1 Cor. 10:21
1 Cor. 11:25
1 Cor. 11:26
1 Cor. 11:27
1 Cor. 11:28

"THIS CUP"

"THAT CUP"

INDIVIDUAL CUPS

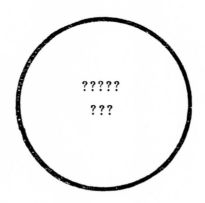

?????
???

And I told him last night, over here in this circle where he has the question marks, that the very minute you will put a passage in there that mentions the plate, I'll put in one that mentions five hundred cups. Well, it's still blank. He hasn't done it yet. Ervin, are you going to try it? I'll tell you what I'll do, Ervin. I'll put one in there that you say means more than one. What do you say? I'll put a reference in there which you say means more than one cup. I Cor. 10:16. (Writes it in the circle). Here is a passage that Brother Waters says means more than one cup. And yet the expression "the cup" is used, for he said that referred to one cup, one drinking vessel at Corinth, and one at Ephesus. Well, there's a passage in your circle, Brother Waters, which you say, although the expression "the cup" is used, means at least two. And furthermore, I would like to have the command and the example, either by Christ and the apostles, or anything of that kind, where they ever used the song books, and I will get to his chart presently.

"Well, why did Brother Porter do this?" He thought better things of him, etc. Well, that's just a play. The fact is, he can't meet the parallels that are drawn; therefore, he tries to run off after something else and do something else, rather than face the issue upon this matter.

The "Cup Of The Lord"—Container Or Contents?

So he goes to a number of books of Composition and Rhetoric, and grammars, and things of that kind, and spends a great deal of his time reading about the figure of speech called Metonymy. And he said, regarding that, that "This is the cup of the Lord" was never the name of the liquid. *That was never the name of the liquid.* "The cup of the Lord" was never the name of the liquid. That cup, he says, is the literal container. Brother Waters, here's your chart.

CHART No. 3—On Communion

(By Waters)

MATTHEW 26:27

"He Took The Cup, And Gave Thanks, And Gave It To Them, Saying, Drink Ye All Of It—(R.V.—A.S.V.—R.S.V., "A Cup")

MARK 14:23

"He Took The Cup, And When He Had Given Thanks, He Gave It To Them: And They All Drank Of It"—(R.V.—A.S.V.—R.S.V., "A Cup")

"A drinking vessel, a cup"................................Robinson P-611
"A cup, a drinking vessel"....................................Thayer P-533
"The vessel out of which one drinks"...................Thayer P-510
"The thing out of which one drinks"..................Thayer P-189

LUKE 22:17

"He Took The Cup, And Gave Thanks, And Said, Take This And Divide It Among Yourselves"   (R..—A.S.V.—R.S.V., "A Cup")
"A drinking vessel, a cup"..............................Robinson P-611
"A cup, a drinking vessel"....................................Thayer P-533

LUKE 22:20

"Likewise Also The Cup After Supper, Saying, This Cup Is The New Testament In My Blood, Which Is Shed For You"

1 COR. 11:25

"After The Same Manner Also He Took The Cup, When He Had Supped, Saying, This Cup Is The New Testament In My Blood"

"A drinking vessel, a cup"................................Robinson P-611
"A cup, a drinking vessel"....................................Thayer P-533
"Cup containing wine"..Thayer P-15
By Metonymy of the container for the contained Thayer P-533
"Metonymy, a cup for the contents of a cup, cup-full, E. G., a cup of wine; So of the wine drank at the Eucharist"—
.... Robinson P-611

1 Cor. 11:26

"As Often As Ye Eat This Break, And Drink This Cup, Ye Do Shew The Lord's Death Till He Come"

"Metonymy, a cup for the contents . . . E. G., A cup of wine".. Robinson P-611

1 Cor. 11:27

"Whosoever Shall Eat This Bread And Drink This Cup Of The Lord Unworthily, Shall Be Guilty of the Body and Blood of the Lord"

"What is in the cup"..Thayer P-510

"Metonymy, a cup for the contents . . .E. G., A cup of wine"—..Robinson P-611

1 Cor. 11:28

"But Let a Man Examine Himself, And So Let Him Eat of That Bread, and Drink of That Cup"

"The thing out of which one drinks" ....Thayer P-189
"The vessel out of which one drinks" ....Thayer P-510

"A cup of wine; So of wine drank at the Eucharist".. Robinson P-611

1 COR. 10:21

"Ye Cannot Drink The Cup of the Lord, and the Cup of Devils"
What is in the cup"..Thayer P-510

"Metonymy, a cup for the contents, E. G., A cup of wine—.. Robinson P-611

"The Cup Of Blessing Which We Bless, Is It Not The Communion of the Blood of Christ?"

1 COR. 10:16

"A cup of wine; So of the wine drank at the Eucharist —.. Robinson P-611

(Bible Dictionary by "American Tract Society—based on Dictionary of Holy Bible by Edward Robinson") ; "The master of the feast took a cup of unfermented wine, and having tasted it, passed it around .... 1 Cor. 10:16"

I helped him look at it awhile ago, and you came back to it also and had something to say about it, but didn't have anything to say about this particular passage. Notice this, Brother Waters. (Pointing to I Cor. 11:27 on chart) "Whosoever shall eat this bread, and drink this cup of the Lord, unworthily, shall be guilty of the body and blood of the Lord." Now you said under each passage you had put the definition. All right, here's your definition: "What is in the cup." Your definition for cup here is "contents," Brother Waters. And you said *the cup of the Lord never means contents,* but on your chart that it does. That it's the *contents* of it, and you have given Thayer and Robinson to prove it. Well, his chart is in conflict with what he said. It's also in conflict with what he said in this little tract about the matter. One time he says the cup of the Lord *is the literal container,* and the next time he says *it's the fruit of the vine.* And then he comes back and says it *never was the fruit of the vine, and* doesn't mean the fruit of the vine under any circumstances. But his chart says that it does; he's got his definition written under there in two different places; the matter is mentioned. In both places he has the *contents* as the definition of it. But in this debate he says it never does mean the contents of it.

Well, he quoted from Williams that he *named something* to *suggest* the *idea intended.* Well, *what* was *intended? The fruit of the vine?* All right, thank you. And "the container is named for the thing contained." That "he *names one thing* that *readily suggests something else."* He doesn't name the thing, but he named something that suggests it. Well, what is suggested then? In these places where cup is named, he says he named that to suggest something else. Well, what's the something else? The fruit of the vine. All right then, the fruit of the vine is the important item in that, *and not the container at all,* because he merely *names the container to suggest the thing itself* that's being considered. I agree with all those statements that he read in the "Rhetoric and Composition" regarding that matter.

"The Cup"—Plurality

But he says, "You can't drink of *the cup,* if you have a plurality." I am still wanting to know, and he has the question there now: Could those babies drink of *the bottle* and still have a plurality? Just what about it? Did they all drink of the same one? Was there just one bottle that served the whole family for twenty years? Just one container and all the babies raised on it? Well, "Paul named the cup of the Lord," and "it was not the fruit of the vine," and "it was a literal cup," and "it was the contents of only one." But that's already taken care of in this matter given.

Reads From His Tract

Then he spent a time reading a lengthy section from his tract when he was reading here all the time about that book. You know he had a book up here with him, Williams' "Composition and Rhetoric," and he read a long statement from it (you remember:), about you "can't name the contents of one cup without naming the container," etc., etc.; or if you named one container, that's the contents of one. You thought all that time he was reading from Williams' "Composition and Rhetoric," but he had folded in Williams' "Composition and Rhetoric" his little tract and was reading from it. (Porter laughs). Now that's what happened; he was reading *from his tract.* (Waters shakes head, "No"). The very words that he read are right here in this tract, word for word, just like he read it. He had his little tract folded in there. Didn't you Ervin? Weren't you reading from your little tract? Weren't you reading from your little tract awhile ago? Didn't you have your little tract folded in Williams' "Composition and Rhetoric?" Tell me! I don't want to misrepresent you. (Waters picks up Williams' "Composition and Rhetoric" and shows it to Porter). You didn't? You were not reading from it? You didn't read from this? Let's see your statement in your tract about that. In your tract!

From Whence Came Individual Cups?

Now, then, going on from there, we come to his chart and his definition under each passage. And we have dealt with that also. And then he came to the individual cups. "From whence came the individual cups?" Well, he said the individual cups came from G. C. Brewer, and he quoted from "Forty Years on the Firing Line," concerning G. C. Brewer's advocating individual cups. Well, *suppose he was* the first to introduce them into the worship; suppose that's true. I might just turn the thing around and say, "Who is the first man to preach on the radio?" The command to preach and the command to teach involve the various methods, and the command to eat and the command to drink involve the various incidentals included in it. So that wouldn't change the thing in the least. Just because some modern day preacher preached on the radio first wouldn't render radio preaching unscriptural, would it? I don't believe it would. Not at all.

Precedents And Incidentals

Now to his blackboard. (Porter pulls down the blackboard). I'm sorry I pulled this down. Do you have a tack, Brother Waters? Now, "Brother Porter talked about the plate last night," he said, "a great deal." But, he said, "His trouble is, he fails to differentiate between an incidental and a precedent." Now a precedent is some word or some deed that was said or done that was to serve as an example or rule to be followed. And Brother Porter failed to distinguish "between the precedent and the incidental." Now in our debate over in Tennessee, Brother Waters, do you remember what you said about that? You said an incidental is not mentioned but a precedent is. I wonder why you didn't say the same thing tonight? Over in our debate in Tennessee he said if it's mentioned, it's a precedent. If it's not mentioned, it's incidental. So he said the cup is mentioned; therefore it's a precedent. The plate is not mentioned; so it's an incidental. And he came along tonight to make his distinction between the two, but he didn't say a word about that. and do you wonder why? Well, I showed, according to his position over there, that since the upper room is mentioned, then the upper room becomes a precedent. According to his application of it, therefore, he would have to have his service in an upper room. Both in the example of Christ and the example of his disciples. When the Lord instituted the supper, it was in the upper room. And in Acts 20:7 they were in an upper room, and on the third floor, Brother Waters. Those things are mentioned, and you said in our former debate, "If a thing is mentioned, it becomes a precedent." You didn't like that so well. You found out that wasn't good debating. You changed it. And so tonight, he has a different set-up for it.

And now he has this (pointing to blackboard), in an effort to show that song books and plates are not parallel with cups, but that cups are parallel with instrumental music.

Chart on Parallels

1. Bread—Eat	(Plate does not violate
	(Beef steak does violate
2. Cup—Drink of it	("Cups" violate "cup"
3. Sing—Make melody	(Song books do not violate
in heart	(Instrumental music does violate

So here he has "Bread" and "eat." And so he said, "Plate does not violate eating the bread." But the beef steak would. Certainly so, because you are adding a coordinate element of food; and the Lord specifies "eating the bread." All right, here he has "Cup" and "drink of." I wonder if I could have a piece of crayon? Now, we drink of the cup, and he said that "cups" violates and substitutes for it. Well, I would like to write on that if I had a piece of crayon. Now here's the thing we drink (writes "fruit of vine") just as here's the thing we eat (pointing to "bread"). We eat the bread; we swallow the bread. The thing we drink is the thing we swallow. And we don't swallow the container; we swallow the "fruit of the vine." I never saw a man drink anything he didn't swallow. Did you? All right, the thing we swallow is the thing we eat; and that's the bread. And whether we do that without a plate or with a plate, we are still eating bread, but if you add beef steak, you add a coordinate element of food; and that's an addition to it. But when we drink, we drink the "fruit of the vine" and not the container; and, therefore, whether we drink that "fruit of the vine" out of *a cup* or out of *cups,* we are still drinking the "fruit of the vine," just like we are eating the "bread." And so it's not a violation, and your cases are not parallel at all, Brother Waters.

Chart As Revised By Porter

1. Bread—Eat	(Plate does not violate
	(Beef steak does violate
2. Fruit of vine—Drink	("Cup" or "cups" do not violate
	(Another liquid does violate
3. Sing—Make melody in heart	(Song books do not violate
	(Instrumental music does violate

And now, here on this other, he said "Make melody." He said there are two ways to make melody—in your heart and on the instrument. It just specifies "in your heart," and then if you make it on anything else, you are violating that. Certainly so. I believe that, because making melody and singing, in this case, cannot refer to the instrument. It cannot be made; it is not included. And when you make music on the instrument, you are doing something besides making melody in your heart, but when you drink the fruit of the vine out of "cups" you are doing nothing but drinking the fruit of the vine. And so they are not parallel at all. You haven't met me on it at all, Brother Waters. You just thought you did. *You just thought you did.* You are going to have to try it over. You haven't touched it—top, edge, side or bottom. For the simple fact, if we drink out of one cup, or if we drink out of a hundred cups, we do nothing but drink the fruit of the vine. If we eat the bread with or without the plate, we do nothing but eat. But when we make music on an instrument we are doing something besides sing. The Lord said "sing." We use the song books—we are singing. We sing with or without the song books— we are still singing. But when we have the instrumental music we have added another music; but it's not true with respect to the fruit of the vine. We drink the fruit of the vine. Whether we drink that fruit of the vine out of "a" cup, or cups, we are still drinking the fruit of the vine; and they are not parallel with the instrumental music at all, Brother Waters. You will have to beat that before you can answer a digressive on his arguments. If you ever undertake to meet them in debate, why, you will have to beat that.

He pledges himself, if we ever have another debate, that he will change his method from what he did before. That he will not try to parallel the Sunday Schools with the Missionary Societies or anything of the kind, but that he will just stick to the Sunday School altogether, and not try to bring in these other ideas. He must be learning. He must be learning. (Porter laughs) Well, the fact is, I brought in other things. Why? To prove that one thing is as Scriptural as something else? No, that's not the idea. He quoted from Brother Foy's tract, or Brother Foy's paper, about proving one thing as Scriptural as something else. I'm not trying to prove one thing as Scriptural as something else. I believe that a plate can be Scripturally used in the distribution of the bread. I believe that the song books can be Scripturally used in the singing of praise to God. In fact, I believe, as Brother Waters said, that you may put a thousand things in there that the Scriptures do not mention. And yet he said many of them would be Scriptural, even though the Scriptures do not mention them. I'm insisting that the cups stand upon the same proposition.

What The Container Pictures

The "cup" is not the vital thing. The "cup" is the incidental matter; the container is not the important thing. The thing that pictures the blood of Jesus Christ is the fruit of the vine, and not the cup, the container. That doesn't picture the blood of the

Lord. The fruit of the vine pictures His blood. Brother Waters agreed that that was so last night. The body is pictured by the bread; the blood is pictured by the fruit of the vine; and he said the container pictures the New Testament. Then I showed, that being true, it cannot be *the cup of the Lord,* because *the cup of the Lord* referred to *the communion of His blood.* The cup of blessing referred to the communion of His blood, according to I Cor. 11; and therefore, the cup of the Lord in that case refers to the contents and not the container. But he said the contents pictures His blood, but the container pictures the New Testament. And do you remember, too, that I showed, according to him, that there could be just one copy of the New Testament to an assembly. He didn't have time to pay any attention to that. He had time to read a lot of other things besides the issue, but he didn't have time to notice what I said about it. Maybe he will in this last speech, when I don't have any chance to reply, but I would have liked for him to say something about it when I would have had a chance to reply to it. I would have liked for him to mention the matter when I had a chance to respond. One New Testament, one volume, to an assembly. Are you going to hell if you have two? Because there's just one? And the "cup" is the New Testament. He makes the literal container picture the New Testament.

Literal Container—Contents Plural

Then he read from Brother Hawley regarding the cup, whether or not there was a literal container, and Brother Hawley said "yes." Wants to know if I would agree. I've never denied that there was a literal container. Certainly, I said all the time there was a literal container. I made that argument from the very beginning. Certainly, a liquid must be confined in a literal container, Brother Waters.

We Drank "From The Bottle"

But I am still wanting to know if the literal container can be referred to to mean the contents of more than one literal container. And I want to know, furthermore, if in drinking from a literal container, we must put our lips to it? Brother Waters, what did you tell me about this bottle? (Pointing to bottle on table). Last night I introduced the statement made by the Lord in which He said, "He that shall give you a cup of water in My name because ye belong to Me, he shall not lose his reward," and I showed that Jesus said, "a cup of water"—just one. Just one cup; and therefore, if the Lord mentioned just one cup, then if you would give him two cups ,you would go to hell. You will lose your reward for it because the Lord said "one cup." And the only reply that Brother Waters made to that was to pour out a cup of water and hand it to me, and I drank part of it. And he wanted to know then if that was one cup or two. Well, but I asked him, "Suppose you give me another; will you go to hell for it?" He hasn't answered yet. And, furthermore, I said, Brother Waters, "You drank water out of this cup, and I drank water out of this cup, and the water came *from this bottle*. And I want to know whether or not we drank *from this bottle*." You haven't said a word about it yet.

Drinking From Jacob's Well

And, furthermore, I gave you Jacob's well, in John, the 4th chapter where Jacob and his sons and their cattle all drank from Jacob's well. I wanted to know if they all put their lips to it, and he said, "Well, there's just one well; there were not a lot of other little wells." But I insisted that he tell us whether there were other containers. Were there other containers besides Jacob's well? And when they drank out of other containers, were they drinking from Jacob's well? He hasn't said a word about that. Maybe he will. He doesn't have time to talk about irrelevant matters. He doesn't have time to get around and talk about the arguments I make, but he can spend a lot of time reading from various books and debates and various things of that kind. He has plenty of time for that. But he doesn't have time to notice what I said. Well, that's up to him about that. But I'm wanting you to keep in mind the fact that the contents of a number of containers can be referred to by the mention of only one. And until he answers that argument, answers that question I have given, why, the thing stands. And I predict it will stand after he answers it.

One Bread And One Cup

But keep in mind this fact, that in all these statements given, I have showed one bread and one cup (I Cor. 10:16). What did he say about that. I showed, according to his own answer to my question, that when Paul said, "The cup which we bless," he referred to two cups. What did he say about that? Nothing—nothing—nothing—nothing—did you, Brother Waters? Did you mention that? I have pressed that into you in every speech. (I. Cor. 10:16). You said that when Paul said, "The cup of blessing which we bless," he referred to one at Corinth and one at Ephesus. I am asking you if that one and one makes two? Paul said, "the cup," and if one cup can mean two, then why can't it mean four? Why can't it mean ten? And why can't it mean two hundred? Why can't it?

The Broken Container Again

And then regarding their congregation being served the fruit of the vine—the vessel is broken, and the contents spilled. He said, "I would get another and serve the remainder of the congregation, or serve the whole congregation." Now when he made that statement, he surrendered the whole issue, because he says under some circumstances two drinking vessels can be used for the same assembly. Two drinking vessels can be used for the same assembly. Brother Waters has said so. All right, Brother Waters, if two can be used, why can't two hundred be used? Will you put that down and tell me? You don't have time to forget that because my time is almost up; you don't have time to forget that, Ervin. Now, you tell us. Since you say that two can be used under some circumstances, for one assembly, then under the same condition, why can't two thousand be used? And if two can be used, then doesn't that give up the idea that *one must be used?* Your proposition says there must be one drinking vessel for one assembly; and if you have more than one, you are going to hell. But he says if I should happen to drop it, "I would get another one" and send the whole congregation to hell. Yes, sir, I would get another one and send the whole congregation to hell, because I would serve the whole congregation again with the second cup. Well, some of them would have two cups. And thus he would send the whole bunch to hell because somebody accidentally dropped the cup. Now, you tell us, Brother Waters, about that. Would one broken cup and one unbroken cup be two cups? I'm wanting to know. I said I would immerse the man who was only partly immersed, but I wouldn't immerse the man who had already been immersed. If I got one completely done, I wouldn't jerk him back in the water and put him under. But Brother Waters, in his answer, has half of the congregation already partaken of the fruit of the vine—then he forces them to do the whole thing over again.

Thank you, Ladies and Gentlemen.

SECOND SESSION

Waters' Second Negative

CUP QUESTION

Brethren Moderators, Brother Porter, Brethren and Friends:
I am happy to stand before you for the last speech of this session of the debate.

I Cor. 10:16 Is Congregational in Application

Brother Porter said that I had not given due attention to his consideration of 1 Cor. 10:16. But you remember last evening in answering his questions concerning 1 Cor. 10:16 that I said, "The cup of blessing which we bless," as used by the Apostle Paul, was used in a *congregational sense.* And I further, in that answer, proved that it was used congregationally by referring to what Paul said in 1 Cor. 11:33, *"When ye come together to eat."* That his instructions pertaining to the communion service in the use of one loaf and one cup obtained "when ye come together to eat" in an assembly is obvious. That an assembly is necessarily involved, and that one cup in an assembly is involved, in the same sense that the Apostle Paul in the same epistle in 1 Cor. 14:31 involves an assembly when he writes to the church at Corinth and all of them at every place that call upon the name of the Lord, 1 Cor. 1:2, and says, "Ye may all prophesy one by one," is easily understood. Who gets the idea that he universally means that we must prophesy one by one all over the world? Does not Brother Porter understand the Apostle to mean that those prophets were to prophesy one by one, "When ye come together," 1 Cor. 14:26? Well, if he can understand that Paul could write to the church universally and say, "Ye may all prophesy one by one," but mean one by one in each assembly, he can also understand that the Apostle Paul could deliver instructions pertaining to the communion service,—and speak of "the loaf" and "the cup," and "a loaf" and "a cup," and the "cup of blessing,",—and yet have reference to an assembly for the communion; he can understand that. If he can understand that we may say concerning the churches, "They prophesy, the prophets prophesy, one by one," because one does so in each assembly, then he can understand why we may speak of *"the cup of blessing"* because each congregation thus uses *"the cup of blessing".*

I told him those things last night. What did you have to

say about my parallel on I Cor. 14, Brother Porter? You talk about having a good "forgetter". Why didn't you say something about 1 Cor. 14:31? Why didn't you? Why didn't you say something about "Ye may all prophecy one by one?" You know it says it. And you know the Apostle Paul was writing to the church universally in every place. Why didn't you deal with that?

-(Porter speaks from seat: "We'll have that tomorrow night".)

Why didn't you deal with that? That was in my answer and you say that I didn't deal with it? Talk about having a good forgetter. I gave that as a parallel, and he didn't have a thing to say about it;—*not one single solitary thing.*

A Cup of Water

Oh, but last night when I handed him *a cup of water,* I said, *"How many did I hand you?"* Well, of course he had to agree that I just handed him *one.* Where he could see it. He said, "What if you had handed me two, would you have received a reward or would you have gone to hell?" No. What if I had handed you a cup of milk, instead of water? Would I have gone to hell, Brother Porter? Huh? Now if he is trying to parallel that with the communion, he knows you have got to use the fruit of the vine in the communion. The Lord said, "a cup of water." Now I want to know if I had handed you a cup of milk, would I have gone to hell? And if I handed you two cups of milk, would I have received a reward? He knows that the Lord Jesus merely mentioned one thing out of a whole class of things, and that we may do a whole lot of things and receive a reward for it. The Lord just mentioned one thing out of a whole class of things. If I'm not mistaken grammatically, you would call that a Synecdoche, in which a part is put for the whole, Brother Porter. (Waters laughs.)

The Bottle

Let's see now about the bottle. The woman said, "I raised all my babies on the bottle." Does she refer to the contents of more than one bottle? You remember last night that I said I believed that sometimes we may have a singular noun to refer to a species. I didn't contest that at all, but I said in order to understand the language involved in the communion, you would have to construct a parallel. And it says, "He took a cup." *If it were said concerning any specific man and any specific cup, "He took a cup,"* how many cups would that be? And if it is said, *"He took a bottle,"* that affirms something, a specific something, of a specific bottle, Brother Porter. There is not a species involved there.

Porter from seat: "What about the bottle?"

Waters: If "he took the bottle," that involves only *one bottle* because if it involved a species, it would mean that he took every bottle on earth with him. You see?

Porter from seat: "The woman didn't use every bottle on earth, did she?"

Waters: Does the language involve one or species, if it is said, "He took 'a bottle'?" The Revised Version says "a cup"; The Kings James says "the cup." I don't believe there's any difference in the meaning of them. Do you contend that there is a difference in "a cup" and "the cup?"

Porter from seat: "You are making the difference." (Brother Porter's followers laugh).

Waters: You are the one who spoke up and said, 'What if it said 'the bottle' instead of 'a bottle'?

Porter: "That was your argument. You were making a difference between the two. That's why I asked you."

Waters: I say that when a *specific statement* is made concerning *a specific bottle,* whether you use *"a bottle"* or *"the bottle"* in the statement, *there's just one bottle.*

Porter from seat. "All right, 'the bottle' means plural. Let's shake hands on that."

Waters: The bottle can refer to species.

Porter: "Plurality?"

Waters: Species.

Porter: "Plurality? Plurality?"

Waters: It can refer to species.

Porter: "Plurality by species? Come on, let's shake hands on that."

Waters: Sir, you have had your time, will you sit down please? (Porter was standing).

Porter: "Won't you shake hands with me?"

Waters: Will you sit down, please?

Porter: "You made the statement and I want to shake hands with you."

Waters: I say will you........?

Porter: "Yes, I want to shake hands with you."

Waters: Will you give me my time?

Porter: (To Moderator) "Hold his time." (To Waters) "Will you agree now? Well, shake hands with me."

Waters: Say, listen!

Porter: "I want to agree with you."

Waters: Do you want to agree with me?

Porter: "I want to agree with you that you said the bottle can mean a plurality by species."

Waters: Do you want to agree with me? Do you want to construct a parallel and say, *"he took a bottle,"* or *"he took the bottle?"*

Porter: "We are talking about what you said." (To Moderator) "I want you to keep his time." (To Waters) "You said 'the bottle' can sometimes mean plurality by species. Is that what you meant? Shake hands on it."

Waters: Well, what do you want to shake hands for?

Porter: "Because you said it and I want to agree with you."

Waters: Do you want to shake hands?

Porter: "Yes."

Waters: Are you going to shake hands with me again then when I question you about this *specific statement?*

Porter: "If I agree with you."

Waters: Well, let's see if you will.

Porter: "Come on."

Waters: Will you shake hands with me on the specific?

Porter: "Yes, if I agree with you."

Waters: All right, then there's not any disagreement between us.

Porter: "Shake hands with me. Sometimes it means plurality."

Waters: If it's specific, it means singular.

Porter: "Sometimes if it's specific, it means singular. Sometimes it can be 'the bottle' and mean plurality."

Waters: When the Scriptures say, *"He took a cup,"* is that *species* or *plurality?*

Porter: "All right, when he says, 'The cup which we bless,' is that specific or species?" (Porter's followers laugh).

Waters: When "He took a cup," did you reply to me? Is that specific or species?

Porter: "Certainly, a cup could be singular."

Waters: Is it there?

Porter: "It may have been."

Waters: I said is it?

Porter: "It may have been."

Waters: "He took a cup."

Porter: "It may have been, but when he said, 'This cup is the New Testament,' and 'The cup which we bless,' that's not specific, is it? It's species, according to your argument."

Waters: "The cup of blessing which we bless" is specific, and refers to *a cup of blessing in each assembly of the saints.*

Porter: "The bottle which my babies were raised on is specific and there's just one bottle." (Porter laughs)

Waters: Let's resume the time, Brethren.

Construct A Parallel

If you construct a statement parallel with the language of the Bible and say, *"The mother gave the bottle to the baby,"* there's not a man on earth who can interpret it grammatically and say that she gave *more than one bottle to the baby.* If you construct a statement parallel with the language of the Bible, you will see this. Now you remember the Bible said, "He took the cup." "He gave it to them and they all drank of it." (Mark 14:23) That's what the Bible says. That affirms a specific something of a specific cup. My brother does not contest the fact that *only one was involved in that language.* He doesn't contest that fact.

Porter Only Found One In Each Congregation

He, furthermore, has not tried to involve a *plurality of cups* with 1 Cor. 10:16 except by involving *one in each congregation. Did you know that?* He has not tried to involve a plurality in 1 Cor. 10:16 except by considering a plurality of congregations with one in each congregation; that is the only way he tried to prove it. Since that has been your argument on 1 Cor. 10:16, one vessel at Ephesus and one vessel at Corinth, that was the basis of your argument in order to get the plurality of cups, but the proposition deals with one assembly, Brother Porter, you have surrendered your position and given up this debate. You had to get a plurality of congregations in order to get a plurality of vessels, didn't you, Brother Porter? Didn't you?

(Porter: "You did that. You said........................")

You have already admitted now that the *Lord just used one.* He said, "I won't deny that that is literal. I won't deny that that is specific." And there is one cup, one literal cup, in one assembly. How did Brother Porter get a plurality of cups, literal cups; how did he do it anyway? To get a plurality of cups he went to First Corinthians to get a plurality of congregations. You didn't get your plurality in one congregation, did you, Porter? Did you? Did you get your plurality in one congregation? *You had to have both Ephesus and Corinth to get two.*

Porter: "You got it in one only when you broke it."

I'll tell you right now, he's hurting; isn't he? (Audience laughs) All right, let's see these questions.

The Cup, One or A Plurality, Is The New Testament?

1st. In Christ's statement, "this cup is the New Testament" (Luke 2:20, 1 Cor. 11:25), does the word "cup" refer to the literal cup or to the fruit of the vine? Well, he says that the container is named to refer to the fruit of the vine. Now you listen to this. He said that Brother Waters says that the cup is the New Testament,—the literal cup is the New Testament. But he says, "Since we may use or have more than one copy of the New Testament in an assembly, why may we not have more than one literal cup?" Isn't that right? All right, Brother Porter says that the cup in Luke 22:20 is the fruit of the vine and that verse says, "This cup is the New Testament." He says that the cup there is the fruit of the vine. Then, according to his argument, if the fruit of the vine is the New Testament and you may have a plurality of copies of the New Testament, you may also have a plurality of fruits of the vine. I want to know if you may have a plurality of cups— what you say the cup is, Brother Porter? Can you have a plurality of bloods? A plurality of fruits? I want to know that. If you are going to say that I may have only one copy of the New Testament if I say the literal cup is the New Testament and contend for only one cup, then you may have only copy of the New Testament per the same argument. And if you insist that I may have a plurality of literal cups because I may have a plurality of copies of the New Testament, I want to know if you may have more than one cup—what you say the cup is? *I am not going to let a man put an argument like that on me that he won't take for himself.* And he won't take it because he says he believes in using just one cup, the fruit of the vine—one blood. He won't take the argument himself, but he wants to put it on me. I won't let a man get away with that.

Accidents Versus Purposeful Action

2nd. If, while passing the individual communion set to the assembly, the set is dropped and broken and the contents spilled, and another communion set is supplied, would you give thanks for this second set before passing it to the remainder of the assembly? Or pass it to them without giving thanks? Well, he said, "I would give thanks for it if no thanks had been given." And, of course, none had been. He said, "I'd give thanks for it." I want you to remember that questions like this deal with accidents. The Bible is not a big enough book to contemplate every accident or every accidental eventuality that may occur. Nowhere could you open the word of God and find out about giving thanks for one set of individual cups, and later on in the communion service giving thanks for another set. After some of them had already drunk, then later getting some more and giving thanks for those, and others drinking! Where would you turn to the word of God and read anything about that? You see? The fact of the matter is you are dealing with an accident, and he tries to make an accident on par with purposeful action. I want to know if it would be Scriptural for the man to just throw down the tray of individual cups and *break them purposefully as a part of worship, and then get some more?* Would it be all right for him to *purposefully* do that? He said it would be all right for him to *accidentally* do it. Would it be all right for him to *purposefully* do it? A man is hard pressed when he goes to accidents to prove something to use purposefully in worship.

3rd. While attempting to baptize a candidate, if because of your slipping or his struggles, you only half immerse him, would you now attempt it again and completely immerse him? Or would you only immerse the half of him not immersed the first time? Well, he said, "I would immerse the whole fellow." All right now, listen! I want to know if a part of that man has been immersed or baptized twice, and the rest of him has been baptized once, Brother Porter. I also want to know if you have two baptisms involved, one complete baptism and one incomplete baptism? One half baptism and one whole baptism? Well, he says, "I would not take him and just immerse the half that had not been immersed. I would take him and immerse the whole fellow because I failed the first time, and if I failed the second, I would just keep on trying until I succeeded." I want you to remember that. Oh, he said, "I wouldn't go back and immerse the fellow that I had already immersed."

The Congregation Is The Unit Of Communion

When we deal with a congregation or *an assembly* of the disciples for the observance of the communion, we are dealing with *the unit of communion*. In baptism *the man is the unit of baptism*. But in communion a man does not go off in a desert and observe it *by himself*. You don't stay at home and observe the communion by yourself, Brother Porter. In order to have communion, you must have *the joint-participation of an assembly of disciples*. In order to have that communion service you must have that unit, and *that unit is the assembly*. In baptism *the unit is the individual*. In the communion *the unit is the assembly*. Just as when that individual over there was half immersed the first time because you just accidentally were not able to immerse all of him, you immersed *all of him the next time*, when *the assembly does not commune*,—when it is not successful in its *joint participation*,—the *next time* it is again going to attempt to have *joint participation*, Brother Porter. It failed the *first time*, and now it wants to get the job done the *second time*, just like you did in immersing that man. Oh! But he says, if you do that, that's on par with purposefully doing it. Would it be Scriptural for you to *purposefully just half baptize a man*, and then *purposefully entirely baptize him the next time*? Is that what you brethren are going to affirm? Are you going to put that which may *accidentally* happen on par with that which is *purposefully* done in service to the Lord of Glory? Is that what you are going to do? Remember that the unit of communion is the assembly. If that assembly is not successful in having joint participation, it must keep trying until it is. Just like you must keep on trying until you are able to baptize that man, Brother Porter.

Porter Admits One Cup Is Scriptural

4th. Aside from other considerations, may an assembly of the Church of Christ use one cup in the distribution of the fruit of the vine and be Scriptural in such practice? He says, "Yes, I cannot say a congregation could not Scripturally use one." Brethren, *our practice is not called in question in this debate.* Our practice is not called in question at all in this debate. Brother Porter will not deny that you may use one cup and be Scriptural in such practice. *Our practice is not questioned.* My opponent's practice is what is in question from the first to the last in this discussion. *Our practice is not in question in either case.* It is my opponent's practice that is called in question. It is not ours. Why? He admits that when I read in the Bible, "He took a cup," or "He took the cup,—and he gave it to them and they all drank of it," *that only one cup is involved.* No wonder that our practice is Scriptural. He also says, "I believe that individual cups are too." But he can't read anything about that.

But he wants to put that on par with the "Order of Worship" question. Brother Phillips can't read *an order of worship* in the New Testament, but I can read where the Lord *took a cup* and gave *it* to them and *they all drank of it.* There's a difference there. You have actually a precedent in the use of one cup, bound by example, by command, by statement, and by necessary inference. And when my brother uses individual cups, he violates those commands, those examples, those statements and inferences in the word of God. When he does that, we cannot go along. We can't do it.

Porter Admits Individual Cups Not Mentioned

No. 5. Is there a Scripture in the New Testament mentioning individual cups in the communion? Answer: *"I am not saying they are actually mentioned."* Yet my brother is affirming that they are Scriptural but will not say that they are actually mentioned. Will you shake hands with me on that, Brother Porter?

Porter: "I will shake hands that they are mentioned the same place song books are.

Waters: Will you shake hands?

Porter: "I'll shake that they are mentioned the same place that the song books are."

Waters: Are you going to let me ask my question?

Porter: "All right, put your question."

Waters: Will you shake hands with me on the answer to the question that the individual cups are not mentioned?

Porter: "If you will shake hands with me that the song books are not mentioned."

Waters: Well, Brother, what are we debating?

Porter: "The cups."

Waters: Are we debating the cups?

Porter: "They are parallel."

Waters: They are *as Scriptural* as the song books, you say. (Waters laughs) Gone back on Foy Wallace!

Porter: "Do you believe song books are scriptural?"

Waters: Are you going to shake hands with me on the answer to that question?

Porter: "Well, do you believe song books are Scriptural?"

Waters: I do.

Porter: "Where do the Scriptures say anything about them?" (Audience laughs) "Read it for me. Come on."

Waters: Are you going to shake hands with me?

Porter: "Are you going to shake hands with me?"

Waters: Are you going to shake hands with me that individual cups are not mentioned in the New Testament?

Porter: "If you will shake hands with me that the same thing is true with the song books."

Waters: Why there is no use to shake hands all night.

Porter: "I'll go fifty-fifty with you."

Porter Follows Digressive Line

Waters: I have never heard a digressive yet but who would try to put the thing he was trying to defend on par with something else. He will do it every time. He will do it every time. He will talk about song books and he will talk about plates. And say, Brother Porter, if you really want to learn a lesson on these things, I want you to hear Burton Barber up yonder at Cedar Rapids next week. You will learn something. Why you haven't even touched the hem of the garment when it comes to bringing in other things. Why you haven't even scratched the surface. Let him hear Burton Barber in defense of instrumental music if he wants to learn to bring in something besides the thing at issue. Oh, your brethren detest those instrumental music folks for doing that, or their attempts to do that. You don't like it. You say that's not fair; that's not debating. But you want to do that when you are debating the individual cups because you can't come up like men and prove the individual cups by the word of God. You simply have to take the position that they are "as Scriptural" as something else. And so then, by association, to try to prejudice the minds of the people. Let me tell you, every thing you can mention has to stand upon its own feet, and stand or fall upon its own merits or demerits. I wonder when people are going to learn in honest and fair investigation to consider the issue that is embraced in the proposition. According to the rules of honorable controversy all matters extraneous to the issues in debate are not even supposed to be mentioned. But he will bring in extraneous matters from beginning to end. *I have never heard a digressive yet that wouldn't.*

Is An Actual Container Named?

Question No. 6. In the metonymy of the container for the contained, is there an actual container named which sustains a relationship to the thing suggested? "I told you," he replies, "a liquid has to be in a container." "Of course a container is suggested." All right, Brother Porter, what about 1 Cor. 11:27, "Whosoever shall eat this bread and drink this cup of the Lord unworthily?" He says, *"Of course a container is suggested."* But he didn't say the *"containers"* are suggested. He said, *"A container is suggested."* One container is suggested, in other words, by that; he didn't say containers. He says, "I told you a liquid has to be in a container. And, of course, a container is suggested." You will never, my brother, be able to *"drink the cup" without "the cup"* until you can *"boil the kettle" without "the kettle."* Until you can "boil the kettle" without "the kettle", a congregation will never be able to "drink the cup" without "the cup." Until you make the statement with reference to something specific grammatically, "she boiled the kettle," and talk about the contents of a plurality of kettles, you will never say "a congregation drank the cup" when they drank the contents of a plurality of cups. Strange that you can understand the one, but some of you cannot understand the other!

Specific or Species?

Again with reference to the species and the singular argument; Brother Porter agrees that, though, when the Bible says, "Go to the ant thou sluggard," it refers to species, if the statement were made, *"The man picked up the ant,"* that would be individual and "one ant." Well, turn to the word of God, and it says, *"He took the cup."* That is *individual and specific.* Turn to 1 Cor. 11:25 where the Apostle Paul delivered that which he had received, according to Verse 23, and of which he said in Verse 2 that we should keep like he delivered, "And in like manner also, *he took the cup."* That is *specific and individual.* My brother constructed a parallel and admitted it. So according to the language of the Bible, it being specific and individual, only one literal cup is involved in the communion service, and he cannot by the laws of language involve more than one in any assembly for the communion. According to the word of God, he can't do it.

CHART No. 3—On Communion

(By Waters)

MATTHEW 26:27

"He Took The Cup, And Gave Thanks, And Gave It To Them, Saying, Drink Ye All Of It—(R.V.—A.S.V.—R.S.V., "A Cup")

MARK 14:23

"He Took The Cup, And When He Had Given Thanks, He Gave It To Them: And They All Drank Of It"—(R.V.—A.S.V.—R.S.V., "A Cup")

"A drinking vessel, a cup"................................Robinson P-611
"A cup, a drinking vessel".................................Thayer P-533
"The vessel out of which one drinks"...................Thayer P-510
"The thing out of which one drinks"...................Thayer P-189

LUKE 22:17

"He Took The Cup, And Gave Thanks, And Said, Take This And Divide It Among Yourselves"   (R..—A.S.V.—R.S.V., "A Cup")
"A drinking vessel, a cup"...............................Robinson P-611
"A cup, a drinking vessel".................................Thayer P-533

LUKE 22:20

"Likewise Also The Cup After Supper, Saying, This Cup Is The New Testament In My Blood, Which Is Shed For You"

1 COR. 11:25

"After The Same Manner Also He Took The Cup, When He Had Supped, Saying, This Cup Is The New Testament In My Blood"

"A drinking vessel, a cup"................................Robinson P-611
"A cup, a drinking vessel".................................Thayer P-533
"Cup containing wine"...................................Thayer P-15
By Metonymy of the container for the contained Thayer P-533
"Metonymy, a cup for the contents of a cup, cup-full, E. G.,
a cup of wine; So of the wine drank at the Eucharist"—
.... Robinson P-611

1 Cor. 11:26

"As Often As Ye Eat This Break, And Drink This Cup, Ye Do Shew The Lord's Death Till He Come"

"Metonymy, a cup for the contents . . . E. G., A cup of wine".. Robinson P-611

1 Cor. 11:27

"Whosoever Shall Eat This Bread And Drink This Cup Of The Lord Unworthily, Shall Be Guilty of the Body and Blood of the Lord"

"What is in the cup"...Thayer P-510

"Metonymy, a cup for the contents . . .E. G., A cup of wine"—
....Robinson P-611

1 Cor. 11:28

"But Let a Man Examine Himself, And So Let Him Eat of That Bread, and Drink of That Cup"

"The thing out of which one drinks" ....Thayer P-189

"The vessel out of which one drinks" ....Thayer P-510

"A cup of wine; So of wine drank at the Eucharist"
.... Robinson P-611

1 COR. 10:21

"Ye Cannot Drink The Cup of the Lord, and the Cup of Devils"
What is in the cup"...Thayer P-510

"Metonymy, a cup for the contents, E. G., A cup of wine—
.... Robinson P-611

"The Cup Of Blessing Which We Bless, Is It Not The Communion of the Blood of Christ?"

1 COR. 10:16

"A cup of wine; So of the wine drank at the Eucharist —
.... Robinson P-611

(Bible Dictionary by "American Tract Society—based on Dictionary of Holy Bible by Edward Robinson") ; "The master of the feast took a cup of unfermented wine, and having tasted it, passed it around .... 1 Cor. 10:16"

He has absolutely mis-applied this chart right here—the definitions. He said, "Brother Waters said that the cup of the Lord is literal." Well, I quoted to him the laws of metonymy which absolutely say that in metonymy you name one thing and suggest something else. And by that metonymy, the thing suggested in 1 Cor. 11:26 and 27 is the thing that's in the cup. That is the thing that is suggested. That is not the thing named. Now, if you had just turned and simply read the references that I gave; I didn't have time to give the entire reference, I put the thing suggested. Thayer says it is "the metonymy of the container for the contained." According to him, the container is there and that is the thing that is named. *The cup of the Lord is the literal container.* That is *named* to *suggest what is in the cup,* or what is *in it.* A cup for the contents. *The cup is there. It is actually there.* And so Waters is *not* against his chart, and the chart is *not* against Waters.

Cups Are Another Way

But what about the chart on expedience? Why he says, "Don't you see here that when you use cups, you are not violating the word of the Lord; you are still drinking the fruit of the vine." But, Brother Porter, it says "He took a cup,——and gave it to them, saying drink ye all of it." (Matt. 26:27) But when you use *cups,* you violate *"a cup,"* and you *violate "all of you drink of it."* *You violate the example. You violate the command.* When you do that, you have inserted something that is a coordinate element. It is another way of doing it other than the way the Lord and the disciples did it. Just like when you use instrumental music, you introduce something else And then he thinks he has met the argument.

CHART No. 2—On Communion

ONE CUP

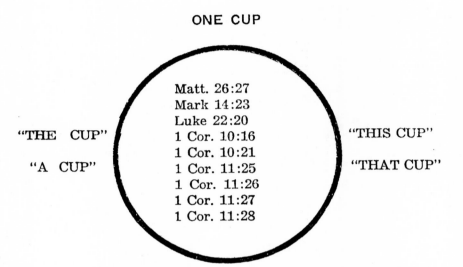

"THE CUP"

"A CUP"

Matt. 26:27
Mark 14:23
Luke 22:20
1 Cor. 10:16
1 Cor. 10:21
1 Cor. 11:25
1 Cor. 11:26
1 Cor. 11:27
1 Cor. 11:28

"THIS CUP"

"THAT CUP"

INDIVIDUAL CUPS

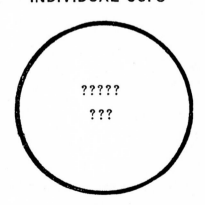

?????
???

I want you people to remember, when this discussion is over, that Brother Porter has utterly failed to produce the Scripture over here that teaches a plurality of cups for an assembly. That is just exactly what his proposition calls for; individual cups for an assembly. He put 1 Cor. 10:16 here, and the only way he tried to get a plurality of cups out of 1 Cor. 10:16 was to involve a plurality of assemblies. His proposition calls for "an assembly." And the only way he could get a plurality of cups was to get a plurality of assemblies. That's the only way he could do it. He has not placed a Scripture in there that involved a plurality of cups in one assembly. But the proposition calls for "individual cups" in "an assembly." Has Brother Porter produced the Scripture? Has anyone heard the Scripture which teaches and authorizes it? When we stand before God in Judgement, we must give an account unto Him for our deeds. When we stand before Him, and the books of the Bible are opened, are we going to have a thus saith the Lord for the things that we have done?

Waters to Moderator: How many minutes do I have?

Moderator Cook: "You have four minutes."

Waters to Moderator: Thank you.

Oh, he says, you will have to beat that to meet the digressives. Well, you are a digressive and I have met you with it.

Porter from seat: "J. D. Phillips says you are."

Waters: And you say Burton Barber is.

Porter "Talks Around"

You know while he was up there I just thought of something that I heard one time. He just talks about so many things besides the thing at issue. It reminded me of what an old lawyer said to a young lawyer. He said, "When you don't have the evidence, talk about the law. When you don't have the law, talk about the evidence. But when you don't have either the law or the evidence,. . . *talk around.*" (Audience laughs) That is just exactly what Brother Porter has done. He has just "talked around."

Porter Produced No Scripture For Cups

He hasn't produced the Scriptures yet which teach the use of a plurality of cups. *He cannot do it.* As far as I know, he's the strongest man on his side of this question. If he cannot do it, *who can do it?* He hasn't done it. Why, he hasn't produced the

Scripture that remotely deals with the use of individual cups. And the only Scripture that he attempted to put in that circle, according to his own construction of it, only involved a plurality of cups by getting a plurality of assemblies. He didn't even begin to try to involve individual cups in 1 Cor. 10:16, and that's the thing that he's defending in this discussion. The church of our Lord Jesus Christ is divided over this question and it is a serious thing. It can only be settled by going to the word of God and by doing what it says.

Why Not Be Strict On This?

It is strange to me that we would be strict about observing the communion on the first day of the week, because Acts 20:7 says so; that we would be strict about using the fruit of the vine because Matt. 26:29 says so; that we would be strict about using bread, because Matt. 26:26 says so; and that some would be so lax and loose as *not to use "a cup" when Matt. 26:27 said to do* so. Are we going to trade what is mentioned for that which is not mentioned? What is taught for that which is not taught? What is revealed for that which is not revealed? What is exemplified for that which has no Bible example? What is commanded for that which is involved in no Bible command? What is stated for that which is not stated? What is implied for that which is not implied? What is safe for that which is not safe? Shall we place our souls in jeopardy by flagrantly abandoning and forsaking the divine and apostolic pattern of observing the communion?

Our Plea

What assurance of divine approbation for our act can be given us? There is none. Our old plea, "Speak where the Bible speaks, and be silent where it is silent," would become a hollow mockery to us when spoken by us. Shall we forsake this Scriptural plea in order to keep in step with the digressives?

We Want Unity

We abhor division. We desire the unity for which our Savior prayed and which the apostles enjoined. It is both good and pleasant for brethren to dwell together in unity. I submit to you the plea, the plan and the practice which will bring unity to our scattered and diversified forces.

I thank you.

Third Session

Waters' First Affirmative

Sunday School Question

Brethren Moderators, Brother Porter, Friends and Brethren:
I am indeed thankful for the opportunity to stand before you tonight in affirmation of the proposition which I believe with all my heart to set forth the truth. I trust, in the consideration of this proposition, that every hearer will be able with unprejudiced and unbiased minds to weigh every Scripture referred to, every argument adduced therefrom and every statement made, and that all of us will endeavor to manifest the spirit of Him who loved us and died for us in the hope that we may be able to resolve our differences.

Need For Discussion

Tonight begins the discussion of an entirely different question,—a different issue than has been discussed during the past two evenings. Over this issue tonight, disciples present and elsewhere are divided. Strife and contention with all of its consequent disfellowshiping has ensued throughout the brotherhood during the past few decades, and when we survey the division existing, the chaos and confusion resulting, we all realize the need of discussing these differences and our attempting to resolve them.

Proposition

The proposition reads, "The Scriptures teach that when the church comes together for the purpose of teaching the Bible, the people must be taught in an undivided assembly by men only."

Definition of Terms

By "Scriptures," I just mean the word of God. By "teach," I mean to convey the thought and impart the instruction. By "the church comes together," I have reference to an assembly, particularly of the church. "For the purpose of teaching," describes the purpose primarily for which this assembly convenes; in other words, convened to study the word of God and to teach the Bible. The people must be taught, that is, they must be instructed. "In an undivided assembly." By "undivided," I simply mean unclassified. By "assembly," I refer to those who have come together. By "men only," of course I mean the male of the species, excluding women or females, for the teaching that is done in that assembly. That is the proposition I am affirming tonight. Brother W. Curtis Porter is denying. Now then, I shall give my attention to a consideration of the proof of this proposition.

I have before me tonight some charts. To the first of these, I presently invite your attention.

CHART No. 1—On Teaching

THE ASSEMBLY

1 Named—James 2:2.
2. Assembles in the name of the Lord—Matt. 18:20.
3. Assembled by the Church—I Cor. 11:18.
4. Called to Order—Acts 14:27.
5. Common meals forbidden—I Cor. 11:34.
6. Not to forsake—Heb. 10:25.
7. Purpose of Assembly.
    (a) To teach all people—Acts 11:26.
    (b) To consider Spiritual matters—Acts 15:6.
    (c) Convince unbelievers—I Cor. 14:24, 25.
    (d) To feed milk to babes I Cor. 14:24, 25.
    (e) Edify all, so strong get meat—I Cor. 14:31.
    (f) Build up and Teach—I Cor. 14:19, 26.
8. Arrangements and Order.
    (a) Tongue speakers spoke by course—I Cor. 14:27.
    (b) Prophets spoke "one by one"—I Cor. 14:31.
    (c) All silent while teacher spoke—Acts 15:12.
    (d) Confusion condemned—I Cor. 14:33.
    (e) Women not to teach—I Cor. 14:35. I Tim. 2:11, 12.
    (f) Same rule in all assemblies—I Cor. 14:33.
9. Dismissal—Acts 15:30.
10. All of this is decent and orderly—I Cor. 14:40.
11. Warning: "If any one does not recognize this, he is not recognized" (I Cor. 14:38 Revised Standard).

We are going to consider a few passages of Scripture which have to do with church assemblies, and find out what we can from the word of God concerning the instructions delivered therein pertaining to this.

The Assembly

In James 2:2, James said, "If any man come into your assembly," and so the church in apostolic days customarily had assemblies. And I read in Matt. 18:20, Jesus said, "For where two or three are gathered together in my name, there am I in the midst of them." So we are discussing primarily and fundamentally an assembly convened, or come together, or assembled in the name of the Lord. In 1 Cor. 11:18, Paul says, "When ye come together in the church," and so we are talking tonight about coming together in the church. In Acts 14:27, we find the Apostle Paul and Barnabas, "And when they were come, and had gathered the church together, they rehearsed all that God had done with them, and how he had opened the door of faith unto the Gentiles." So they gathered the church together; they called the assembly to order. The Apostle Paul said in 1 Cor. 11:34, "If any man hunger, let him eat at home." Of course, the assembly of the church was not for the purpose of feeding the physical man, but the spiritual man. Now in Heb. 10:25, "Not forsaking the assembling of ourselves together, as the manner of some is." So these assemblies which are called by the church are not to be forsaken by the members thereof.

Purpose of Assembly

Next, we consider the purpose for which we may have such church assemblies.

(a) To teach the people. In Acts 11:26, "And they assembled themselves with the church for a whole year, and taught much people." They assembled themselves with the church for the purpose of teaching much people.

(b) They came together in such assemblies to consider spiritual matters. In Acts 15:6, "The apostles and elders came together for to consider of this matter." The context shows that the church was present.

(c) We come together in such assemblies to convince, teach, and convert the unbelievers. In 1 Cor. 14:24,25, "But if all prophesy, and there come in one that believeth not, or one unlearned, he is convinced of all, he is judged of all." In such an assembly the unbeliever may be convinced.

(d) We come together in such assemblies to instruct the unlearned or, in other words, to feed the babes. For the same verses in 1 Cor. 14:24,25 say, "If there come in one that believeth not, or *one unlearned,"* and *"one unlearned"* would be *one unskillful in the word of righteousness.* He could be taught in such an assembly.

(e) We further come together to edify all because we read in 1 Cor. 14:31, "For ye may all prophesy one by one, that all may learn, and all may be comforted." In such an assembly all learn, unbelievers and unlearned, and those, of course, who otherwise may be taught or instructed, and who may be *needing* what is considered to be *strong meat.*

(f) Next we come together in such an assembly to build up and to teach the church, for we read in 1 Cor. 14:19, "In the church I had rather speak five words with my understanding, that by my voice I might teach others also, than ten thousand words in an unknown tongue." So we come together that we may teach others, and, further, the apostle said in verse 26, "Let all things be done unto edifying," or building up the church. Those are some of the purposes for which we come together in a church assembly.

Divine Arrangements

But now then, let us find out some of the divine arrangements, and something about the divine order, regulating such an assembly.

(a) The tongue speakers were those who spoke in unknown tongues, or foreign languages, in the apostolic age and they were to speak "by course". 1 Cor. 14:27, "If any man speak in an unknown tongue, let it be by two or at the most by three, and that by course; and let one interpret." So then, they spoke in consecutive order.

(b) Then we learn that the prophets spoke one by one, 1 Cor. 14:31, "For ye may all prophesy one by one, that all may learn, and all may be comforted." And these instructions obtained according to verse 26, "When ye come together." When ye come together the apostle says ye may all learn and all be comforted,—all both old and young, those who are learned and unlearned,—by all prophesying one by one.

(c) But we read in Acts 15:12, that when the assembly came together and the speaker spoke, "all the multitude kept silence." The hearers remained silent while the teachers spoke.

(d) Confusion in such an assembly is condemned, 1 Cor. 14:33, "For God is not the author of confusion, but of peace, as in all churches (assemblies) of the saints."

(e) In that assembly the women are not to teach. In 1 Cor. 14:35, Paul said, "For it is a shame for women to speak in the church."

(f) The rules that are here given applied to *all assemblies of the saints* for 1 Cor. 14:33 says, "For God is not the author of confusion, but of peace, as in *all churches (assemblies) of the saints.*" These things then apply to all assemblies of the saints. In Acts 15:30, we read where they were dismissed. All of this which I read tonight concerning that done in the assembly was decent and in order. 1 Cor. 14:40, "Let all things be done decently and in order."

And again we read in 1 Cor. 14:38 from the Revised Standard Version that was published in 1946, "If any one does not recognize this, he is not recognized." Those who *fail to recognize* these divine arrangements, instructions, and rules of order laid down by apostolic injunctions *are not to be recognized.*

I call your attention next to the Second Chart.

CHART No. 2—On Teaching

ASSEMBLED ALL TOGETHER UNCLASSIFIED MEN TAUGHT Women LEARNED IN SILENCE I Cor. 14:35. II Tim. 2:2. I Tim. 2:11-12.	Lk. 4:14-15, 16-28. Lk. 4:31, 36; Lk. 8:4; Acts 3:11. Acts 6:2. Acts 11:26. Acts 14:1. Acts 15: 6, 22, 25 Acts 17:2. Acts 20:7. I Cor. 11:18, 33 Heb. 10:25.	Lk. 5:15. Acts 2:1, 6, 7, 12, 14, 36. Acts 4:31. Acts 10:27, 33. Acts 13:14-16. Acts 14:27. Acts 15:30. Acts 17:19-22. I Cor. 5:4. I Cor. 14:26. James 2:2.

On this chart we have some more Scriptures pertaining to coming together and how the teaching was done when they came together.

How Jesus Taught

I call your attention to Luke, the fourth chapter, beginning with verse 14. We are going to inquire into the personal ministry of Jesus and see how He taught the assemblies. "And Jesus returned in the power of the Spirit into Galilee: and there went out a fame of him through all the region round about. And he taught in their synagogues, being glorified of all." (Luke 4:14,15) When Jesus taught, He was glorified of *all*. They all heard Him in that synagogue because He was glorified of *all*. In verse 16, "And he came to Nazareth, where he had been brought up; and, as his custom was ,he went into the synagogue on the sabbath day, and stood up for to read. And there was delivered unto him the book of the prophet Esaias. And when he had opened the book, he found the place where it was written," and He read it. In verse 20, "He closed the book, and he gave it again to the minister, and sat down. And the eyes of all them that were in the synagogue were fastened on Him." So *all of those who were present* had their eyes on Him.

Next we read that He came down to another place, beginning with verse 31, "And came down to Capernaum, a city of Galilee, and taught them on the Sabbath days. And they were astonished at His doctrine." And verse 36 says, *"They were all amazed."* If they were all amazed, they all heard Him just as they did at Nazareth.

Well, we turn to Luke 5:15, "But so much the more went there a fame abroad of him; and great multitudes *came together* to hear, and to be healed by him of their infirmities." Now I want you to notice, as we refer to these passages of scripture, that time after time we have people *assembling together* and *remaining in one undivided and unclassified assembly* to be taught by *men only.*

We next call your attention to Luke 8:4, "And when much people were *gathered together*, and were come to him out of every city, he spake by a parable." They were *gathered together*.

Together On Pentecost

We next turn to the book of Acts for some more matters of history. Acts, the second chapter, beginning with verse one, "And when the day of Pentecost was fully come, they were all with *one accord in one place*. And suddenly there came a sound from heaven as of a rushing mighty wind, and it filled all the house where they were sitting. And there appeared unto them cloven tongues like as of fire, and it sat upon each of them. And they were all filled with the Holy Ghost, and began to speak with other tongues, as the Spirit gave them utterance." And verse six says, "When this was noised abroad, the multitude came together." The apostles were all with one accord in one place. When this was noised abroad, *the multitude came together*. Verse seven says, "they were *all amazed*." Verse twelve says, "they were *all amazed*," and verse fourteen says, "Peter, standing up with the eleven, lifted up his voice, and said unto them, ye men of Judea, and all ye that dwell at Jerusalem, be this known unto you, and hearken to my words." And in verse thirty-six, the apostle Peter said, "Therefore let all the house of Israel know assuredly, that God hath made that same Jesus whom ye have crucified, both Lord and Christ." So there we have *one undivided assembly*.

Some Assemblies

We turn to Acts 3:11, "And as the lame man which was healed held Peter and John, all the people *ran together* unto them in the porch that is called Solomon's, greatly wondering. And when Peter saw it, he answered unto the people."

In Acts 4:31, "And when they had prayed, the place was shaken where they were *assembled together*." I want you to notice that time after time you find the people *assembling together*. No where do you find them being divided asunder into classes or being thus classified by anyone.

In Acts 6:2, "Then the twelve called the multitude of the disciples unto them."

In Acts, the tenth chapter, when Peter had come down to the household of Cornelius, having been brought from Caesarea, we read in verse twenty-seven, "And he went in and found many that were *come together*." We next read in verse thirty-three, "Immediately therefore I sent to thee; and thou has well done that thou art come. Now therefore are we *all here* present before God, to hear all things that are commanded thee of God." We are all here to hear these things.

In Acts 11:26, "And when he had found him, he brought him unto Antioch. And it came to pass, that a whole year they *assembled themselves with the church,* and taught much people." They taught much people by assembling themselves with the church.

In Acts 13:44-46, "And the next Sabbath day came almost the whole city *together* to hear the word of God." Also verses fourteen through sixteen. Next, in Acts 14:1, "And it came to pass in Iconium, that they went *both together* into the synagogue of the Jews, and so spake, that a great multitude both of the Jews and also the Greeks believed."

In Acts 14:27, "And when they were come, and had gathered the *church together,* they rehearsed all that God had done with them."

Next we read in Acts 15:6, "And the apostles and elders *came together* for to consider of this matter." Verse twenty-two said, "Then pleased it the apostles and elders, with the *whole church,* to send chosen men of their own company to Antioch with Paul and Barnabas."

In Acts 17:2, "Now when they had passed through Amphipolis and Apollonia, they came to Thessalonica where was a synagogue of the Jews: And Paul, as his manner was, went in unto them, and three Sabbath days reasoned with them out of the scriptures."

Come Together

In Acts 20:7, "And upon the first day of the week, when the disciples *came together* to break bread, Paul preached unto them." They *came together* to break bread. In 1 Cor. 15:4, the Apostle Paul mentions, "when ye are gathered together." In 1 Cor. 11:33, *"when ye come together."* 1 Cor. 11:28, *"when ye come together in the church." 1 Cor. 14:26, "when* ye come together." *Heb. 10:25,* "not forsaking the assembling of *ourselves together."*

No Women

We have already learned that it is a shame for women to speak in the church (1 Cor. 14:35), and in 1 Tim. 2:11,12, Paul instructed, "Let the women learn in silence with all subjection. But I suffer not a woman to teach, nor to usurp authority over the man, but to be in silence."

But Faithful Men

In II Tim. 2:2, the Apostle said, "And the things that thou hast heard of me among many witnesses, the same commit thou to faithful men, who shall be able to teach others also."

How We May Teach Effectively Without Classes

Now then, I am going to briefly illustrate how we may teach the word of God effectively, just as has been outlined by these many passages of Scripture. I call your attention to Colossians,

the third chapter and beginning with verse 17, "And whatsoever
ye do in word or deed, do all in the name of the Lord Jesus, giving thanks to God and the Father by him."

Wives

Verse 18 is to the wives and absolutely applies to nobody
else.   Yet the apostle Paul incorporates all these instructions in
the *same chapter* in the *same epistle* written to the *same church*.
When we all assemble together in one assembly, we have *wives
present*.   *It is not necessary* for me to classify, or segregate the
wives to themselves, and read this verse to them and instruct them
accordingly, because they are present.   When I read this verse,
they get it. "Wives, submit yourselves unto your own husbands."
There are women and girls here who are not wives, and this verse
is not to them; but since some day they may be wives, we want
them to hear this.   And, furthermore, there are husbands present, and while this verse is not to them, we want them to know
what to expect of their wives.

Husbands

Verse 19, "Husbands, love your wives." This is not to boys
who are not married, and yet we want those boys to hear it because they may be married some day, or hope to be married, and
we want them to know their duty when they are married, "Husbands, love your wives." We want the wives to hear that so they
will know what to expect of their husbands.

Children

In verse 20, "Children, obey your parents in all things." This
is to children, but we want the parents to hear so they will know
what to expect of their children.   We want the children to hear
it, but we don't have to segregate them, get them aside in a class,
and read it to them because they get it here.

Fathers

Verse 21. "Fathers, provoke not your children to anger, lest
they be discouraged."   There are some husbands who are not
fathers, but who may be fathers some day, and they need to hear
this.   And, of course, those who are fathers are also husbands,
and we have two verses here now which apply to them, and they
need to get both of them.   They are all here and, when this
teaching is given, they all get it.   So we learn now that when the
word of God is taught everyone gets what is for them.

Porter Misrepresented

I want to call your attention to a misrepresentation or two made last evening that I neglected to get to. My brother Porter claimed last evening, or alleged, that I did not read from Williams' "Composition and Rhetoric," but that I just read from my tract. He said that I had it folded in Williams' "Composition and Rhetoric," or he thought that I did. Actually, I *did not* have my tract or any portion of it folded in Williams' "Composition and Rhetoric," and I did read in at least three places directly from Williams' "Composition and Rhetoric" last evening. I did, however, at another time read some from a *page or two* that I had torn out of my tract and had *in my notebook,* but *not* in Williams' "Composition and Rhetoric." When he saw me pick up that book, I read *directly from it.*

And next, he tried to misrepresent me about what I said concerning the missionary society, which he claimed I said in the last debate I had with him. I don't remember having said anything about it there; maybe I did. But, as I said and if I did, he had already for several nights been talking about plates and song books and various other extraneous matters. I told him I would be very glad to make him a proposition that in a future debate neither one of us would mention any extraneous matters and just simply deal with the issue under consideration. He said, "Well, Brother Waters seems to be learning something." If I am, I am not learning it from you.

Four Members And Three Classes In One Room At Quincy

Now then, I would like to mention, since the discussion here exists as a consequence of a challenge issued by Brother Porter's brethren who meet here in Quincy, that his brethren conduct their services on Lord's Day and Brother Porter is going to have to either defend their practice or repudiate it during this discussion. And I would like for him to come to close grips right now and not wait until tomorrow night. Let us get to it because I am eager.

These brethren come together. There is one man and three sisters who are members of his congregation and who meet in this city regularly. (1) They come together. (2) They have some songs. (3) They read the lesson. (4) They have prayer. (5) After prayer they go to the three classes and these three classes are all held simultaneously in the same room. These four members divide into classes, three classes. Sister Bybee teaches the oldest child of Brother Harrison Herman, the nine year old. Sister Herman teaches the two youngest, five and three in ages. That leaves one sister to be taught by Brother Herman.

Confusion At Quincy

Now we have two women and one man speaking in one room at the same time. Talk about confusion!—1 Cor. 14:33, "God is not the author of confusion." And there are three simultaneous classes being conducted in one room! Now you get that.

(6) Then they come back together to observe the communion and the contribution, and in some way dismiss.

Will Porter Defend It, Or Repudiate It?

Now I want Brother Porter to tell us whether or not he endorses that procedure, or whether or not he repudiates it, and if he does repudiate it, upon what grounds.

Tonight I have affirmed the proposition: "The Scriptures teach that when the church comes together for the purpose of teaching the Bible, the people must be taught in an undivided assembly by men only." I have given you chapter and verse, time after time, which absolutely proves that our practice is apostolic, —that our practice is Biblical. But my brother will not be able to refer to Scriptures which authorize the practice of his brethren at this place.

And I thank you.

Third Session
Porter's First Negative
Sunday School Question

Brethren Moderators, Brother Waters, Ladies and Gentlemen:

I appear before you for the purpose of replying to the speech to which you have just listened for the past thirty minutes, in which an effort has been made by Brother Waters to prove that all teaching, when the church comes together for the purpose of teaching, must be done in an undivided assembly. The first thing I shall mention is the last thing he mentioned regarding the classes being taught by my brethren in Quincy.

The Classes In Quincy

He said there are three classes in the same room. I do not know anything about the arrangement of the classes, or anything of that nature, but if those classes are near enough to each other for the teaching of one to interfere with the other, certainly it should not be. So just keep in mind, I do not know, but the teaching of one class should certainly not interfere with the teaching of the other class.

Questions For Brother Waters

But now I have some questions for Brother Waters before I go on. We note the fact in his proposition here that it reads, "The Scriptures teach that when the church comes together for the purpose of teaching the Bible. the people must be taught in an undivided assembly by men only." Originally the proposition read like this: "The Scriptures teach that when the church comes together for the purpose of teaching, the people must be taught in an undivided assembly by men only," but before Brother Waters signed the proposition, he took his pencil and wrote in the words "the Bible." If the church comes together for some other teaching, you would not have to remain in an undivided assembly. So I am wanting to know something about that. So these questions will bring out that and some other things.

1st. If the church should come together for the purpose of teaching musical science, could classes be arranged for the teaching without violating any principle of Scripture?

2nd. If the church should call together its members for the purpose of teaching a singing school, would such a group constitute an assembly of the saints?

3rd. Can two men Scripturally preach from two radio stations, operating on different kilocycles, from different rooms of the same building, at the same time?

4th. Can a sister Scripturally call a group of sisters to her home and teach them?

5th. If two separate groups from the same congregation were to go to separate places, without first meeting in an assembly, could they be Scripturally taught at the same time?

6th. What percentage of the membership must assemble before it becomes a church assembly?

7th. Is it a sin to take a group away from a larger group and teach it?

8th. Does the command to "sing" ever include playing an instrument of music?

9th. Does the command to "teach" ever include methods of teaching?

10th. When the church comes together for the purpose of teaching the Bible, can a woman do any type of teaching or speaking in this assembly?

11th. Can a woman Scripturally be a teacher over a class of men?

12th. (This will be right down his alley because he brought up Quincy) Can two groups from the same congregation, because of contention, Scripturally meet for simultaneous worship and teaching in separate rooms on the second floor of the Labor Temple in Quincy, Illinois? (Porter laughs)

Disfellowship And Order Of Worship

And now we will see what he says. The first thing I want to call your attention to now, after having given the questions, is with respect to the idea of strife and contention, of disfellowship, that Brother Waters mentioned awhile ago. On this, as on other things, there are strife and division, contention, disfellowship, and it is a sad state of affairs, as he has already said. He claims that in this matter his practice is not called in question, and that it is only my practice that is called in question, but his is not. And, therefore, I should give up my practice in order to eliminate disorder and contention and disfellowship. But, bear this in mind, that we have not disfellowshiped Brother Waters. Brother Waters and his group have disfellowshiped us. And such men as Joe Blue and the lamented C. L. Wilkerson, if he were living today, and J. C. Roady and Gus Winters and numbers of others with whom you are acquainted, if they were to go into an assembly of brethren identified with Brother Waters, they would not be allowed to preach or be allowed to lead a public prayer or have any part in the service whatsoever, because they disfellowship us as digressives. So he said his practice is not called in question.

But I called attention last night to the fact that J. D. Phillips, the editor of "The Truth," advocates what is called the order of worship. That in our worship, first, there must be the apostles' teaching; second, there must be the contribution, or fellowship; and third, there must be the Lord's Supper or breaking of bread; and fourth, there must be prayer. And Brother Waters admitted in this paper, which I read from last night, that he had no objection to that order, for he said right here in this issue I read last night that when Phillips asked the question, " 'If it doesn't make any difference, what difference does it make "' " he meant that "if, as we say," (that's Brother Waters now) "as we say one order is as good as another," why have anything to say when they press their order on' the brethren. Now Brother Waters says "one order is as good as another." The practice of Brother Phillips is not called in question by Brother Waters, and if they are divided on that (there are divisions, strife and contention among them), it is not Brother Phillips' position that is being called in question. He admits the other is all right. Then why not give his up? You say you do not find his order of worship in the Bible, but Acts 2:42 gives it in the very order he's contending for: "And they continued steadfastly in the apostles' doctrine and fellowship, and in breaking of bread, and in prayers." Now, the very order (the very things in the order Brother Phillips is contending for) is mentioned in Acts 2:42. And now then, Brother Waters, can you find the things mentioned *in the order in which you use them in your assembly?* You say one is as good as the other; it makes no difference. But there is division between you. Then Brother Phillips' order is not being called in question. It's Brother Waters there that is being called in question; and, therefore, as the idea presented, he is the one that should give it up and go back to Brother Phillips for the sake of unity.

His Offer To Compromise

Another thing he mentioned just at the close, I want to mention now, is with respect to the deal he tried to offer me and get me to make that in future debates he would make no mention of instrumental music, and missionary societies, if I would not mention the song books and the plates for the communion and things like that. I am not making any compromise with Brother Waters on that thing at all, for the simple fact that I am willing for my practice to be tested. If I were meeting a Christian Church preacher in a debate, and he brought up song books, plates, and radios, tuning forks and things of that kind, I would not try to make a deal with him to get him to say nothing more about them. If I use them, he has the right to bring them up. If he can make a parallel of them with his instrumental music, he will show that I am inconsistent in rejecting the one and accepting the other; and the same thing is true with

Brother Waters. If I bring up the plate and song books and things of that kind and show that they are parallel with the things that he accepts, then I show he is inconsistent by rejecting one and accepting the other. Then it is perfectly legitimate for me to bring up things of that kind. *I am not afraid of my practice.* I am not going to enter into any kind of agreement and any kind of conciliatory movement in this matter, in order to keep him from saying anything about these things in future debates. Let him say what he wants to about it—I am willing to take care of it. I am willing for my practice to be questioned, and I am willing to question his. He doesn't want me to say anything about anything except the cups and the classes—that's all he wants me to mention. He doesn't want any parallels drawn along with those other things in his practices—forget about his other practices—but I don't intend to do it. I am going to let you know that his practice is inconsistent; and if you will see these matters, you will give up this inconsistent stand and quit agitating these hobbies that have caused division and strife and contention throughout the brotherhood today.

CHART No. 1—On Teaching
THE ASSEMBLY

1 Named—James 2:2.
2. Assembles in the name of the Lord—Matt. 18:20.
3. Assembled by the Church—I Cor. 11:18.
4. Called to Order—Acts 14:27.
5. Common meals forbidden—I Cor. 11:34.
6. Not to forsake—Heb. 10:25.
7. Purpose of Assembly.
 (a) To teach all people—Acts 11:26.
 (b) To consider Spiritual matters—Acts 15:6.
 (c) Convince unbelievers—I Cor. 14:24, 25.
 (d) To feed milk to babes I Cor. 14:24, 25.
 (e) Edify all, so strong get meat—I Cor. 14:31.
 (f) Build up and Teach—I Cor. 14:19, 26.
8. Arrangements and Order.
 (a) Tongue speakers spoke by course—I Cor. 14:27.
 (b) Prophets spoke "one by one"—I Cor. 14:31.
 (c) All silent while teacher spoke—Acts 15:12.
 (d) Confusion condemned—I Cor. 14:33.

(e) Women not to teach—I Cor. 14:35. I Tim. 2:11, 12.

(f) Same rule in all assemblies—I Cor. 14:33.

9. Dismissal—Acts 15:30.

10. All of this is decent and orderly—I Cor. 14:40.

11. Warning: "If any one does not recognize this, he is not recognized" (I Cor. 14:38 Revised Standard).

Now, then, to his chart.   (Refers to Waters' Chart No. 1) First, he has the chart on 'The Assembly," and he's trying to prove by this chart that when the church comes together for the purpose of teaching, the people *must be taught in an undivided assembly.*   Now keep that in mind.   His proposition says, "The people must be taught in an undivided assembly."   The "Scriptures teach that."

No Scriptural Demand For Undivided Assembly

Brother Waters, where do the Scriptures say anything like that?   You have been wanting details; you are demanding details for all of these things; now give us some.   Where do the Scriptures say anything about "must be taught in an undivided assembly?"   *Is it there?*   Not in any passage that he gave.   There's *not a word in any of those passages* which said *anything* about you *must remain or be taught in an undivided assembly.*   Not a word.   *It just isn't there.*   But Brother Waters is demanding that a thing be found in so many words in the Scriptures.   Give it to us, Brother Waters; I want to see it.   I want to show it to this congregation—any passage from your chart, any chart you have there—which says in any sort of words anything about the congregation or assembly *must remain in an undivided assembly.*   Where is it, Brother Waters?   Point out the Scripture that says that.   Is it on the chart?   If it is, I missed it.   I think I got every one of them down, and I noticed them carefully as you referred to them and quoted them and read them, but you didn't read a word about that, and you didn't quote a word about that.   There wasn't a statement, in any passage that you gave, that said one thing about remaining in an undivided assembly, or being taught in an undivided assembly.   He says the Scriptures teach that it must be; it must be taught in an undivided assembly.   Where is the Scripture teaching that?   He's the man who has been demanding details—now let him give us some details.   And let him

find something about that in the Scriptures.   The Scriptures say
nothing about that.

Undivided Assemblies And Upper Rooms

He found where some teaching was done in undivided assemblies, but he didn't find in any of them where the teaching must
be done in undivided assemblies.   Now I could follow the same
plan.   If he took every example of every assembly in the New
Testament record, and found that in every assembly the teaching was done in an undivided assembly, and yet he found no
statement that said teaching must be done in an undivided assembly, his proposition would stand unproved.   Because the two
examples we have of the assembly for communion in the New
Testament, we find the record declaring they assembled in an
upper room.   Yes, when the Lord instituted the Lord's Supper,
the Scripture tells us in two of the gospel records, Mark and Luke,
that they were in an *upper room*.   And in Acts 20:7, the one example we have of the disciples' observing that institution in the
New Testament days, we learn they did it in an *upper room*.   All
right, those two assemblies for the Lord's Supper are revealed to
us in the New Testament, and in both of them, the assemblies
were in upper rooms.   Therefore, I can conclude, according to him,
that when the church comes together for the purpose of communion, they must assemble in an upper room.   Now that's just
as sensible, just as reasonable, just as logical, just as Scriptural,
as the conclusion he's drawn, from finding some teaching done
in undivided assemblies.   If I should take a position like that,
what would Brother Waters do?   He would say, 'Yes, you may
find places where they did assemble in upper rooms, but find the
place which says that it must be done that way."   That's what
he would say.   And one of his brethren could start a hobby on
that, and I would not be surprised if one of them does.   And
when he would start a hobby on that he would say, "Now, we
have got to meet in an upper room for the Lord's Supper."   What
would Brother Waters do?   Ah, he would say these assemblies
are all right in upper rooms; those examples are there all right,
but there is no statement made in connection with these which
says that it *must be in an upper room*.   All right then, Brother
Waters, in every assembly that you have, have you found a statement anywhere which says the teaching *must be done in an undivided assembly?* Not one. I demand that he produce the sort of

proof that he demands the other fellow to produce. Let us have it. Now then to the chart.

First, we have James 2:2—the assembly is named, "If one come into your assembly wearing gay clothing, etc." Nothing said in that about *remaining in an undivided assembly* to be taught. Not a word.

All right, then, in the second place, they "assembled in the name of the Lord." (Matt. 18:20) "Where two or three are gathered together in My Name." The Lord promised to be there, but there nothing is said about how the teaching is to be done, whether they are to remain in one assembly to be taught, or if they must remain in an undivided assembly. Not a word said about it. That's what he's trying to prove by it.

And then, in the third place, (1 Cor. 11:18), they were "assembled by the church." I don't know what he meant by "assembled by the church." What did you mean by that, Ervin? You didn't read it that way when you read it. In fact, it doesn't read that way. It doesn't say one word about *being assembled by the church.* "When ye come together in the church." It didn't say, "by the church." He read it correctly, but he has it written incorrectly on his chart. He must have copied that from somebody, and failed to discover the fact that he had the thing fixed wrong. No, it doesn't say "by the church," Ervin. The passage says nothing about "by the church." It says, they assembled "in the church." Now where does he get the idea of being assembled "by the church?" And what do you mean by "assembled by the church?" We want to know about that.

All right, then, in the fourth place, "Called to order." (Acts 14:27). "Called to order." That proves that if it is *called to order,* then all teaching *must be done in an undivided assembly,* you see. (Laughing at Waters) Yes, sir, if you call the assembly, that proves all the teaching must be done in an undivided assembly. Now that's the kind of proof that Brother Waters is offering for his proposition tonight.

And then, in the fifth place, "Common meals are forbidden." (1 Cor. 11:34). And since *common meals are forbidden* in the Lord's day worship, why, then, of course, that *means* that *all teaching must be done in an undivided assembly.* Can't you see the logic in that? Can't you see the connection? That's beautiful, isn't it?

All right, and then in the sixth place, (Heb. 10:25), "Forsake not the assembling of yourselves together as the manner of some is." All right, here is a command not to forsake the assembly, but does that say *anything* about all the teaching being done in an undivided assembly? Not a word. It's not even hinted at. Nothing said about the matter at all there.

All right then, we come to the seventh, the "purpose of the assembly." First, he says it's "to teach all people." (Acts 11:26). Well, that passage says they "taught *much* people," but I guess I will let him get by with the word "all." It says "much." "They taught much people." So it's to teach all people. And since they assembled to teach all people, that means *all people must remain in an undivided assembly.*

And then next (b), "to consider spiritual matters.' (Acts 15:6). They came together here to consider spiritual matters. What were the spiritual matters? Some Judaizing teachers had gone from Jerusalem down to Antioch and tried to bind circumcision of the law of Moses on the Gentiles. They came up to Jerusalem about it, and they called the church in to consider that matter. That's not the assembly of your proposition, Brother Waters. Your proposition says, "When the church comes together *for the purpose of teaching the Bible."* It doesn't say when it come together to consider spiritual matters. They did come together to consider matters of that kind. They did not come together for the purpose of teaching the assembly. It was for an entirely different purpose—that assembly was. But nevertheless, whatever the purpose was, that proves that whenever the church comes together for the purpose of teaching the Bible, the teaching *must be done in an undivided assembly.* It makes no difference whether it says anything about that or not—that's what it proves.

All right, then, in the next place (c), "to convince unbelievers." They couldn't be convinced unless *they remained in an undivided assembly,* you see. You can't divide the assembly if you are going to convince unbelievers. You couldn't do it anywhere else.

And then (d), "to feed milk to the babes.' (1 Cor. 14:24, 25). And next, "to edify all so the strong will get the meat." I thought you brethren didn't know any difference between meat and milk. When we make the argument about feeding milk to babes and feeding meat to those who had their senses exercised to discern the good and evil, why, Brother Waters' brethren have come back and said, "You can't tell anything about it. What's the milk, and what's the meat?" They have oftentimes asked the question, "What's the milk and what's the meat?" Brother Waters said that's what we have got to do. We've got to feed the babes the milk. Now, if you do not know which the milk is, maybe you will feed the milk to the grown folks and the strong meat to the babes—if you don't know which is which.

Then in the next place, "to build up and to teach." (1 Cor. 14:19,26). And since the teaching is for the purpose of edifying, of course, the church must remain in an undivided assembly; you couldn't be edified any other way. And that proves my friend's proposition, you see.

And then to his arguments on order and arrangement.

First, "The tongue speakers spoke by course," but, of course, he doesn't have any tongue speakers. And the second place, "The prophets prophesied one by one." Of course, he doesn't have any prophets. And neither of them is found in the assemblies of my Brother Waters. He doesn't have them. And next, "All were silent when the teachers spoke." Acts 15:12. "All silent when the teachers spoke." Well, that referred to an assembly where Paul and Silas were rehearsing some matters. And only two of them on that occasion were rehearsing the matters; everybody else keep silent, men and all. If that proves that silence is enjoined in an unlimited sense, then only two speakers could ever speak according to that. That won't fit 1 Cor. 14:31, because there he has two or three. All right, then, again, 1 Cor. 14:33—"Confusion is condemned." And since confusion is condemned in the assembly of the saints, then in order to be taught the Bible, you *must remain in an undivided assembly.* You couldn't do otherwise. If you taught any other way, you would have confusion; and so you have to remain in an undivided assembly in order to prevent confusion. "Confusion is condemned." That *proves* my friend's proposition. And in the next place, "Women are not to teach." And I will pass that until he gives us some answers to the questions. And next, the "same rule in all the assemblies." I don't know whether my friend meant to say by that that this rule that governs tongue speakers governs his assemblies or not. I don't know just what he meant by that. We will wait and see.

And then the "dismissal," in Acts 15:30. The assembly was dismissed; here the assembly was dismissed. Here was an arrangement for the assembly. Here's the dismissal. All right, first, *named, assembled in the name of the Lord, by the church, called to order,* and then these other things in between, and, finally, *they were dismissed,* and that's the end of it. They were through; the assembly is dismissed; and that concludes the assembly. All right, Brother Waters, if we meet together in a common assembly, in an undivided assembly, and we engage in a number of services to God, and then after while we *dismiss the assembly,* could different groups *then go to various places* and be taught the Bible? Now tell us. After the assembly has been dismissed—*after the assembly has been dismissed,* Ervin—could the people who comprise that assembly go to various places and study the word of the Lord? Some to one place, and some to another? I want to know. We will wait and see if he tells us.

And then his 11th one, "If any one does not recognize this, he is not recognized." (1 Cor. 14:38 from Revised Standard Version) "If one does not recognize this, he is not recognized." Personally, I recognize everything the apostle Paul said in 1 Cor. 14, but I don't recognize my opponent's application of a number of things in 1 Cor. 14. I am certain that when Paul said, according to the Revised Standard Version, that "if a man does not recognize this, he is not recognized," he was not referring to Ervin's application of it. I know he didn't mean that. Paul was talking about things he had said, and not about things Brother Waters has interpreted him to mean. I wonder if he means that you must have all these things in all of your assemblies or otherwise you don't recognize it. If so, then that forces Brother Waters to have tongue speakers. If not, he doesn't recognize what Paul said. Paul goes right on in the following verse and says, "Forbid not to speak in tongues." And right in connection with what is said about this—"If any man does not recognize this, he is not recognized," he said, "Forbid not to speak with tongues." Well, if someone would make an attempt to speak with tongues in Brother Waters' assemblies, would he make an effort to stop it? Would he do anything about it? Would he oppose it? Well, he says, "If any man does not recognize this, he is not recognized." Now that's right in the same connection, Ervin, and so I want to know if you mean that we must have everything in the assemblies today that you find in 1 Cor. 14. We will wait and see.

Now then to his next chart (No. 2).

CHART No. 2—On Teaching

	Lk. 4:14-15, 16-28.	
	Lk. 4:31, 36;	Lk. 5:15.
ASSEMBLED	Lk. 8:4;	Acts 2:1, 6, 7, 12, 14, 36.
ALL TOGETHER	Acts 3:11.	Acts 4:31.
UNCLASSIFIED	Acts 6:2.	Acts 10:27, 33.
MEN TAUGHT	Acts 11:26.	Acts 13:14-16.
Women LEARNED	Acts 14:1.	Acts 14:27.
IN SILENCE	Acts 15: 6, 22, 25	Acts 15:30.
I Cor. 14:35.	Acts 17:2.	Acts 17:19-22.
II Tim. 2:2.	Acts 20:7.	I Cor. 5:4.
I Tim. 2:11-12.	I Cor. 11:18, 33	I Cor. 14:26.
	Heb. 10:25.	James 2:2.

Jesus In The Synagogues

We come to his second chart. And here he gave a number of instances in which he endeavored to show how Jesus taught during His personal ministry. Luke 4:16, where He went into the synagogues, and (verse 20) when in the synagogue all eyes were fastened upon Him, (verses 31-36)—they were all amazed; therefore they all heard. And Luke 5:15—the multitudes came together. And so we find here where there was an assembly, or they came together, and things of that nature. He concludes that that proves that in teaching the Bible, we *must remain in an undivided assembly*. Brother Waters is making a law where God hasn't made it. It's not there in God's book. We don't read anywhere in the Bible where a congregation must remain in an undivided assembly. Brother Waters, is that "must" as strong as it was in the other proposition? In that other proposition, you said the word "must" meant "obligatory"—no way around it—although you did give us a way around it before we got through. But in this case, does it mean the same thing? "They must be taught in an undivided assembly." The "Scriptures teach" that it must be. Now I want to know where is the passage that says a word about it. He hasn't found it so far. I'm waiting for him to find it.

Did Not Remain In Undivided Assembly

And in these statements made concerning Jesus' teaching in

the synagogues, is there *anything* in *any of them* that *says anything* about the teaching must be *done in an undivided assembly?* No, not a word. Not a word. *Not even mentioned.*

Then he came to Luke 8:4, where the great multitude was gathered together unto Christ; so all teaching must be done in an undivided assembly. But that's an unfortunate passage for Brother Waters, because we find in that assembly gathered there, which the Lord taught, it was not only the multitude which came but His disciples also. And in the 13th chapter of Matthew, Matthew records the same incidents—the multitudes coming together, and the teaching which Jesus did to the multitudes in parables. And then verse 36 of the 13th chapter of Matthew, the Revised Version, tels us that "Jesus left the multitudes," "went into the house," "His disciples came unto Him," and He taught them. Now then, here's where some teaching was done where the assembly *did not remain* in an undivided assembly. Right here in the teaching of the Lord; the Lord taught them. There was the great multitude there, and the Lord taught them; but Matthew later says, "He left the multitude, went into the house, and His disciples came to Him." The multitude was left behind, and He explained matters to the disciples. He taught them there. So Jesus did not do all of His teaching in an undivided assembly. There "He left the multitude;" He left part of them behind and took some of them into another place, and there He taught them in a house. So instead of proving what Brother Waters tried to prove by it, it just proves the reverse.

The Pentecost Assembly

Then he came to Acts 2—"the multitude came together," and they were amazed. And they heard Peter speak as he said, "Hearken unto my words" when he addressed *all Israel* (verse 36). Yes, Peter spoke to the whole crowd, but *before that speaking was done,* there was *much other speaking* done in a number of different languages. And the men said in that connection, "How *hear we* every man in our own tongue in which we were born?" "We hear them speak the wonderful works of God," present tense, and the very language indicates that there was simultaneous teaching even in Acts 2. For it did not say, "we heard" them speaking in our own tongue, but we "hear" them. "How *hear we* every man in our own tongue?" And it says, "There were *dwelling* at Jerusalem devout men, Jews out of every nation."

"Dwelling at Jerusalem." Does that mean at the same time? Or some in one year and some in another? "And filled all the house where they were *sitting."* Does that mean some of them were sitting one day and the others the next day? All right, we hear them *speaking.* If *dwelling* means at the same time, and *sitting* means at the same time, why wouldn't *"speaking,"* in the same connection, mean at the same time? And there we have simultaneous speaking indicated right there in Acts 2 that he gave. He gave Acts 3:11, but Acts 3:11 is an entirely different assembly, Brother Waters. There they came together because of curiosity, wondering about the man who had been healed of his lameness. And then he came to Acts 4:31 where they were assembled, but not a word was said about their being assembled for the purpose of teaching.

The Appointment Of The Seven

Acts 6:2 is another that he gave, but they came together there to appoint the seven men to look after the daily administration; nothing said about teaching. He has the wrong assembly. That proves, because they came together into one assembly to appoint men to look after their daily administration, that all teaching must be done in an undivided assembly. That's what it proves! And I know it does, because Ervin says so.

Thank you.

Third Session

Waters' Second Affirmative

Sunday School Question

Brethren Moderators, Brother Porter, Brethren and Friends:

I am happy to be here for the second affirmative of this session.

Is It A Class?

Just before Brother Porter closed his speech, he dealt with Matt. 13:2-3, "Great multitudes were *gathered together* unto him, so that he went into a ship, and sat; and the whole multitude stood on the shore. And he spake many things unto them in parables." He alleges that after Jesus teaches the multitude, He separated a smaller group from the larger group, classified and segregated them, and went into a house and taught them. He then said, "That's authority for our classes." I want you to understand that Matt. 13 does not even remotely have anything to do with the division and segregation of any assembly whatsoever into classes. It doesn't say so.

Porter Thinks He Sees Classes

And the main fault with Brother Porter and his brethren in trying to use such references to prove classes is just this; that they want the word of God to teach classes so badly that they just think they can see a class everywhere they turn. Just anywhere you find anyone talking about the Bible, or spiritual matters, with anyone else, they think that's a class. Whether it be found out by the way, whether it be found over here incidentally, informally, and privately in somebody's house or wherever it is, why they think that constitutes a class parallel with their class system. They do that.

What Really Happened

The Lord Jesus taught the multitude which *came together*. Now then, let's see what happened after the teaching here. Jesus sent the multitude away and went into the house (Matt. 13:36). The service is over; the teaching is over. I want you to understand that the multitude which *came together had not been classified and segregated* in any respect whatsoever by the Lord, or by anybody else. They assembled down there and nothing was said about classification and segregation whatsoever. Nothing was said about it. The Lord just went into a house and His disciples came unto Him. In other words, he just went into somebody's house. And now the disciples come unto Him and say, "Declare unto us the parable of the tares." Lord, explain this to us. Tell us something about this. And now then, because after the Lord taught the multitude, He goes into somebody's home and the disciples come to him and ask Him a question, why Brother Porter says, "There's a class. There's a parallel for our classes." There is our authority for coming together in an assembly of the church, such as you have here at Quincy, and singing and reading and praying, and dividing and segregating into classes. He says, "That's it." Now what do we have here? Why he just has the Lord going into a home and some disciples coming unto Him and asking Him a question. He answers it, and Porter says, "That's it." He just thinks he can see a class, parallel with the classes he has, everywhere he turns. He does. And I'll just challenge him to find some more like this. They will be just about like this, Brother Porter.

It Does Not Resemble His Classes

It doesn't even remotely resemble the classes that you and your brethren have. This does not parallel the class system utilized by Brother Porter and his brethren at all. It just doesn't parallel it. But they think they can find a class almost anywhere they look.

Were There Classes On Pentecost?

All right, but just before he sat down, he referred to Acts, the second chapter And you know in Acts, the second chapter, he tried to find classes. He just thinks he can see classes everywhere he turns. I'm going to turn and read it. "Now when the day of Pentecost was fully come, they were all with one accord in one place. And suddenly there came a sound from heaven as of a rushing mighty wind, and it filled all the house where they were sitting. And there appeared unto them cloven tongues like as of fire, and it sat upon each of them. And they were all filled with the Holy Ghost, and began to speak with other tongues, as the Spirit gave them utterance." (Acts 2:1-4) Do you see classes there? Do you see the twelve apostles divided into twelve classes? Now I ask you, do you? Can you even look between the lines and imagine it? Now was it there? Brother Porter said, "They must have had them." Does it say anything about the classification of an assembly in the second chapter of the Acts of the Apostles? Do you read about segregating into various groups? *No.* But how do we know they did it? *Because W. Curtis Porter said so.* But you can't read it in the word of God.

They Were Together

"And there were dwelling at Jerusalem Jews, devout men, out of every nation under heaven. And when this was noised abroad, the multitude *came together*." (Acts 2:5-6). Now what does the Bible say? *"The multitude came together."* What does Porter say? "After they came together, they were divided into classes." But I haven't read that verse yet, Brother Porter. I haven't found that one yet. Now I found where they *"came together,"* in verse 6. Now will you read me where they divided asunder into classes, Brother Porter? Will you do it? If you will, just turn over there and read it. Just read, now, where they divided the assembly into classes. Verse 6 said they "came together." Now if you will just turn over and read it, I will just let you stand up on my time, and, *without any comment,* read it. Be glad to on my time. Will you do it, Brother Porter?

Porter speaks up from seat: "Will you read where it says for us to remain in an undivided assembly?" (Audience laughs)

Waters: Listen, "And when this was noised abroad, the multitude *came together*." *I* want you to remember that I'm considering an argument in answer to Brother Porter awhile ago. Brother Porter said that they had classes in the second chapter of Acts. No wonder he's trying to evade the thing. He said they had classes in the second chapter of Acts. I've given him the opportunity to just stand up and read *without any comment,* now, on my time. And what does he do now? He just goes and brings up something else. You know Brother Porter has fallen short of my estimate as a debater in this way. I have never seen him, I have never known of him, *speaking up from his seat as many times as he has during this debate.* I have never known him to.

Porter speaks from seat: "Beg your pardon, Brother Waters. I thought you meant for me to answer."

Waters: I said, *"Without comment,* will you turn over and read it?" Now when you ask me another question, you have no authority whatsoever to do it. In your speech, you can ask as many questions as you want to.

Porter Can Not Find Where They Classified

Now then, I said that you claimed in Acts, the second chapter, that they divided up into classes. You said it. You said that the apostles spoke simultaneously in the second chapter, and they spoke to classes. Now I just want him to read it; just read where they divided into classes. Brother Porter said they divided into classes. The Scriptures said, "The multitude came together." Well, has the multitude gathered? Were the Apostles together? Brother Porter says the apostles were separated and the multitude was separated into classes and he can't read either one. I'll tell you right now that a man who can see those things between the lines like that is not a reliable instructor of the word of God. He can't read either one of them.

Classified Without Students According To Porter

"And they were all amazed and marvelled, saying one to another, Behold, are not all these which speak Galilaeans? And how hear we every man in his own tongue, wherein we were born?"

Porter says, "How hear we every man? They were hearing them all speak; therefore, they were all speaking simultaneously. And they must have been divided into classes." Well, he said there were not some of them sitting at one time and some of them sitting at another time. So I want to show you the position he has gotten himself into now. Verse 1 says, "And when the day of Pentecost was fully come, they were all with one accord in one place." Verse 2, "And suddenly there came a sound from heaven as of a rushing mighty wind, and it filled all the house where they were sitting." Now he says they were all sitting simultaneously. Remember that now. He says where the word "speaking" is found, they were all speaking simultaneously. Verse 4, "And they were all filled with the Holy Ghost, and *began to speak* with other tongues, as the Spirit gave them utterance." "*Began to speak* with other tongues." That means they were all speaking simultaneously, and they were divided into classes according to Porter. I want you to understand that, according to that construction, the twelve apostles were divided into twelve classes *before there was even a multitude there to which to speak.* There are twelve apostles now, dividing themselves with no classes to speak to. Now that's just exactly the fix that Brother Porter has himself in on the second chapter of the Acts of the Apostles. He cannot read classes in Acts, the second chapter.

Porter's Predicament

Verse 1 says, "They were all with one accord *in one place.*" Verse 6 says, "The multitude *came together,*" and Verse 14 says, "Peter, standing up with the eleven, lifted up his voice, and said unto them, Ye men of Judea, and *all ye that dwell at Jerusalem.*" They were *all there.* Oh, but he says they were divided into classes! Listen! And think about it. Were these people who had crucified the Son of God, unbelievers, having no faith whatsoever in the apostles, docile and humble enough now, to let twelve apostles divide them into classes, to teach them for awhile, and then to bring them back together? And yet they are unbelievers; they are the bloodthirsty people who had crucified the Son of God. He thinks they were docile and humble to let the twelve Apostles divide them into classes, to teach them. That's Brother Porter's position. *Talk about reading between the lines!* And when we read in verse 36, "And let all the house of Israel know assuredly." How many? "All of them." All right, *he did not find classes* in the second chapter of Acts of the Apostles. That's as close as he will ever come to finding his classes.

No Classes In New Testament

But now then, what has he done? Well, he has referred to some of the Scriptures on my chart, and he would take one Scripture, you know, and would say, "Well, does this Scripture mention this? Does this Scripture mention that?" I didn't say all the truth was found in one of them. But I want you to get this: In Matthew, Mark, Luke, John and Acts, the first five books of the New Testament, there are, if I remember correctly, approximately 150 references to teach, and you *cannot in those 150 references find an assembly ever segregated and classified into groups for the teaching of the word of God.* It is passing strange, indeed, if inspiration would make mention of a matter so important as teaching 150 times and leave unmentioned a system as important as Brother Porter thinks his is! Why doesn't he turn to the word of God and read it, if he can find it?

Questions

Now then, we are going to consider some questions which Brother Porter gave me tonight. I expected about the number he gave me the other night. We didn't have any agreement on the number of questions. He handed me about six then, and that's not too unreasonable. Tonight he handed me twelve. I just don't know what to think about that. I have never entered a debate yet and handed a man that many questions unless he first handed me that many. Twelve questions Not just five or six, but twelve! That's for me to consume a lot of my speech now in answering twelve questions. All right, he'll get *twelve* from me tomorrow night, and I'll receive none.

1. If the church should come together for the purpose of teaching musical science, could classes be arranged for the purpose of teaching and not violate any principle of Scripture?

Answer: *Teaching musical science is not the work of the church.*

2. If the church should call together its members for the purpose of teaching a singing school, would such an assembly constitute an assembly of the saints?

Answer: *Such teaching is not the work of the church.*

3. Can two men scripturally preach over two radio stations,

operating on different kilocycles in different rooms of the same building at the same time?

Answer: Perhaps. If parallel with your classes, can a sister teach over one? Another sister over the other?

4. Can a sister scripturally call a group of sisters to her home and teach them?

Answer: If you are discussing such a class as embraced by your proposition tomorrow night, no. But could she call a group of men to her home and teach them?

5. If two separate groups from the same congregation were to go to separate places without first meeting in an assembly, could they be scripturally taught at the same time?

Answer: If these groups are such groups as embraced by your proposition tomorrow night, no.

6. What percentage of the membership must assemble before it becomes a church assembly?

Answer: Well, I know definitely, if this assembly is intended to be a church assembly. If so understood, if so announced, if so arranged, if two of them came, it would be a church assembly.

7. Is it a sin to take a group away from a larger group and teach it.

Answer: It is a sin to teach such classes as you brethren have and as are embraced in the proposition which you are to affirm tomorrow night.

8. Does the command to sing ever include the playing of a musical instrument of music?

Answer: No.

9. Does the command to teach ever include methods of teaching?

Answer: *It includes those authorized by the Bible.*

10. When the church comes together for the purpose of teaching the Bible, can a woman do any type of teaching or speaking in this assembly?

Answer: She may sing.

11. Can a woman scripturally be a teacher over a class of men?

Answer: No, or women either, if you use the word "class" in the sense in which it is used in your proposition.

12. Can two groups from the same congregation, because

of contention, scripturally meet for simultaneous worship and teaching in separate rooms on the second floor of the Labor Temple in Quincy, Illinois?

Answer: Get this. *No!* Either both are wrong in such circumstances or one is wrong. If only one is in the wrong, then one can meet scripturally, but *if both parallel your classes, then your classes are public, and women may publicly teach them.*

Will Porter Endorse It?

Let's consider again the practice of Brother Porter and his brethren here at Quincy, Ill. They come together, first; they sing songs, second; they read the lesson, third; they have the prayer fourth; and then these four members divide into three classes along with three children who are too young to be members. One sister teaches one nine-year-old; one sister teaches one five and one three-year-old; and one brother teaches the remaining sister. All of these three classes are conducted simultaneously in the same room. Now through the years in which I have engaged in discussion those of like persuasion with Brother Porter, I have never had one single solitary representative of his brethren to take the position that you could have more than one class being taught simultaneously in the same room. Twenty years ago, twenty-five years ago, his brethren defended that almost universally, but they learned better than that years ago. Time after time I've had their preachers in discussion to say, "We will not defend that. That's why we built the classrooms in order to avoid and eliminate the confusion." Now Brother Porter just kind of hedges around. Of course, he doesn't want to come out in this discussion and say, "Brethren, I don't endorse that." And so he said, "If those classes are close enough together to interfere, I don't endorse them." But you go down yonder and look at the room in which these classes are convened. And you remember that three teachers have to speak in that room, *that small room,* loudly enough to be heard by those classes. He says, "If they are closely enough together to interfere, I do not endorse them."

I, personally, witnessed this year three classes, just a little larger than those, being conducted simultaneously by his brethren in a room no larger than that one, and I know they had confusion. *They had confusion! Every student could hear every teacher.* A student in any class could hear all three teachers, and it takes pretty good concentration to tune out two and listen to one. I want to know. Will Brother Porter endorse that procedure? Brother Logan Buchanan a year ago at Dallas, Texas, said, *"I will not endorse it!"* Will Brother Porter endorse it without any equivocation or circumlocution? Will he just come out and tell us? *Will he endorse it?*

Porter Versus Watson On Disfellowshiping Me

He says, "We have not disfellowshiped Brother Waters. They have disfellowshiped us." He wouldn't have you to believe that the Sunday School and Individual Cups brethren fellowship me, would he? Brother, I want to know; do you and your brethren fellowship me? Do you? Why you said you hadn't disfellowshiped me. Now have you? Now I want to know, have you? Quite a difference from what his moderator told me last year in our discussion at Clio, Mo. He said, "Let us not beat around the bush, Brother Waters. You know that I believe that you're going to hell, and you believe that I am." (Watson nods—audience laughs). Brother Sterl A. Watson. That's just exactly what he said. Brother Sterl says, "You know that I believe that you are going to hell." Brother Porter says, "We have not disfellowshiped Brother Waters." But, according to his moderator, I'm on the road to hell! And he says he hasn't disfellowshiped me? Now I want you to get that. You brethren better get off and talk about this thing. Do you fellowship me, Brother Porter? *Do you fellowship me?* Do you *believe I'm on the road to hell?* You brought up the fellowship question. What about it?

Oh, he makes an appeal for sympathy. He says that we brethren wouldn't call on Joe Blue, and Brother C. L. Wilkerson of sainted memory, and other brethren, if they should come into our assembly. Most of our brethren don't know any of those men, but we wouldn't call upon them, or my respondent, or his moderator, more particularly (audience laughs), if they should come into our assembly. That's right. Why? Because they endorse, and they use, individual cups in the communion. They have not one iota, one scintilla, one jot or one tittle of authority for it. And because they use the Sunday School. They divide the assembly of the church into classes and segregate them. *They have no Bible authority for it.* They permit women to teach in such assemblies. They have no Bible authority for it. And those practices, endorsed and utilized by these brethren, have become the bone of contention and the wedge of division among the disciples of Christ. Their advocates do not endeavor to keep the unity of the spirit in the bond of peace. They do not speak where the Bible speaks and they are not silent where it is silent.

Order of Worship Not Parallel With Classes

And he refers to J. D. Phillips again, and to the order of Worship. I just mentioned to him that Brother Phillips could not find the order of worship in the New Testament. But I have found time after time where people came together, and where they were taught in unclassified assemblies by men speaking one at a time and the women remaining silent during the teaching and instruction of the church. He has not found any assembly in the New Testament classified and segregated into classes for the purpose of teaching, such classes as are utilized by him and his brethren.

Quibbling By Porter

About Acts 15:6, one of the proof texts on my chart, he said, "Why that didn't say they came together to study the Bible." He protested that they came together to consider the subject of circumcision. My brother, *is circumcision a Bible subject?* Is the subject of circumcision a Bible subject? Is it a Bible matter? Oh, such quibbling, Brother Porter!

Why, he says, "You mentioned milk and meat. You said that in that assembly the unlearned could get milk and that those who were learned could get the meat." That's right, and I didn't say anything about dividing the milk from the meat either. Now did I? Huh? Did I say anything about dividing the milk and the meat? Not a thing! It's you brethren that talk about dividing it. I didn't say anything about dividing it. Now, whenever you come to an assembly, you have those in there who are unskillful and those who are skilled. You teach them the word of God and the unlearned will get milk and the learned will get meat. I didn't say anything about dividing it. Now if he thinks he can, he's welcome to try it. I'll be right along with him to show him he can't. You brought it up. I want you to tell me how your brethren divide the milk from the meat in these three classes here, the classes that your brethren have here, the classes that your brethren have here in Quincy. I wonder what three grades they divide that milk and meat into. I want to know more about that. You brought it up.

Does I Cor. 14 Apply Today In Principle?

Of I Cor. 14:31, "Ye may all prophesy one by one," No. 6 on the chart, he said, "You don't have any prophets today. That's the rule of order that was laid down for those teachers who were inspired." Well, *is there any reason at all why inspired teachers should teach one by one and uninspired ones should not teach one by one?* Is there any principle which would make it mandatory upon the inspired teachers that they teach one by one, that would not apply to the uninspired teachers? What does Brother Porter mean? But, he says, "You don't have any tongue speakers." Well, we don't have anyone today speaking foreign languages miraculously, but we have them all over the earth speaking languages which we cannot understand, that they have learned. The principle that is given in 1 Cor. 14 would apply to them. And if we had a foreigner in our assembly, who was even a member of the church but couldn't speak English, and who wanted to teach, that foreigner would have to remain silent so far as teaching us is concerned unless we had someone present who could interpret the speech to us. *The same principle applies.* What's the matter with Brother Porter? Does he think that someone can get up and teach us in an unknown tongue, or foreign language, without an interpreter and it be Scriptural? *I'm not afraid to tell you what I believe about it.* Are you?

What Would Porter Do?

But in 1 Cor. 14:33, the apostle Paul said God is not the author of confusion, but of peace as in all churches (assemblies) of the saints. If the brethren here in Quincy have three classes in one small room and three teachers teaching those three classes simultaneously and that is not confusion, *will you tell me what is confusion?* And Paul says, "Ye may all prophesy one by one that all may learn and all may be comforted." According to Paul's instructions here, we can all learn and all be comforted in an undivided assembly where we speak one at a time. If they could so learn nineteen centuries ago, *we can so learn today.* He says, "Would Brother Waters stop a tongue speaker today." *I would.* If we had someone present speaking in a foreign language without an interpreter, and we could not understand him, *I would certainly apply and invoke the principles here. Would you?* Now you come back and tell me, *would you?* And that without any evasion whatsoever.

Tonight I have affirmed the proposition which has been read and I have gone to the Scriptures to prove it. I again call your attention to Chart No. 1 and Chart No. 2.

CHART No. 1—On Teaching

THE ASSEMBLY

1 Named—James 2:2.
2. Assembles in the name of the Lord—Matt. 18:20.
3. Assembled by the Church—I Cor. 11:18.
4. Called to Order—Acts 14:27.
5. Common meals forbidden—I Cor. 11:34.
6. Not to forsake—Heb. 10:25.
7. Purpose of Assembly.
   (a) To teach all people—Acts 11:26.
   (b) To consider Spiritual matters—Acts 15:6.
   (c) Convince unbelievers—I Cor. 14:24, 25.
   (d) To feed milk to babes I Cor. 14:24, 25.
   (e) Edify all, so strong get meat—I Cor. 14:31.
   (f) Build up and Teach—I Cor. 14:19, 26.
8. Arrangements and Order.
   (a) Tongue speakers spoke by course—I Cor. 14:27.
   (b) Prophets spoke "one by one"—I Cor. 14:31.
   (c) All silent while teacher spoke—Acts 15:12.
   (d) Confusion condemned—I Cor. 14:33.
   (e) Women not to teach—I Cor. 14:35. I Tim. 2:11, 12.
   (f) Same rule in all assemblies—I Cor. 14:33.
9. Dismissal—Acts 15:30.
10. All of this is decent and orderly—I Cor. 14:40.
11. Warning: "If any one does not recognize this, he is not recognized" (I Cor. 14:38 Revised Standard).

CHART No. 2—On Teaching

	Lk. 4:14-15, 16-28.	
ASSEMBLED	Lk. 4:31, 36;	Lk. 5:15.
ALL TOGETHER	Lk. 8:4;	Acts 2:1, 6, 7, 12, 14, 36.
UNCLASSIFIED	Acts 3:11.	Acts 4:31.
MEN TAUGHT	Acts 6:2.	Acts 10:27, 33.
Women LEARNED	Acts 11:26.	Acts 13:14-16.
IN SILENCE	Acts 14:1.	Acts 14:27.
I Cor. 14:35.	Acts 15: 6, 22, 25	Acts 15:30.
II Tim. 2:2.	Acts 17:2.	Acts 17:19-22.
I Tim. 2:11-12.	Acts 20:7.	I Cor. 5:4.
	I Cor. 11:18, 33	I Cor. 14:26.
	Heb. 10:25.	James 2:2.

Take down those scriptures and read those scriptures and you will find the instructions that will obtain in the assemblies of the church. You will see that it will be impossible for you to find any division of an assembly into classes for the purpose of teaching the word of God. We have no authority whatsoever to divide into classes. I want Brother Porter to tell us how he would divide an assembly. Would he do it according to *physical age. Spiritual age?* Amount of knowledge possessed? Or *intelligence quotient,* ... I. Q.? *How would he divide people into classes?* If the Bible authorizes such, we ask him to tell us *how to do it.* When he tells us how he thinks it should be done, or can be done, I'll show him that every time he thinks he has them classified systematically, he has them *unclassified some other way* and that he has not accomplished that which he thinks he has accomplished.

I thank you.

Third Session
Porter's Second Negative
Sunday School Question

Brethren Moderators, Brother Waters, Ladies and Gentlemen:

Just thirty minutes more and this session of the debate will be over. During that thirty minutes, I want to pay attention to the things that Brother Waters said during the speech that just preceded this. He complained about my speaking up from my seat. I don't often do that. I thought he wanted me to. He said, "Why you just read it without comment," and then turned around and said, "Will you do it?" Well, when he asked me if I would do it, I thought he wanted me to tell him. That's why I spoke up from my seat. I thought he wanted to know. If he hadn't said, "Will you do it?" I wouldn't have made any response. But he turned around and asked me whether I'd do it or not. That's when I responded.

Another Question For Waters

In regard to the number of questions which I gave him, I didn't say he had to answer all these questions to-night. I gave them early in the debate so I wouldn't have to give any more. Perhaps I could have scattered them along through the debate, but I thought I would give them to him early in the debate, and he could answer them whenever he wanted to. I didn't insist that he answer them in one speech. But now, for full measure I'll just give him one more to be liberal with him. Ervin, *would you divide a church spiritually over how it is arranged physically?* He can answer that tomorrow night, if he wants to.

Disfellowship And Division

Now regarding the matter of fellowship. He had a great deal to say about the fellowship business and whether I disfellowshiped him or he disfellowshiped me, and what I thought about that. He asked the question, "Do you disfellowship me?" He stated that Brother Watson said in his debate with him that "I believe you're going to hell, and you believe I'm going to hell." Brother Watson said, "That's right," And Brother Waters said, "Yes." So Brother Waters thinks we're going to *hell*. Why? Because we divide the church *physically* for the purpose of teaching. Brother Watson thinks *he's* going to hell because *he divides the church spiritually*. That's why. There's the difference. There's the difference. If we just arrange them physically into classes, Brother Waters thinks we're going to hell. Brother Watson thinks he's going to hell, not because he teaches one class, but because *he divides the church spiritually* over how it should be arranged physically. That's why Brother Watson things that. That's right, isn't it Sterl?

(Brother Watson answers: "That's right.")

Porter: I hadn't asked him, but I knew that was right. And so he's the one who drew the line of disfellowship, when he began to oppose us to the extent that he was willing to divide the church over it. That's the point. And that's why I say he disfellowships and not us. But, of course, when he draws the line and disfellow-ships and divides the church spiritually over the matter, why then, of course, we think he's doing wrong. As Brother Watson said, "He's on the road to hell," because he's making law where God hasn't made it. Just like you think J. D. Phillips did. I'll get to that, too, presently. But does he mean to say that he doesn't — that his brethren do not-fellowship anybody that may be on the road to hell? I wonder about that.

A Joint Statement Concerning Marriage And Divorce

I have a copy here of a joint agreement signed by two editors of the Old Paths Advocate. This is taken from the February issue, 1946. It says, "We, the undersigned editors of the Old Paths Advocate, desire to publish this joint statement relative to the marriage and divorce question. With a view to bringing about unity and cooperation among all the faithful brethren, thus demonstrating that all can work together, we sincerely think if a division ever comes over this matter, we will have no part in it. We have never suggested nor recommended division. We have never suggested a separation. We have never suggested a withdrawal from one who is divorced and remarried, nor have we refused to worship and cooperate with them. We have never refused to baptize anyone who wanted to be baptized. We shall continue to love all of our preaching brethren and work with all who will let us. We do not advocate divorce and remarriage, but if it occurs, it is them and their God for it. So why should there be division among us?" And that's part of the statement. The rest of it goes on and says what they will try to do to prevent that. Let's suppose we just take that much of it and substitute classes and cups. What if it should read this way: "We, the undersigned editors of the Old Paths Advocate, desire to publish this statement relative to the class and cups question. With a view to bringing about unity and cooperation among all the faithful brethren, thus demonstrating that all can work together, we sincerely think if division ever comes over this matter, we will have no part in it. We have never suggested nor recommended division. We have never suggested a separation. We have never suggsted a withdrawal from those who use classes and cups, nor have we refused to worship and cooperate with them. We have never refused to baptize anyone who wanted to be baptized. We shall continue to love all of our preaching brethren and work with all who will let us. We do not advocate cups and classes, but if it occurs, it is them and their God for it.

So why should there be division among us?" Now, will Brother
Waters and his group take the same stand relative to cups and
classes that they take regarding adultery? These men, editors of
the Old Paths Advocate, said they will not disfellowship anybody
over the matter of divorce and remarriage. "We'll work with them.
We'll cooperate with them. We'll worship with them; everyone who
will let us. We will not draw any lines. But if you just teach a
class, you're going to hell. We'll disfellowship you, and we won't
have anything to do with you. You use cups and we'll cut you off,
but divorce and remarry all you want to, and we'll still fellowship
you." That's what the editors of the Old Paths Advocate said. I
wonder if Ervin would endorse that.

Annual Boys' Meeting

Then, by the way, another thing I want to get to just here
while we're on this matter. He's had a great deal to say about
Sunday School and classes. "You can't find it in the Bible" and
things of that kind. He demands that the Sunday School be named
in the Bible. Now, here are two other copies of the Old Paths Advocate (the one published by the brethren who stand with Brother
Waters) and on page 6—this is the Old Paths Advocate, issue December 1, 1948—we have this announcement: "We will have our
new church building finished, the Lord willing, by the time our
winter meeting begins December 26th. Brother Clovis Cook is to
do the preaching." That's his Moderator (pointing to Brother
Cook). "Saturday, January 1, 1949. That's the time set for the
Annual Boys' Meeting." Now, Brother Waters, I want to know
where you read in any of those assemblies anything about a "Boys'
Meeting" Come on! I'll give you a minute of my time, or two
minutes of my time, Ervin, to get up and read the passage. Now
will not do it? Here's the "Annual Boys' Meeting"; Did you ever
read in any of these assemblies about the *Annual Boy's Meeting?*
I wonder who started that. (Audience laughs).

Then here's another one, February 1, 1949, page 6, also, of this
issue. Here's an article headed "Meeting For Young Men." "On
Saturday evening, January 1st, at the Church of Christ in Heald-
ton, Oklahoma, the Annual Meeting of the Young Men of the
Faithful Brotherhood of Oklahoma convened." Who did that?
These fellows who say you can't read a class in the Scriptures.
They are the ones. It further says, "This was the third of such
events." That's an annual affair, you see. "And they are growing
progressively better with the years. Brother M. Lynwood Smith."

That's this brother right here (pointing to Lynwood Smith) who is recording the debate. "Brother M. Lynwood Smith, one of our adopted Oklahoma young men, is to be commended for playing the leading role in these meetings." I wonder if he started them. He is commended for the *leading role* in these *Boys' Meetings,* the *Annual Boys' Meetings.* Now, of course, Brothers Waters doesn't want me to say anything about any of his practices. That isn't good debating. He doesn't want to defend his practices.

And now, Brother Waters, I'll tell you what I'll do. If you will read me the passage tomorrow night that says anything about the Annual Boys' Meeting, I'll read ten passages that say they divided into Sunday School classes and taught simultaneously. What do you say? I'll give you enough time right now if you want to read the passage that speaks of the Annual Boy's Meeting. Brother Waters, do you endorse the Annual Boys' Meeting? Your Moderator does, and Brother Smith does. I wonder if you do. The Annual Boys' Meeting! Do you read, in any of these assemblies that you have on the board, about the Annual Boys' Meeting? Well, he says if you can't read about the class or Sunday School in the New Testament, you're going to hell. Then you're going to hell for an Annual Boys' Meeting because you can't read that in the Scripture, Ervin. *Can you? Honestly* now, Ervin, *can you?* I wish I knew. (Audience laughs). Tell me! Nod your head, Ervin, and tell me if you can. Don't let me wonder about it till tomorrow night; maybe I won't sleep any. Well, let me wonder about it till tomorrow night; then find me the passage if you can do it. The Annual Boys' Meeting, conducted by these brethren who say you're going to hell for the Sunday School because you can't read the "Sunday School" in the Bible.

His Answers To My Questions

Now, then, to the questions. He said he'll give me twelve questions tomorrow night. That's all right. If I don't give him any nearer twelve answers than he gave me, he'll not get many answers —I'll tell him that. If I answer his questions like he answered most of mine, there won't be many answers given.

The first question was: "If the church should come together for the purpose of teaching musical science, could classes be arranged for the teaching without violating any principle of Scripture?"

And the second goes along with it, "If the church should call together its members for the purpose of teaching a Singing School (he doesn't want that mentioned though), would such a group constitute an assembly of the saints?" To both he says that "it's not the work of the church."

They Belong To The S. S. Brethren

Now when you brethren have Singing Schools, who is doing the work? Who is doing the work? Who's doing the work, Brother Waters? They refer to us as "S. S. Brethren." Read their papers. Read the Old Paths Advocate. You'll see it spread all over their papers. Well, they are the "S. S. Brethren," too, because that stands for Singing Schools just as much as it does Sunday Schools. Therefore, Brother Waters is identified with some of the "S. S. Brethren." And he says that teaching the "S. S." or the Singing Schools, or arranging for it, is not the work of the church; but *you brethren* do it. How do you pay for it, Ervin? Do you pay for it out of the church treasury? Do you use church money to pay for that which is not the work of the church? And if it's not the church at work, then *who's doing the work?* You preachers are doing it. Brother Homer L. King, the editor of this Old Paths Advocate, is almost constantly engaged in a Singing Schools, here and there. I read his reports all the time. He is teaching Singing Schools all over the country. And then, since he is teaching Singing Schools all over the country, is he teaching them for the church, or what's he teaching them for? Just who is sponsoring the work anyway? They have their Singing Schools, but he can't find, my friends, in any of these assemblies of the saints that he read, anything about a "Singing School." *It just isn't there.* But he thinks you will go to hell if you have a Sunday School class, but he can have a Singing School class and go right along to heaven.

Simultaneous Teaching On Radio Stations

Third, "Can two men Scripturally preach over two radio stations, operating on different kilocycles, from different rooms of the same building, at the same time?" He says, "Perhaps." "Perhaps!" Well, why didn't you just say "yes" or "no?' Either they can or they can't. He says "Perhaps" they can. "Perhaps" they can. "Can two men Scripturally preach from two radio stations, operating on different kilocycles, in different rooms of the same building, at the same time?' He says, "Perhaps." Brother Waters has *simultaneous teaching* in the same building.—two rooms of the same building. Teaching at the same time, by two preachers, in the same building. Then he says we are going to hell if we have two teachers in diferent rooms of the same building at the same time. We're going to hell for it. But he says you can do it on the radio.

"Perhaps" you can. "Perhaps." But, he says, "Brother, I'll ask you a question. Since you are making that a parallel with your classes, can a sister teach over one of them?" I'm not afraid to answer your question, Ervin. Why didn't you answer mine? Inasmuch as teaching over one of them would be just the same as preaching publicly to a congregation of mixed people, I say "No." Now you tell me "yes" or "no." If there were only women listening in, I would say "Yes."

Teaching A Group Of Sisters

All right: "Can a sister Scripturally call a group of sisters to her home and teach them?" He said, "Not if they are like the ones you have." Well, a group's a class. Can a sister Scripturally call a group or class of sisters to her home and teach them? "Not if it's like the class you have." Now then, Brother Waters, I want you to tell what kind of class *she can teach.* Now, you indicate that she can teach some other kind of class; she can't teach one like the kind I have. I want to know, then, *what kind can she teach?* You indicate that she can teach one of some kind. Now what kind can she teach? Now he wants to know, "Can she call a group of men?" I would say the same as I did of the other, "No."

Teaching Without A General Assembly

Fifth. "If two separate groups from the same congregation were to go to separate places without first meeting in an assembly, could they be Scripturally taught at the same time?" He said, "No, not if they are like yours." Now then, if they are not like mine (if he had them arranged some other way, and I don't know just what the arrangement would be, perhaps he will tell us), why then, they could. Two *separate groups from* the *same* congregation could go to *different places,* if they didn't first come together in an assembly, and teach *at the same time,* providing those classes were not like mine. Well, I would like to know then, Brother Waters, *what kind of classes could they teach under those conditions?* You admit they could teach some kind. Now, what kind?

What Constitutes A Church Assembly?

Sixth. "What percentage of the membership must assemble before it becomes a church assembly?" He said, "Well, if it's announced, only two persons will do it." But, of course, if it is not announced, two thousand persons would not make one, you see. In other words, the singing and teaching in these matters, and dividing the assembly and having different classes, cannot depend upon the idea of simultaneous teaching or anything of that kind; *it depend upon whether the announcement was made or not.* If you announce the meeting, then two persons will constitute an assembly; if you don't announce the meeting, if it's not advertised, why then you can have two thousand people gather together, and it's not a church assembly. Don't you see? Then if we want to have our classes, our Sunday School classes, the thing to do is just don't announce it. Then Brother Waters will go along hand in hand with us, because he says *you can do it if you don't announce it.* "If you don't announce it." So the sin is not in the teaching. The sin is in the announcing.

Not Sinful To Separate Groups

Seventh. "Is it a sin to take a group away from a larger group and teach it?" He says, "It's a sin to teach in classes like yours." Now then, you *can* take a group away from a larger group and teach it, if it's not like mine. I want to know what that group is that you can take away and teach. Brother Waters, *what kind of group* is it you can take away from another group and teach, if it cannot be like mine? I want to know what the characteristics of mine are that you say must be eliminated in order to teach this group that you say *can be taught.* Tell me. Brother Waters, tell me Now I want to know what kind of classes. I want to know *what kind of classes can be taught* by taking one group away from another group. He says you can't "if it's like mine." Well, tell us *what kind.* We'll find out what kind it is, and we'll bring about unity, and follow that kind, and eliminate ours, Brother Waters. We *can teach some other kind of classes,* if they are not like ours, at the same time. You tell us what they are, and we'll just see if we can't get together on this question and stop this division. *Will you do it?* What kind of group can you get away from another group, and teach the group that you take away? And what kind of classes can you go to and teach, without coming to the assembly first, that are not like mine? That's what I want to know.

Instrumental Music And Methods Of Teaching

Eighth: "Does the command to 'sing' ever include playing an instrument of music? And he said, "No." Well, thanks for that good confession. We'll have use for that some day, perhaps.

Ninth. "Does the command to 'teach' ever include methods of teaching?" He says, "It includes those authorized by the Bible." "Those methods authorized by the Bible." I thought you said the Bible didn't authorize but one method. Now you say, "Those *methods* authorized by the Bible." "Well, I want to know what those other methods are, Brother Waters. You've got a plurality here as sure as you're born. You said, "Those authorized by the Bible."

Women Can Teach

Tenth. "When the church comes together for the purpose of teaching the Bible, can a woman do any type of teaching or speaking in this assembly?" He says, "She may sing." *Let that sink in.* "She may sing." All right, if she sings, does she teach? Paul says, *"Teaching* and admonishing one another in psalms, hymns and spiritual songs." If she sings, does she speak? Paul says, *"Speak-*ing to yourselves in psalms, hymns and spiritual songs." (Col. 3:16; Eph. 5:19). And in these passages, Paul said when people sing, they both *speak* and *teach.* Brother Waters says that a woman can teach by way of singing; she can speak and sing and teach in these assemblies that he has on these charts—right there in the assembly where she is told to keep silent. Therefore, the rule that requires women to keep silent is not unlimited. He makes provision for some sort of teaching and some sort of speaking even in those assemblies.

I'm insisting that, for Brother Waters to be consistent, she must not be allowed to sing. If he makes that rule unlimited and universal in its application—that "it's a shame for a woman to speak in the church"; that she cannot under any circumstance speak and under any circumstance teach in that assembly—then *she cannot sing.* Because if she does, why, she's *speaking and teaching.*

And she cannot confess Christ. If she does, she is speaking and teaching. And if some woman should respond to Brother Waters' sermon on Sunday morning when he gives an invitation, and that woman comes forward, she can't confess Christ; because if she does, she is *speaking in the assembly.* She will go to hell for it. What has to be done? Brother Waters will have to take her out on the front steps and take her confession; and when he does, he divides the assembly. And that will send both of them to hell. Don't you see? That's the inconsistencies and absurdities of the position for which he contends tonight.

A Consistent Man Among Them

But I'm glad I have found one man who is consistent. I have a statement here made in The Truth (September 1950). That's one of the papers published by the anti-class brethren—Brother J. D. Phillips we were talking about awhile ago. And here is the heading of a statement which says, "Brother King Makes His Statement." This is not Homer L. King; but Warren T. King. (Audience laughs) All right, the statement says, "Dear Brother Phillips: I wish to state to the brotherhood that after studying the matter, I have decided that for a woman to sing or to make a confession while assembled for public worship would violate I Cor. 14:35, and hence I oppose women singing in the public worship of the church." Signed, "Warren T. King, Box 131, East Gadsden, Alabama." Now there's a man who has reached consistency. And that's where Ervin Waters will have to go in order to stay with his position. He'll have to say the same thing, for he makes an unlimited application of his rule in all of the assemblies of the saints, that the women are not to teach or speak. But when she sings, she both teaches and speaks. Therefore, he'll have to say that it's not unlimited or occupy Brother Warren T. King's position and say, "I oppose women singing in the public worship of the church." The sooner they all go there, the sooner they will reach consistency. Thank you.

Simultaneous Teaching In Quincy, Illinois

Number Twelve. We will skip Number Eleven. Number Twelve: "Can two groups from the same congregation, because of contention, Scripturally meet for simultaneous worship and teaching in separate rooms on the second floor of the Labor Temple in Quincy, Illinois?" I tried to copy what he said, but he had a long answer, and I couldn't get every word of it. But I think this represents what he said: "No; either both are wrong in such circumstances, or one is wrong and the other is not. If only one is wrong, then the other can." Was that right, Brother Waters? That's the gist of what I got from what you said. "If both of them are wrong, it cannot be done; if one of them is wrong, the other can." Then, if you want to have simultaneous teaching, just get a little fuss of some kind, and it will be all right to have it. That's all. Get a confusion started, and some of you get in the wrong, and rest of you keep out of it; and when you get the confusion started, then some of you can get off into one place and some into another and the one who isn't in the wrong can teach while the other group is teaching. Well, then, the sin *is not in simultaneous teaching*, Brother Waters. The sin is not in simultaneous teaching. And if you have one group teaching while the other group is teaching, you will have simultaneous teaching. Therefore, it's not wrong to have simultaneous teaching. And all his arguments against it goes with the wind. The thing that makes it wrong or not is whether somebody has been wrong—in a fuss or not. It's not the teaching at all that determines the matter. Thank you, Brother Waters.

The "Order Of Worship" Brethren

Now then, I have just a little time. I want to see if there's something I have overlooked. Oh, yes, the "order of worship." He says, "Phillips cannot find his order in the New Testament." But Acts 2:42 says, "They continued steadfastly in the apostles' doctrine and fellowship, and in breaking of bread, and in prayers." And he takes *that very order* that's mentioned there and follows that and *makes a law* that *it must be done that way*. And Brother Waters said that *all must remain in an undivided assembly*, but he can't read that in any shape, form or fashion in the New Testament. So Brother Phillips is far ahead of him on it.

Milk And Meat

And then to the milk and meat. He didn't know about the milk and the meat—how to divide the milk and the meat. He said just feed it out to them and let them get what they want. That wasn't what Paul said he did. He said, "I have fed you with milk, *and not with meat;* for hitherto ye were not able to bear it" (I Cor. 3:2). So he didn't just dish it all out to them and let them get what they wanted. He said, "I have fed you with milk, and not with meat." So Paul must have recognized there was a difference. Whether I know or not, there's a difference there, and Paul said I have fed you with one, and not with the other. If he had dumped it all out to them, he could not have said this. But Brother Waters says, "Just preach the word. Just preach the word." Why didn't Paul do that and let them get what they wanted?

Tongues Speakers

Regarding tongue speakers, Brother Waters said we don't have them here in our assemblies, but we have them all over the earth, who speak in tongues. Where are they, Brother Waters? "We have them." I was talking about your brethren, the assemblies of your brethren. Where do you have them all over the earth? "We have them all over the earth that are doing that." I wonder where they are. What country are they located in? Give me the address of some of them. Then he said he would stop a tongue speaker, and wanted to know if I would. Why, certainly so. Yes, I would, because I have said that there are many things in I Cor. 14 that do not apply. You admit that that's so. Absolutely so.

The Pentecost Assembly

And now then, to Acts (refers to chart). Acts, the 2nd chapter. Here's the question. (To Moderator: "Now how much time do I have?" Moderator: "Two minutes.") Acts 2, I want to read that hurriedly. Second chapter of Acts of the Apostles. He said, "Porter thinks he sees some classes; he's seeing things." And Brothers Waters reads it, and he thinks he sees a statement there which says they must remain in an undivided assembly. But I never have seen that. I have looked for it, but it isn't there. But he sees it. He's looking for a thing like that and so he sees it everywhere—just everywhere he looks. But it isn't in the Book. Now, then, he turned to Acts 2 and he started to read, "When the day of Pentecost was fully come, they were all with one accord in one place." All right. "And suddenly there came a sound from heaven as of a rushing mighty wind, and it filled all the house where they were sitting." He read on down to the 4th verse, and then he skipped on down to verse 14. Why did you skip so much, Brother Waters? In these verses you skipped, there's a number of people represented from various parts of the country that spoke different languages, and they *were divided according to tongue.* And they said, *"We hear* every man in our own tongue wherein we were born." Not that "we heard," but "we hear." I want to know if Peter spoke in all of those languages at the same time? Or did each man deliver a sermon upon that occasion in each language represented upon that occasion? Or did some man speak to one group in the language that he understood, and somebody hear somebody else in the language he understood? So he skipped the whole thing, and came down to verse 14, in order to find where Peter addressed the whole multitude. Yes, but *this was before Peter ever stood up to address the whole multitude.* Before that ever happened, they heard them speaking, "How hear we every man in our own tongue?" And "We do hear them speak in our tongues the wonderful works of God." Every man heard them speaking in his own language. Yes, "We *hear them spaek* in our tongues the wonderful works of God." He skipped all of that. "We hear them speak"—not "we heard them speak." "We hear them," present tense.

Thank you, Ladies and Gentlemen.

Fourth Session

Porter's First Affirmative

Sunday School Question

Moderator Watson:

Now in just a moment I shall read the proposition that will open the discussion. First, however, I think we can congratulate ourselves upon the fact that we have enjoyed many of the good things of this life. In the fear of the Lord we are now assembled to have the closing session in this meeting. In about two hours now, the evidence will all be yours, and these discussions will be a matter of history. I think that all of us (that is, those who have been listening to these brethren from night to night), if we expressed ourselves to them, would say to them that we certainly appreciate the fine, dignified manner in which they have ordered these discussions. I know that they have been keen critics of the things believed and practiced by each other, and all of that; but at the same time it has been in the kindest way possible, and we certainly have had splendid discussions and good behavior on the part of these brethren.

Both of them tell me that they are bothered with a little throat irritation here tonight and we regret that.

The audiences have been fine from night to night. Of course, things a little amusing come up once in a while that provoke us to smile and maybe laugh a little, but we do not want to be disturbed by that. I fully concur with Brother Cook, in a statement that he made last evening, to the effect that it was his intention or desire that a man be permitted to order the course of his part of the discussion in his own peculiar style, or words to that effect. Because of the fact that we both feel that way about it, Brother

Cook and I have had very little to do in this discussion, and I certainly commend these brethren.

Now I will read the proposition for the discussion tonight.

Proposition: When the church comes together for the purpose of teaching the Bible, it is Scriptural to divide into classes for the teaching, some of which may be done with both men and women. Brother W. Curtis Porter affirms; Brother J. Ervin Waters denies.

Fourth Session
Porter's First Affirmative
Sunday School Question

Brethren Moderators, Brother Waters, Ladies and Gentlemen:

The subject as revealed in the proposition which Brother Watson has just read pertains to the same issue that was under discussion last night; but, of course, in this case I am in the affirmative, and the question or proposition has been reversed. Brother Waters takes the negative. Both the propositions have to do with the idea of teaching; just how that teaching is to be done; whether it could be class teaching or whether it *must be otherwise*. Things of that kind are involved in it. Very little definition, I presume, is necessary to get the meaning of the proposition before you, because it is simply expressed. By "when the church comes together" we mean an "assembly of the church," when it comes together in what we may call "congregational capacity" for the purpose of teaching the Bible. Of course, by "the Bible" we mean the Word of God, the Old and the New Testaments. And by "teaching" we mean to impart the instructions found therein or to get the information to the people that is revealed therein. "For the purpose of teaching." We mean that's the purpose or motive of the coming together. And by "dividing into classes" we mean arranging into groups, separate groups, for the teaching; and that "some of this teaching may be done by both men and women." That is, that this procedure is Scriptural, that it is not contrary to Bible principles or Scriptural statements, but in perfect harmony with the things taught in God's Book.

The Classes In Quincy

Now, then, passing on to an investigation of the things I want to get before you tonight, I wish first to mention briefly the Quincy affair. I shall pay my attention to the things that Brother

Waters said last night regarding the classes taught in the assembly of the brethren who stand with me on this issue. And he mentioned tha Sister Bybee had only one person in her class, but he's mistaken about that. There's a little Hebrew girl coming to her class, in whose home there never was even a copy of the Bible prior to the time when she started, but whose home now has a Bible. And his charge was that there was confusion in a little room where about three classes are assembled in the same room. He asked if I would endorse three classes in the same room, and I said that it depended upon whether one class interfered with the teaching of the other class. If the room is small enough and the classes are large enough to cause interference, then of course not. But we might enclose a forty-acre field out here somewhere within a wall of some kind. I believe that three or four classes, or half a dozen, can meet in that field, on the inside of the same wall, as long as the teaching of one does not interfere with the teaching of the other. I feel sure the statement made by Brother Logan Buchanan would exactly correspond with my idea along that line. Brother Buchanan indicated that he meant simply that if the teaching of one interfered with the teaching of the other, certainly he would not endorse it. Well, so much for that particular thing just now.

Dividing The Assembly

In this proposition, you will note the fact that I'm affirming that it is Scriptural to arrange or divide into classes. There seems to be on the part of Brother Waters, and those associated with him, an idea that it is a sin to divide the assembly; that if we come together for the purpose of teaching, it is a sin to divide the assembly, that is, to arrange the assembly at different places for teaching. So it's the old idea that it's a sin to divide the assembly. Brother Waters oftentimes, no doubt, divides the assembly. Suppose, for example, he is preaching some Sunday morning in a building, and he extends the invitation. And when the invitation is given, four people respond to the invitation to obey the gospel—two men and two women. They come down to the front, and he asks them to confess Christ. Even the women do, and *speak in the church,* which he indicates is the thing they are not allowed to do *under any circumstances.* And after he has taken their confession—we'll say there is a baptistry in the building; I don't suppose he opposes one. I never heard of their taking any position against one. And there's a dressing room on each side. I don't suppose he objects to dressing rooms. And when these confessions are made, then some sister comes and takes the two women into one room to make preparation for the baptism, and *divides the assembly.* Brother Waters takes the two men into the other room, *and divides the assembly again.* Then he leads one of these men down into the baptistry to baptize him, and *he divides the assembly* again. So I suppose that after all it is not a sin to divide the assembly, if that's the thing he's getting at. So we might have something from him along that line.

The Assembly Of Acts 15

Now, regarding the statement in Acts 15:6, when the assembly came together for the purpose of considering spiritual affairs. I insisted that this Scripture does not indicate that they came together for the purpose of teaching the assembly, and Brother Waters asked, "Is circumcision a Bible subject?" Certainly so, but they did not come together on the occasion *to speak to the assembly* anything about circumcision. It was a matter they were considering, that a decision might be sent to the church over in Antioch and other places. And in that connection I might ask him this question, "Is singing a Bible subject?" Is singing a Bible subject? When we come together for the purpose of teaching singing then, is that a church assembly? He said last night that teaching a Singing School was not the work of the church; that it is not the work of the church at all. Well, we want to know more about that tonight. We want him to tell us, then, just how his Singing Schols are conducted by the church, if it is not the work of the church.

And then, too, in Col. 3:17-21, we have wives and husbands and children all mentioned. Brother Waters said that all of them are present. It doesn't say anything about it in the passage given. It does not say that the husbands and wives and children and fathers must all be present when this teaching is done. He simply read that intto it. I mention those points because I missed them in my notes last night. So I pass on now to some affirmative arguments that I want to present.

Generic Commands

So in the next place, I call your attention to the fact that we have *generic terms* or *generic commands.*

The Command To "Go."

In the first place, in Matt. 28:19, the Lord said unto the apostles, "Go ye therefore, and teach all nations, baptizing them into the name of the Father, the Son and the Holy Spirit." Now note the fact that here is the command to "go." "Go ye therefore, and teach all nations." The Lord gives the command to "go." That's a *generic* command. He does not limit them as to *how* they may go. He does not specify a number of ways as to how they might go; but he said, "Go ye into all the world and preach the gospel to every creature," or "Go ye therefore, and teach all nations." Men might go in various ways. The apostles might have gone in various ways. And when we go today we may go in various ways and thus obey that command to "go." I might walk across the country, or I might ride in a chariot as some of the early men did, or I might go in a boat, or I might go on a train, or I might ride in an automobile, or I might ride on an airplane; but there's nothing said in the Book of God about riding on a train or an automobile or an airplane either. Yet I believe that I could Scripturally ride on a train; I could Scripturally ride in an automobile; or I could Scripturally ride in an airplane and thus obey the command that says, "Go." I believe that I could do that. I believe that it is perfectly Scriptural to do a thing of that kind—it is not contrary to any Scriptural principle. But suppose someone would arise and start some hobby on that and say, "Now, I don't believe a man has any right to go by riding in an airplane, because the Bible doesn't say anything about one. And if someone rides in one, I will draw the line, and I will disfellowship him and consign him to hell, according to my way of thinking, because he is riding in something the Bible says nothing about." Well, that's parallel with the position occupied by Brother Waters tonight in this matter.

The Command To "Sing."

And then, in the second place, we have the command to "sing." We have some *limitations* placed on us as to *what we sing,* for in Eph. 5:19 and Col. 3:16, we are told to "sing psalms, hymns and spiritual songs." So we have a limitation placed on us as to what we sing, but we do not have limitations placed on us as to *how we sing.* We must sing with sincerity; certainly, we must sing that way. All worship must be done from the heart. There must be sincerity in all worship. But as to whether I use a song book when I sing, or sing without a song book; whether I sing alto or soprano, bass or tenor, are simply matters left up to my judgment. And I can sing bass and be Scriptural, although the Scriptures say nothing about singing bass. I can sing with a song book and be Scriptural, although the Scriptures say nothing about the song book. The command to sing involves *singing,* and when I sing with a book or sing without one—when I sing bass or tenor or alto, or whatever it might be—I am still singing, and that's what God said. It's a *generic term.* And it is from that particular commandment that Brother Waters and the brethren who stand with him get their authority to teach a Singing School. They can't get it anywhere else. The New Testament says nothing about teaching such Singing Schools. But they teach them. And even that "Annual Boys' Meeting of the Faithful Brotherhood of Oklahoma" would have to come from some similar passage that says "teach" or something similar to that. And consequently, even though those things are not specifically mentioned in the Scriptures, they may be done Scripturally because the Bible says "to sing." Therefore, we have that *generic commandment given.*

The Command To "Teach"

The Bible says "to teach," and we have that also. And so in this third place, we have the word "teach." The Lord said, "Go ye therefore, and *teach* all nations." Matt. 28:19. And II Tim. 2:2: "The things which thou hast heard of me among many witnesses, the same commit thou to faithful men, who shall be able to *teach* others also." We are *limited* as to *what to teach.* In Mark 16:15 Jesus says we must preach "the gospel." In I Peter 4:11, Peter says we must "speak *as* the oracles of God." We are *limited* as to *what we preach,* but the *various methods* of preaching are not prescribed nor limited in the Book of Almighty God.

And so if I teach by means of a chart, I am doing what the Lord says. We have a chart up here—one that belongs to my opponent. He has been teaching by means of a chart. I wonder where he reads about it in the Bible. Can he find a Scripture in all of God's Book that says anything about a chart for the purpose of teaching? Or a blackboard? Well, he's been using both of them, and he insists to you now that there must be a command, an example, necessary inference, or statment. I want him to find the command for the chart in the Bible. I want him to find the example for the blackboard or chart for teaching. I want him to find the necessary inference or statement in God's book about them. Yet he uses them without any question and without any scruples of conscience whatsoever. So whether we teach by means of charts, blackboards, printing presses or radios, or by means of classrooms or whatever it might be, we are still teaching. If we teach the truth, we are doing what the Lord said. We are doing nothing but "teach," and the Lord said do that.

Things Admitted By Brother Waters

And then before I go into the next point, I want to call your attention to some things which Brother Waters has already admitted.

In answers to the questions given last night, Brother Waters has admitted that *two men can do simultaneous teaching over two radio stations operated in the same building on different kilocycles,* and *these two men can be in separate rooms of that building.* Now, then, if that's true, we have simultaneous teaching; we have two different teachers teaching at the same time. Brother Waters has admitted, in answering those questions, that such can be done. All right then, his objection is not to simultaneous teaching, because he has here agreed that simultaneous teaching can be done over two radio stations operating on different kilocycles in separate rooms of the same building. So his objection is not to that.

He has *admitted,* in the second place, in answering those questions, that *a sister can call a group of sisters to her home and teach them,* provided they are not like mine. Now, I don't know just what the difference must be; so it's up to him to show us the difference. If she calls a group of sisters to her home to teach them, and she can do that Scripturally as he intimates, then I want to know the difference between that group and my group, as he refers to it. So the issue is not there, and the debate is not over that; he's agreed on that particular thing.

Third, Brother Waters has *admitted* that *two groups from the same congregation, if no assembly was first held, can be taught in separate places at the same time,* if the groups are not like mine. Now, then, I figure that is simultaneous teaching of two groups from the same congregation, but they do not go to the common assembly first. Yet that can be done, *provided those groups are not like mine.* So I am wanting to know what we must give up in our groups to make it like the groups that he says can be taught from the same congregation at separate places at the same time.

Brother Waters has *admitted,* in the fourth place, that *two persons would constitute a church assembly if that assembly is announced and advertised.* So we have learned what it takes to make a church assembly; it must be announced and advertised. If no announcement is made of it, it is not a church assembly. If two people assemble by way of announcement, it *is* a church assembly. But they *announce* their Singing Schools, and if as many as two come, they will have a *church assembly* in spite of everything. But if no announcement is made of it, then two hundred may come, or two thousand may come, yet it will not be a church assembly, according to Brother Waters.

In the fifth place, he has *admitted* that *he would take one group* or *you can take one group from a larger group and teach it.* And it is not a sin to do so, *if the group is not like mine.* So I am wanting to know more about that.

He has admitted, in the sixth place, that *more than one method of teaching is authorized by the Bible,* for he referred to "those methods" which the Bible authorized. He has been giving us the lecture method during this time. Now I want him to tell us something about the "other methods" the Bible authorizes.

In the seventh place, he has *admitted* that *the command to sing never includes the use of a musical instrument.* And in making that admission, he *admits* that *musical instruments are not parallel with the methods of teaching.*

In the eighth place, he has *admitted* that *women can teach by singing when the church comes together for teaching.* The issue, therefore, in the remainder of this debate, is not over a woman's teaching, and not even the teaching in the assembly when they assemble for the purpose of teaching, because Brother Waters admits that a woman can do *some of the teaching,* and my proposition says that "some of it" may be done by women. That's exactly what he has admitted can be done.

In the ninth place, he said that *one group can teach at the same time of another group in two rooms of the same building—* the Labor Temple—*if there is something wrong in one of the groups.* So he has agreed to *simultaneous teaching* as goes on in this very building. His brethren are taking part in it, some of them *in* one room and some of ours in another room *just across the hall.* They are teaching and worshiping *at the same time,* and he says that his group can Scripturally do that. All right, his objection then *is not* to *simultaneous teaching*. It depends on whether one congregation is wrong about something as to whether simultaneous teaching can be done. So he is not against simultaneous teaching. You keep those things in mind.

Simultaneous Teaching In Judging Israel

Now, then, we pass on to another thought. This principle which I have just given you on the *generic term* is a principle involved in both the Old Testament and the New. In the Old Testament, God commanded Israel to *teach* His law (Deut. 4:1-9). And sometimes, according to Deut. 31:11-13, they assembled in one congregation for such teaching. That was once every seven years as the context shows in that case. And on some other occasions, we find that some other methods were followed. So I want to turn and read you just a few verses here from the Old Testament in which there was another method of teaching done. This is found in Exodus 18, and beginning with verse 13, "And it came to pass on the morrow, that Moses sat to judge the people; and the people stood by Moses, from the morning unto the evening. And when Moses' father-in-law saw all that he did unto the people, he said, What is this thing that thou doest unto the people? Why sittest thou thyself alone, and all the people stand by thee from morning unto even? And Moses said unto his father-in-law, Because the people come unto me to inquire of God: when they have a matter, they come unto me; and I judge between one and another, and *I do make them to know the statutes of God, and His laws.*"

Now Moses there was teaching "the statutes of God and His laws" - making them *known*. That's verse 16. And his father-in-law said that he would wear himself out, and would wear the people out, by following that method, and so he suggested something else. He said, "Hearken now unto my voice, I will give thee counsel, and God shall be with thee: Be thou for the people to God-ward, that thou mayest bring the causes unto God: and thou shalt *teach them ordinances and laws,* and shalt *show them the way wherein they must walk,* and *the work that they must do.* Moreover thou shalt provide out of all the people able men, such as fear God, men of truth, hating covetousness; and place such over them, *to be rules of thousands,* and *rulers of hundreds, and rulers of fifties, and rulers of tens.*" Verses 19-21.

Now these judges were teachers, because they were to "teach

them ordinances and laws," and "show them the way wherein they must walk and the work that they must do." So here we have teachers. And he suggested to Moses that he place certain judges over thousands, over hundreds, over fifties and over tens, and thus help to divide that work of teaching and the responsibilities. And it was done, as the other verses show in the connection.

Now when we stop to think about it, what do we have? Well, in that group of people, the congregation of Israel, from twenty years old and upward, men who were able to go to war, that were numbered, there were "six hundred thousand and three thousand and five hundred and fifty," according to Numbers 1:46. All right, taking just that, besides all that were under age and the women - people of that kind - and we have here six hundred three thousand, five hundred and fifty. One teacher placed over a thousand would make 603 teachers. And then that subdivided into groups of hundreds. We would have over those groups of hundreds 6,035 judges or teachers. And then over fifties, as they were further divided into groups, you have 12,071. And then over tens, you have 60,355. The combined total of those teachers or judges placed to teach men the Law of God numbered 79,064. I insist that when that exercise was carried on, when that arrangement was made, there *had to be simultaneous teaching* with that many men involved in the matter in order to keep the people from wearing themselves out as well as Moses. Well, I pass on. And I suggest this: that if the command to "teach" in the Old Testament could cover an arrangement of that kind, why could not the command to "teach' in the New cover a few small groups such as we have in our class teaching today?

The Example Of Jesus

All right, in the next place, I learn that Jesus took one group out of another group and taught it. A number of times this was so.

First, on the way to Jerusalem, He took the twelve disciples apart from the multitude. Luke says in Luke 18:31-33, that "He took unto Him the twelve," and He taught them about his coming crucifixion and resurrection, the record shows. And Mark says in Mark 10:32-34, "He took *again* the twelve." That shows He had done it before. This wasn't the first time He ever followed this arrangement. "He took *again* the twelve." And Matthew says in Matt. 20:17-19, that "He took the twelve disciples apart in the way." Now then, note the fact. Here's a class of twelve, a group of twelve. Jesus took them away from the rest and taught them after He separated them from that other group. Jesus taught them the things concerning His rejection, His crucifixion, and His resurrection. And so I say that Jesus often took a smaller group away from the larger group and taught the smaller group that He took away.

Well, in the second place, we learn that He also took Peter, James and John up into a high mountain. I want to read along here just a few verses. And it's found in the 9th chapter of the book of Mark. Here we have given us the statement by the gospel writer, beginning with verse 2, "After six days Jesus taketh with Him Peter and James and John, and leadeth them up into a high mountain apart by themselves: and He was transfigured before them." Now note the fact that He takes three men, a class of three, away from the rest of the multitude and the disciples and their associates. All right, He took them away from the group. He took three of them, Peter, James and John, up into a high mountain *by themselves*. And then the transfiguration scene occurred, and Moses and Elijah appeared, and God's voice spoke, and there was teaching done. And then in verse 9 we read, "As they came down from the mountain, He charged them that they should tell no man what things they had seen, till the Son of man were risen from the dead." And then verse 14, "When He came to his disciples, He saw a great multitude about them, and the scribes questioning with them." Here Jesus Christ took a group away from another group and taught the group that He took away. There was teaching going on in the group that He left behind. Because when He came back to that group, He found them engaged in teaching. There were those gathered about them, "questioning with them." Not "questioning them," but "questioning *with* them." And the Revised Standard Version, which my opponent introduced last night says, "arguing with them." Certainly they did not argue by themselves. And so we have teaching going on in the group that Jesus left behind. He took one group away and taught that group, and the group that was left behind was also taught.

And thus we have a parrallel in principle with the things we do today in teaching more than one group at the same time. Then in verse 28, we find after that it says, "And when He was come into the house, His disciples asked Him privately, Why could not we cast him out?"

All right, and then another time, I call your attention to a statement in Mark, the 7th chapter, where Jesus divided the "called assembly." In the 14th verse of this chapter, we are told that "when He had called all the people unto Him." Now, here's a called assembly. Not just one that happened, but here's one that Jesus called unto Him. "He said, Hearken unto me every one of you, and understand." And then He taught them about what defiles a man. And then, verse 17, it says, "And when He was entered into a house from the people," or as the Revised Standard Version, which he gave, reads, "left the people." All right, "when He left the people, His disciples asked Him concerning the parable." Then He explained unto them about that matter. So Jesus called the assembly together - He called the people to Him; He separated His disciples from that assembly that He called together; and taught them when He took them away. All right, so there's where Jesus *divided the assembly*. So I suppose if a man goes to hell for dividing a called assembly, then the condemnation would rest upon Jesus.

And then again in Matt. 13. We had that last night. Brother Waters introduced the first verse where the multitude came to Jesus and He taught them there by the seaside as He stood in the boat. And I call attention to the fact in verse 36, that the record says that He "left the multitude, and went into a house" and there taught His disciples. So He took one group away. And Brother Waters says that shows that the assembly was over before He taught the disciples. So I asked last night - I'm asking again tonight: If we dismiss the assembly - when we come together and have an assembly - if we dismiss the assembly, if that assembly comes to an end, then can we take the groups out somewhere and teach them? I want to know about that. But dropping back, we find that Jesus did some teaching to a separate group before the assembly was over. Or dropping back to verses 10 to 17, and before Jesus left the multitude, the record tells us that His disciples inquired of Him about some matters and he explained the matter to them - speaking to that group directly and teaching them directly, before that assembly was dismissed, if you please. All right, but I move on.

To Moderator: I have about three minutes?

Moving Assemblies Toward Each Other

Now, then, I want to make this statement. We are going to say there are two congregations meeting in Quincy, Illinois—meeting six blocks apart. There are two assemblies there. There are two groups that meet at the two different places for the purpose of teaching. Brother Waters has admitted that they can do that, even though the groups are from the same congregation, *if they are not like my groups*—that those groups can meet there if they don't have a common assembly first. So we will say that one group goes to one place and another group goes to another place, without first having a common assembly, and they can teach if they are not like my group. I don't know if he means that they must not look like them or just what. Anyway, there must be some difference between them and my group, but they can be taught in those two different places, six blocks apart. Well, suppose we start moving those two houses together? We move them two blocks apart. Can the teaching still be done Scripturally? Yes. Well, suppose we move them again. We have them only one block apart. Can they still teach at the same time in those different buildings? Yes. Well, suppose we move them to within a half block of each other. Can they still do it? Yes. Well, just how close can they get before the thing becomes unscriptural? Ordinarily Brother Waters' brethren say, "Why, when you get them in the same building." "When you get the two buildings joined together," or something of that kind. But he can't say even that, because his group teaches in this same building while another group is teaching across the hall—thus doing simultaneous teaching. Consequently, he cannot even take that position, but I want him to tell us something about that.

Faithful Men To Teach

Then with respect to the women teaching, and we haven't much time for that, we have already agreed on it that she can do some teaching when they come together. But he gave II Tim. 2:2 last night on his chart. You have it over here (pointing to chart), I Cor. 14:35, II Tim. 2:2, and I Tim. 2:11-12, referring to the fact that men must teach. "Commit thou to faithful men, who shall be able to teach others also." I understood him to mean to say that by "faithful men" it means the male sex. I want him to tell us if that's what he meant by it. I insist that it's a generic term and is not limited to the male sex.

Women Commanded To Teach

Then in Titus 2:3, 4, we have a statement where the Lord commanded, by the Apostle Paul, that women be teachers. Titus 2:3,-4—"teachers of good things;" that the older women teach the younger women, etc., "the good things" there referred to. There's the command for her to teach. "The aged women likewise, that they be in behavior as becometh holiness, not false accusers, not given to much wine, teachers of good things; that they may teach the young women to be sober, to love their husbands, to love their children, to be discreet, chaste, keepers at home, obedient unto their own husbands, that the word of God be not blasphemed." And so women are *comanded to teach.* And since she is not allowed to teach a group of women, and she is not allowed to teach a group of men, I want him to tell where she can teach and whom can she teach? And in I Tim. 2:12, which he gave, Paul said, "I suffer not a woman to teach nor to usurp authority over the man."

Thank you, Ladies and Gentlemen.

Fourth Session
Waters' First Negative
Sunday School Question

Brethren Moderators, Brother Porter, Brethren and Friends:

I'm thankful for the opportunity to stand before you tonight in denial of a proposition which I disbelieve with all of my heart. I'll take up some of the last arguments of Brother Porter first.

Is Tit. 2:2-4 To All Aged Women?

He mentioned Tit. 2:2-4 where the Apostle Paul instructed Titus to instruct the aged women to teach the young women. The word "teach" there is rendered in the Revised Version "to train." It means *"to curb, control, or to discipline."* It is that type of training or teaching which could not be done thirty minutes or forty-five minutes a week. It is that kind of instruction which the older women are to give the younger women constantly as they are being around them. And as they are brought up. But I would like to question Brother Porter. Is the command in Tit. 2:3-4, pertaining to the aged women teaching the younger women, to every aged woman in the congregation, or *is it to only one of the aged women?* Few of his congregations even have such a class as he thinks these verses contemplate. But where they do have such as he seems to think they contemplate, they try to permit that teaching to be done by one aged woman in that one congregation. I want to know if that woman would be the only woman in that congregation *fulfilling* her duty. If she is not the only one fulfilling her duty, then there are other aged women in the congregation fulfilling their duty without teaching such a segregated class as his proposition calls for. Now, *if every one of his women except one* in the congregation can *fulfill their duty without teaching in a class* such as his proposition contemplates tonight, *I maintain that every one of ours can.*

Not Whether But Where Women May Teach

But, now then, I call your attention to II Tit. 2:2, "The same commit thou to faithful men, who shall be able to teach others also." He took the position that the word "men" there is generic and includes both men and women. *If that be the case,* it has no bearing whatsoever on the question at issue tonight, simply because *I do not deny that women may teach.* It is *where they may teach* that is under consideration. The question is not *whether* or not they may teach, but *where they may teach.* But there is some doubt about this word meaning both men and women everywhere it is used. The word is the Greek word "anthropos." You turn to Matt. 19:10, after Jesus had said in Verse 9, "Whosoever shall put away his wife, except it be for fornication, and shall marry another, committeth adultery," and the disciples said, "If the case of the *man* be so with his wife, it is not good to marry." The word "man" there is from the Greek word "anthropos" and *this man had a wife.* I wonder if it was *a male of the species.* You turn to John the 7th Chapter, and there the Lord Jesus said, Verse 22, "and ye on the Sabbath day circumcise a man." And there the word "man" is translated from the Greek word "anthropos," and it's a man that is to be circumcised. I wonder whether you circumcise men or women, Brother Porter. "Anthropos" doesn't always mean "men and women," or "men or women." But if it means "men and women" in II Tim. 2:2, it has no particular bearing on the proposition tonight.

In Goes The Female Ministry!

Then he mentioned two congregations in Quincy, Illinois, six blocks apart, and he asked if these two congregations were moved up closer together, closer and closer, until finally they are in one building, would that be all right? Now he's trying to parallel these congregations, which he knows are public assemblies, with his classes. And I want to thank you, Brother Porter, for *admitting in that parallel that your classes are public assemblies.* He paralleled his classes with *public congregational assemblies* in that instance. I want to thank Brother Porter for that. He admits that his classes are public, but notice that in his proposition he affirms that women may teach some of these classes. Now then, since these classes which he is defending tonight are on par with congregations meeting in different parts of the city, and women may teach some of these classes, I want to know which women are teaching *some of your congregations, according to your illustration.* Why, don't you see that he has a *female ministry! If the parallel means anything, then it's all right for you to have some women ministers and teachers teaching these various congregations, with which he attempts to parallel his class system. In goes the female ministry,* Brother Porter. *Keep her out if you can with that illustration.* Do you get any solace and comfort out of that?

In Go Men To The Classes Taught By Women!

All right, but now he went to several places in the four gospels, for instance to Matt. 13:2, where the mutlitude "came together" and the Lord instructed them. Verse 36, "Then Jesus sent the multitude away, and went into the house." *No segregating, no classifying involved, and Brother Porter knows it.* "He went into the house; and his disciples came unto him, saying, Declare unto us the parable of the tares of the field." Now the Lord went into a private home, His Disciples came to Him, asked Him a question, and He answered it. Brother Porter says that parallels his class. But I want you to notice now. Brother Porter says that *women may not teach men* in such circumstances and classes as his proposition contemplates; but *under the same kind of circumstance that Matt. 13:36 has under consideration, a man might come into a house and ask a question of a woman, and she could answer that question.* But if she could answer that question, and that parallels his class, *then he could have women teaching men in his classes.* Thank you, Brother Porter.

But we come to Mark, 7th Chapter, and we consider again. Mark 7:14, "And when he had called all the people unto him, he said unto them, Hearken unto me everyone of you, and understand." And in verse 17, "When he was entered into the house from the people, his disciples asked him concerning the parable." The same kind of case as before. Could a man, or could men, in a similar house or private home, ask a woman a question, and *could she answer it.* That's the same kind of circumstance as is under consideration here. If she could answer the question, and that parallels his class system, then he could have women teaching men in his classes. But Brother Porter says *she can't do it.* Thank you, Brother Porter. Your illustration wasn't worth anything to you, was it?

Mount of Transfiguration

But, now then, let's consider Mark 9:7 where Jesus took Peter, James and John up to the mountain and was transfigured before them. Why, he said, "That was a class." Why, you just think about it! I told you last evening that Brother Porter thought he could see a class everywhere he looked. And now the Lord takes Peter, James and John, and they walk up a high mountain. He says, "That's a class." According to him, if you just walk along the way, or climb a mountain with anybody, and even begin to talk about spiritual matters, you have a class. I wonder, Brother Porter, if under the same circumstance a woman and three men were up on top of a mountain somewhere, or were to go up a mountain somewhere, could she talk to the men and, if she knew something they didn't know, I wonder if she could teach them anything? If that kind of circumstance parallels your class system, then you could have women teaching men in classes. But Brother Porter says, "Not so." I thank you, Brother Porter. The illustration wasn't worth anything, was it? But that's what he has to introduce to try to find his classes. Now that's just as close as he can get. But he says they came down from the mountain, and when they came down, there was a multitude with some of them questioning the disciples and the disciples talking to them. He said, "There's another class." Don't you see? He can find a class just anywhere, he thinks. Why, if he has a group of people out here who are just standing by the road, and they're talking, Brother Porter says, "There's a class." And here's some more coming down from the mountain,—you read Luke 9 and you will find that they came down from the mountain the next day after they went up there—and he says, "That's a class." Well, what you need then, my brother, if that's a class, is not a classroom built on your building, but a catwalk. Well, you just think about it! *Walking down a mountain,* and he says, "There's a class." And *here's some of them out here by the road,* and he says, "There's another class." Now you think about it! *Walkie-talkie class,* I guess. Now that's just as close as he can get to proving his proposition. See? Think about it! If he had any better, I'm sure he'd give it to us. He'd be glad to.

Exodus 18 Is Too Much For Him

We turn to Exodus 18. He said that he would find classes over in Israel because Moses put judges over thousands and hundreds and fifties and tens, and he said, "There are my classes." Now you think about that! "There are my classes." All right, let's look at that thing. Remember, now, that the judge over the thousands was a superior judge, in other words, an appellate court, and under him there were ten judges over hundreds, and twenty judges over fifties, and a hundred judges over tens. Now then, if that person in that ten is taught by the judge over tens and that's a class, that same person, who is in the class of ten, is also in the class of fifty and he's under the judge of fifty, *so he's taught by two at the same time.* And, then, he's also a part of a hundred over which another judge is placed a little higher up. If that equals your class, then he's taught by the judge of ten, the judge of fifty, and the judge of a hundred at one time. Then he's also a part of the thousand over which that judge judges, and Porter says he is being taught by him, and then that thousand is a part of Israel which Moses judges; and so then he's being taught by the judge of tens, the judge of fifties, the judge of hundreds, the judge of thousands and Moses. *That's five teachers teaching one man at one time.* Think about it! And remember that within that thousand, according to him, he's trying to get a hundred and thirty-one simultaneous teachers, and *every man being taught by at least four of that thousand,* judges of tens, of fifties, of hundreds, and thousands, and *every man being taught by at least four at the same time.* Now you think about that! And he says "there's my class system. There it is." Do you think it looks like it? It won't do him any good, if it does. Talk about confusion! *He would have it,* wouldn't he?

Questions For Porter

I want to ask Brother Porter some questions:

1.   Is it Scriptural to divide a congregation spiritually because it refuses to be divided physically?

2.   Is the teaching in a Sunday School public teaching?

3.   Did the "silence" of 1 Cor. 14:35 prohibit the women to whom it applied from singing where it applied?

4.   May the colleges operated by your brethren Scripturally be supported out of the church treasury?

5.   Is teaching grammar school a work of the church?

6.   May a woman teach the rudiments of music to a college

class or a high school class composed of both male and female?

7.   May a woman in a private, informal, and individual way teach men, or a man, the word of God?

8.   Do you endorse or oppose the missionary combinations among your brethren, such as many churches channeling their funds through one church whose elders over-see the work and the spending of the money in the distant field?

9.   What would make it right for a woman to privately, informally, without announcemnt, teach men in her home, but wrong for her to call a group of men to her home and teach them? He said she couldn't call a group of men to her home and teach them.

10.   Do you believe that a Christian can go into the armed services of the nation and with carnal weapons shed the blood of his fellowmen on the battlefield?

11.   Is it Scriptural for three classes to be taught simultaneously in one room as is done by your brethren in Quincy?

12.   What percentage of the membership must assemble before it becomes a church assembly?

Boys' Meeting

Now then, he mentioned "boys' meetings" last night. You know, Brother Porter really didn't know what that was. He didn't have any idea what that was. But I want you to remember this, that last evening I had Chart No. 1 with the rules and regulations governing an assembly of the church. In this meeting that was called a Boys' Meeting, there was in the assembly a heterogeneous group of people composed of men, women, boys and girls, old and young. *Everybody was there. The teaching at that particular time was done by young men.* The assembly in *every way* observed every rule of order laid down in my Chart No. 1 and in Chart No. 2. Remember that. Brother Porter just didn't know what it was all about and he had to have something to talk about.

Singing Schools

All right, but again he mentioned the singing schools and asked me about the singing schools. I said that teaching the rudiments of music is not the work of the church. Well, he said, "Do you support that out of the church treasury?" Then, "Do you believe in doing it?" *I do not believe it.* I do not believe in supporting singing schools out of the church treasury anymore than I believe in supporting grammar schools out of it. Teaching the musical characters is no different in principle from teaching the letters of the alphabet. You learn the letters of the alphabet to read language and learn the musical characters to read music. After you learn to read the music, you may praise the Lord with your knowledge or you may not do it, and after you learn to read, you may read the Bible or you may not do it. You may read that which you ought not to. But I'd like to just mention this. As far as I know, there's not a preaching brother present here tonight, who agrees with me on the issue under consideration, who believes in supporting singing schools out of the church treasury. Isn't that right? Brother Fred Kirbo? (Brother Kirbo: "That's right.") Brother Lynwood Smith? (Brother Smith: "Right.") Brother Clovis Cook? (Brother Cook: "Right....."). Nelson Nichols? (Brother Nichols:: Right.") Johnny Elmore? (Brother Elmore: "Right.") Authur Wade? (Brother Wade. "Right.") Tommy Shaw? (Brother Shaw: "Right.") Billy Orten? (Brother Orten "Right.") Larry Robertson? (Brother Robertson: "Right.") *There you are.* What's he got?

Now then, I want to call your attention to Chart No. 3.

CHART NO. 3   On Teaching
By Waters
Porter Has Not Found The Elements of His Proposition

      (1.)   Church Come Together
      (2.)   To Teach The Bible
      (3.)   Divided Into Classes
      (4.)   Both Men And Women
              Teaching These Classes

Porter Has Not Found Elements Of Proposition

Porter has not found the elements of his proposition. First, the church came together. Second, to teach the Bible. Third, divided into classes. Fourth, both men and women teaching his classes. Why hasn't he produced the command, or the example, or the statement which authorizes the four elements of his proposition? There they are. There's the proposition analyzed and put down. *He hasn't found it.*

CHART NO. 4   On Teaching
By Waters
Porter Has Not Found In Bible

      (1.)   Name of Sunday School
      (2.)   Practice of Sunday School

(3.) Idea of Sunday School

(4.) Regulation For Sunday School

Chart No. 4. Porter has not found in the Bible: First, *the name of Sunday School*. Second, *the practice of Sunday School*. Third, *the idea of Sunday School*. And fourth, *regulations for the Sunday School*. He's not found any of those.

CHART NO. 6   On Teaching

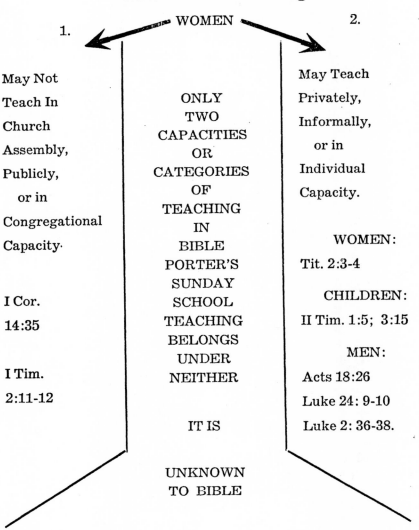

WOMEN

1.

2.

May Not Teach In Church Assembly, Publicly, or in Congregational Capacity.	ONLY TWO CAPACITIES OR CATEGORIES OF TEACHING IN BIBLE PORTER'S SUNDAY SCHOOL TEACHING BELONGS UNDER NEITHER	May Teach Privately, Informally, or in Individual Capacity.
I Cor. 14:35		WOMEN: Tit. 2:3-4
		CHILDREN: II Tim. 1:5; 3:15
I Tim. 2:11-12		MEN: Acts 18:26
	IT IS	Luke 24: 9-10
		Luke 2: 36-38.
	UNKNOWN TO BIBLE	

Now, I want to call your attention to Chart No. 6. Remember this now, that there are only two classes, or categories, of teaching in the Bible. Porter's Sunday School comes under neither one of them according to him. Now you get that.

Women May Not Teach Here

Women may not teach in the church assembly, publicly, or in congregational capacities, I Cor. 14:35, "For it is a shame for women to speak in the church." I Tim. 2:11-12, "Let the women learn in silence with all subjection. But I suffer not a woman to teach, nor to usurp authority over the man, but to be in silence." She can't teach there. But Brother Porter says she can teach in the Sunday School. So Sunday School doesn't belong there then, does it? All right, let's try again.

Women May Even Teach Men Here

We turn over here, and find that women may teach privately, informally, and in individual capacity. She may teach *women* (Tit. 2:3-4) in that capacity. In that same capacity she may teach *children* (II Tim. 1:5). The unfeigned faith that was in Timothy was first his grandmother, Lois, and his mother, Eunice. And I Tim. 3:15, "And that from a child thou has known the holy Scriptures," -known them, having been taught them, of course, as the implication is in the epistle, by his mother and grandmother.

Then we have *a man* taught by a woman in this capacity because Aquilla and Priscilla, a man and a woman, took Apollos aside and taught him the word of the Lord more perfectly (Acts 18:26). He says, "She can't do it in my Sunday School class." So the Sunday School doesn't belong in that category then.

Women may teach men privately (Luke 24:9-10). The women told the eleven apostles or disciples about the resurrection of Jesus. There are women talking to or teaching men. He says, "She can't do it in my Sunday School class." So then his classes don't belong in that category.

And in Luke 2:36-38, Anna, the prophetess, "Spake of him *to all that looked for redemption in Jerusalem.*" But that would include men, as well as women, and he says, "She couldn't do that in my Sunday School class." In other words, his Sunday School classes don't belong in either category according to him. I challenge him to find one place in the New Testament where women taught that cannot be placed under one of these two categories. Why, he would have you believe that I don't believe that women can teach at all. But he's the one who has the teaching capacity that does not fit the word of God. He's the one that has it. Let him try to put his Sunday School somewhere. Let him put the Scriptures out now that will bring the Sunday School under it. He argues for a third capacity of teaching, or a third category of teaching, *that cannot be found in the word of God.*

The Marriage Question Introduced By Porter

Last night, Brother Porter went so far adrift from the subject, as usual, and even brought in the marriage question. Yes, and referred to an agreement signed by Brother Homer L. King and Brother Homer A. Gay several years ago on the marriage question. The agreement, not being worded as specifically as it should have been worded, had to do simply with a controversial matter in the brotherhood, a difference existing over whether or not one could put away a companion for the cause of fornicaton and remarry. There was difference existing. But those two brethren, differing on that one point, agreed that there would be no division between them over it, and no disfellowshiping over it, and that was the thing under consideration. I wonder if Brother Porter is gentleman enough to accept that.

What John O'Dowd Says About Porter's Brethren

But since he's tried to make out that we just endorse everything, endorse adultery, and that we will fellowship anything. go along with anything, and since he intimates now that his brethren are *so* good and pure, I want to read a little from Brother John O'Dowd from the October issue of The Vindicator, 1950. John says, "We are living in days of growing apostasy. (John O'Dowd is one of his brethren and has debated this question many times.) The church is fashioning itself more and more after the world. The Scriptures speak of 'perilous times,' when 'evil men and seducers shall wax worse and worse, deceiving and being deceived.' Did God intend for the church to conform to the world, or to re-form humanity? Who is to blame for the condition of the world today? Everywhere selfishness is growing in the churches. Preachers are self-satisfied, with good salaries and comfortable surroundings, and this in the midst of the growing alarm of things. They are sleeping instead of watching; whitewashing sinners instead of warning men of impending dangers.

When I go to work for a man I need to know what his plans are. Every architect has his 'blueprint' and he studies it step by step in building. If he makes a mistake he does not let it go, but he corrects it immediately. All the mechanics today are required next to perfection in all their particular jobs.

The Lord has given a perfect 'Blueprint' to guide us in the work that He wants done. Instead of following it to the letter, we are butchering and remaking the blueprint to fit our notions and opinion." Brother O'dowd is talking about these brethren. "We need to stop changing the plan and go to work changing our lives to harmonize with what the Lord demands. We have studied far too long without making the practical application. *We are accomplishing very little according to God's ways, but a multitude of things according to man's garbage borrowed from Denominationalism.* What is the aim and end of all the labor put forth? The modern pulpit is becoming more and more the agency for incorporating denominational practices into the Way of the Lord. It has for an object the borrowing of those who are the enemies of God—their worn-out 'Daily Vacation Bible Schools,' with punch, play, and praise of men. They are seeking to remedy the existing conditions of the world by making the church a recreational center, playground, and competing Sectarian ball-players. Swiftly reverting to pianos, choirs, quartets, with smooth-mouthed preachers condoning brethren who dishonor God, turning their eyes from the God of life to the men of death. They are more concerned about the environment of earth than the power of God's Gospel. We have the founts of art, science, human philosophy, memorials of heathenism, buildings costing hundreds of thousands of dollars, filled with disgusting and debased men and women who are guilty of every sin, shame and sorry phase of life. Brethren are craving and seeking something different than the simple Gospel of Christ. *We are crumbling today with our own inward decay.* Brethren are boasting of Titles, Degrees, and Recommendations; but all these are worthless when they have left the solid foundation and are building on sinking sand.

On every hand we note increasing lawlessness; drinking, gambling, dining, and dancing, and people rushing like animals to slaughter. It is much too strong for these anemic brethren who are following the ritualism of the educated, trained, courteous preacher-pastor, who is far too nice to oppose anything. Churches are empty, except when the kitchen is blasting at full force to give their stomachs another feed. Schools and colleges are permeated with corrupt, diluted, apologetic teaching and restraints

on morals are becoming fewer and fewer. Infidelic preachers
and modernistic, worldly practices are growing at an alarming
rate. Men are boasting today of their big buildings, successes in
D. V. B. S., few days preachers' meetings, Doctored preachers,
but it is all without sanction or support from God. 'They have
not God or Christ.' (John 9:11) What delusions have gripped the
hearts and made them fearful of the false gods and false reli-
gions.

We need some of the pioneer stock of preachers today. Men
who can be stirred with inidignation against nudism, communism,
laxity and disregard of the Scriptures; men who can be aroused
to open their mouths and protest against all sin.

The brethren are being harrassed by hireling preachers and
over-Lord elders who are without Bible qualifications. There is
a definite need for God-fearing laborers. Christ was sympathetic
toward the people who were shepherdless, but unmerciful when it
came to the hirelings and religious leaders.

Are we jarred, moved and alarmed at the conditions in the
church, to say nothing of the world and its sinfulness? *The church
is undisciplined?* Is expressing itself in congregational and Christian delinquency? There is a wave of these evils all over the
country. Read and believe 2 Tim. 3:1-5."

And then he continued on and said, "How shocking the
thought! Why does the church refuse to return to God? Why go
further into the darkness of heathenism, Catholicism, and so-
cialism? What are YOU doing where you worship to stem the
tide of apostasy?"

And he ends and says, "God pity us, if we fail to give heed
and take warning. The rising generation will never know the
pure and simple Way of Gospel preaching and living, if we fail
to teach and warn them.'

*That's what one of his main preachers has to say about the
conditions in their brotherhod. I'll teach him to stay on the subject in a debate.* (Audience stirs.)

C. R. Nichol On Deaconesses

All right now, I want you to notice something else. Brother
C. R. Nichol, who has had more debates than any living man in
his brotherhood, in the book God's Woman has an entire chapter
on Deaconesses, and takes the position that the church today
ought to have not just Deacons, but Deaconesses. And he said, on
page 166, "The church must carry on and to properly function

under divine direction, there must be Elders and Deacons doing the work assigned to them, and as *there was need for the Deaconesses in the early days of the church, so there is now."* "Phoebe," page 159, *"Was a servant, a Deaconess at the church in Cenchrea."* Well, that's what Brother Nichol says about it. I want to know what Brother Porter has to say about that.

Relief And Charity Committee

All right, but here's something else. Here's a church bulletin from the congregation at East Main and Academy in Murfreesboro, Tenn., where Brother George W. DeHoff is the minister. It has the Elders named, the Deacons named, and *the Relief and Charity Committee.* That's a part of their congregational organization. I wonder what Brother Porter thinks about that.

Elements of Proposition Not Found

He has during his speech absolutely failed to produce the essential elements of his proposition. *He has not found those elements and I want you to notice that.* If he *could* find them, *he would* find them. *But he has not found them.* He has not found the church come together for the purpose of teaching, and divided into classes with women teaching some of those classes. He has not found that in the word of God. And until he finds that in the word of God, his practice must stand on the shifting sands of human opinion. When he stands before God in judgment, he will not have the word of God in any way whatsoever to back him up. *How is it going to be then?* When he is shorn of his sophistical reasoning and he has to face the books which are opened in the Day of Judgment?

God Not The Author Of Quincy Practice

And I want to warn you brethren who come and divide into classes. You have no authority for it. And you have three classes here at Quincy. They are public. You come together and sing, read, and pray; and *then you have three classes in one room right in the middle of your service.* You come back together and observe the communion. So that is the main assembly divided, and you have three classes taught simultaneously in one small room. Paul said in I Cor. 14:33, "God is not the author of confusion, but of peace, as in all churches of the Saints." *So God is not the author of the condition here.*

Thank you.

FOURTH SESSION
Porter's Second Affirmative
Sunday School Question
Brethren Moderators, Brother Waters, Ladies and Gentlemen

The Condition In Quincy

The first thing that I want to call your attention to is the last thing you heard, the condition in Quincy. When they meet together, they sing, they pray, they have three classes, they have communion. I understood him to say the communion was divided; I don't know whether I got that right or not. Is that what you said, Brother Waters. Did I misunderstand you? I understood you to say the communion is divided. Oh, you mean into individual cups; I beg your pardon. I thought maybe you meant that some of them took it in different rooms or something. I didn't know just what he was talking about. All right, he said, " 'God is not the author of confusion.' (I Cor. 14:33), and, therefore, God is not the author of the condition that exists here."

Well, there wasn't any confusion here until you brethren started it. The congregation in Quincy was begun in Sister Bybee's home. Somebody shakes his head; but she put ads in the paper and advertised for people that might come in with them, and they would be together. And after they started meeting here, or in some other public building (maybe it was this same one, I don't know), then the agitation began. Someone brought in somebody to preach against the idea of classes and cups, and the agitation began and confusion resulted. If God is not the author of it, then your brethren are the ones who stand guilty, because they are the ones who started the agitation against the matter and endeavored to change the whole thing from what it was originally.

And then, besides all of that, Brother Waters has a divided communion in another way, because when we are having communion in one room, his group is having communion in another. And while there's teaching in one room, his group is teaching in another, and they can do that all right if there's something wrong in one of them. But if both groups are composed of Christians, it's wrong to do it. If one of them is composed of Christians and the other has something wrong, then they can. So it's not the simultaneous teaching that's wrong. It's not even the simultaneous communion that's wrong, according to Brother Waters. It's

whether or not there's something wrong in one of the groups
that determines whether the thing is right or not. And so that's
the set-up in this thing now. Now then, back to the first.

Answering Waters' Questions

"1. Is it Scriptural to divide a congregation spiritually because it refuses to be divided physically?"

Physical Arrangement and Spiritual Division

Ervin, where is your answer to that question I gave you
last night? Did you think that I would forget about that? I
handed him the question last night, "Would you divide the body
of Christ spiritually over how it may be arranged physically?"
And he didn't say a word about it, but he came around and handed me one on the other side. Why didn't you answer mine? Now
then, since you didn't answer mine, I'll treat yours with the same
respect with which you treated mine—on that particular one.
You completely ignored mine. You didn't say a word about it.
You let on like you didn't even have it. *You didn't even mention it.*
It's too late now, because in your last speech I have no chance to
notice what you say. So he skipped the thing completely. "Would
you divide the body of Christ spiritually over how it may be arranged physically?" What did he say? Silence; perfectly infinite
silence; that's all. But he wanted to turn around and ask me one
on the other side. Well, why didn't you answer mine? You expected me to answer yours on the same thing.

Is Class Teaching Public Teaching?

"2. Is the teaching in the Sunday School public teaching?"
Well, that altogether depends on what you mean by "public." If
I knew what you mean by "public," I could tell you what about it.
If by "public" you mean that every body is invited to that par-
ticular class, No. Everybody is not invited to that particular class.
The very word "class" restricts. Is that what you mean, or what
do you mean by "public?" That would help us to understand about
that.

The Extent Of Silence

"3. Did the 'silence' of I Cor. 14:35 prohibit the women to
whom it applied from singing where it applied?" No. And the
"silence" of I Cor. 14.34, 35 does not prohibit the women to whom
it applied from teaching women where it applied. Absolutely not.
Now then.

Colleges And The Church Treasury

"4. May the colleges operated by your brethren be Scripturally supported out of the church treasury?" I thought Brother Waters had pledged himself to never bring in extraneous matters any more. He says that's not good debating; he would never do a thing like that any more. And then he turns around here tonight and spends almost all of his questions on matters that have no reference under the sun, nor the moon, nor the stars, to the proposition we are discussing. But he does not intend to do that kind of debating any more. "It's not good debating," he said. So he quit it. "May the colleges operated by your brethren be Scripturally supported out of the church treasury!" The colleges operated by my brethren are individual affairs, and I do not believe in supporting them out of the church treasury.

The Church And Grammar School

"5. Is teaching a grammar school the work of the church?" No. But in teaching a Singing School, you teach singing, and singing is the work of the church. Absolutely so. You teach them about whether a song is Scriptural or whether it is not Scriptural. You discuss this thing and that thing about those matters, and, therefore, you discuss the teaching of the Scriptures in your Singing Schools. So it's not parallel with your grammar schools.

Women And Rudiments Of Music

"6. May a woman teach the rudiments of music to a college class or a high school class composed of both male and female?" Maybe so. I'm not running or having anything to do with high school classes. I have no connection with them. And the high school has no connection with the church. And the church members are not operating it. But the Singing Schools which you brethren operate are being operated by you preachers and your church members. All right, Brother Waters: May women teach the rudiments of music in the Singing Schools which you brethren operate? Now tell me whether they do or not.

Women May Teach Privately

"7. May a woman in a private, informal and individual way teach men, or a man, the word of God?" Yes.

Centralized Control And Oversight

"8. Do you endorse or oppose the missionary combination among your brethren, such as many churches channeling their funds through one church whose elders oversee the work and the spending of the money in a distant field?" And if I said "yes" or "no," that would either prove that it's a sin to divide into classes or prove that all must remain in one class. Now Brother Waters doesn't deal with extraneous matters. He confines himself to the issue. He wouldn't think about turning aside to something that has no relation to the subject. Why the very idea! Trying to make that parallel *with what*, Brother Waters? You ought to tell us what you are trying to make that parallel with. Are you trying to make that parallel with the Bible classes, or what is it anyway? Personally, I do not endorse any centralized oversight of congregations by one congregation, if that will help him any.

Formal And Informal Teaching

"9. What would make it right for a woman to privately, informally, without announcement teach men in her home, but wrong for her to call a group of men to her home and teach them?" I Tim. 2:12 says she must not be a teacher nor usurp authority "over the man." I will get to that again presently.

Christians And Carnal Warfare

"10. Do you believe that a Christian may go into the armed services of the nation and with carnal weapons shed the blood of his fellowmen on the battlefield?" Whatever my answer to that may be, teaching in classes is sinful and will send you to hell. What did he try to parallel with that? Nothing; nothing; not a thing on earth. He thought that he might arouse some prejudice. If I said "yes", and if I said "no", it wouldn't make any difference. He just hoped he might arouse some prejudice before somebody. If I said they can't go, why, somebody who believed that his boys who died on the battlefield were not murderers, would get it in for me. Then if I said that they could go, why then, somebody who is a conscientious objector would get it in for me. So he is trying to reason that way; and there's no connection. There's no connection with anything that we have in this discussion, Brother Waters. Did you think that that would prove one way or the other?

Now then, Brother Waters, what do you believe about it? I wish you would tell me now, because I won't have any chance to notice your reply later. Do you believe that a Christian may go into the armed services of the nation and with carnal weapons shed the blood of his fellowman on the battlefield? If you believe that, then there will be people in this audience who will say, "Why you are teaching murder, and I'm opposed to you and I won't accept any such thing." And if you say you don't believe that, the boys who die on the battlefields are dying murderers, and there may be someone in this audience whose boy died on the Korean battlefield. And Brother Waters, you would be into it. So you tell me what you believe about it. What connection does that have with the proposition anyway? Any? If I said "yes," would that have any effect on the teaching question? If I should say "no," would that have any effect on the teaching question? What relation is there? . None. None. Why did he ask it? Because he "sticks with the issue." He sticks with the subject. All right.

Class Teaching In Quincy

"11. Is it Scriptural for three classes to be taught simultaneously in one room as is done by your brethren in Quincy?" I thought I had answered that already. I said as long as the teaching in one class does not interfere with the teaching of another.

What Constitutes A Church Assembly?

"12. What percentage of the membership must assemble before it becomes a church assembly?" Well, Brother Waters says two, if it's announced; two thousand wouldn't if it's not announced. But Matt. 18:20, that he gave us there last night, says, "Where two or three are gathered together in My name, there am I in the midst." He put that as a church assembly. I'll endorse Matt. 18:20 as a church assembly, if he wants me to.

Teaching Away From The Assemblies

And he came to Titus 2:3, 4, and I want to go to that. "The aged women likewise, that they be in behavior as becometh holiness, not false accusers, not given to much wine, teachers of good things, that they may teach the younger women to be sober, and to love their husbands, to love their children, to be discreet, chaste, keepers at home, good, obedient to their own husbands that the word of God be not blasphemed."

Brother Waters says that the word "teach" in this case means "to train" and the word "train" means to "curb, control, discipline." And it's that kind of instruction that she gives constantly away from the assemblies, don't you see? Well, if it's instruction, it's teaching. Why do you go all the way around to come back to where you started? It said "teach" in the first place. Why did he go all that circuitous route there to get back to where he started? He said it means "teach." Well that's what I said—that's the way I read it to begin with. Then why define the word "teach" to mean "train," and the word "train" to mean "discipline, curb and control," and then get back to the idea that the words "discipline, curb and control" mean "to instruct?" He gets right back where he was. So why go all that way around? He ought to just take it like it is to start with.

But that's the teaching that she does constantly *away from the assemblies*. In other words, this is a duty, this is a law, this is an admonition, this is a commandment, given to women *with respect to their conduct away from the assemblies*. Now then, let's read. "The aged women likewise that they be in behavior as becometh holiness." That means that holiness in which they constantly engage *away from the assemblies*. Of course, if they are in the assemblies, they don't have to conduct themselves that way. They don't have to act in behavior as becometh holiness *in the assemblies*. That's just away from the assemblies. And also it says "not false accusers." That means, of course, in all relationships *away from the assemblies*. Of course, if she is *in the assemblies,* she can make all the false accusations she wants to because these are home duties, these are duties away from the assembly. And not only that, but "not given to much wine." That means, of course, that she must not be given to much wine in all those relationships *away from the assemblies*. But if she is *in the assembly,* she can drink her fill of it; it wouldn't matter, because these are home duties, or duties away from the assembly. And if he limits all of this, if he confines all of this, to duties away from the assemblies, then the drinking of the wine and the false accusations and the behavior go right along with the teaching. It's all right there together. Now, if I had limited that to the public teaching, or assembly teaching, or whatever he wants to call it, and said this refers to women teaching *in an assembly and nowhere else,* he could turn the thing around. And he could say, "Now if that's true, then they could be false accusers away from the assemblies, but not in the assemblies. Away from the assemblies they would not have to heed. They could not be false accusers in the assemblies, but away from the assemblies they could be. And they could not drink much wine in the assemblies, but away from the assemblies they could, etc. Well, *if I had limit-*

ed it that way, he could turn it around; but *I have not limited it that way.* He limits it to the teaching away from the assemblies. I have not limited it to any teaching anywhere. Absolutely not. And any such turn certainly will not work, for the simple fact that I have not made any such limitation upon it.

The Command Of Titus 2:3

"13. "Is the command in Titus 2:3 that the aged women teach the younger women to be obeyed by every aged woman?" "If that's so, then only the women who are teaching are fulfilling their duty." Well, let's turn that around, Brother Waters. When the Lord commanded men to preach the gospel, does that command come to every man? And if not (public preaching is involved), every man that is not doing public preaching is not doing his duty, and all are going to hell except public preachers then. All of the men will go to hell on the same proposition on which you send the rest of the women to hell. They are exactly parallel.

Teaching By Faithful Men

Then II Tim. 2:2. He said now that they teach "faithful *men* who shall be able to teach others also." He said, "Now if that's general, if that be the case, then that does not pertain to the proposition." But he says that's from the Greek word "anthropos," and he said that doesn't necessarily mean male or female. Well, I have a higher authority than Brother Waters. I have a copy made here from higher authority than he that speaks about this matter, and he makes these statements regarding the matter. We have a definition given by men who knew the meaning of the word. We have this statement on page 46 of Thayer's Greek-English Lexicon. If he denies it, I have one out in the car, and he may have one. I'm sure he has one somewhere. Thayer says "Anthropos," which means "without distinction of sex, a human being, *whether male or female.*" Now that's what Thayer says about it on page 46 of his Lexicon, and Thayer is the greatest New Testament lexicographer the world has ever known. That's what he says about it.

Well, he brought up some passages here that say, (Matt. 19:10), "a man and his wife;" (John 7)—"circumcise a man." And in both of these places the word "man" comes from "anthropos." So he wants to know if that means the female sex. Well, it so happens that Mr. Thayer covered that idea, too. And he goes right on to say. "With reference to the sex (contextually), the male." In other words, when the context shows or uses a female in contrast with it, then it refers to the male. Thayer says, "With reference to the sex (contextually), the male." Yes, if there's something in the context that identifies or applies the word to a male, all right; if not, it applies to both male and female. And there's nothing "contextually" in II Tim. 2:2 that can make it apply to the male, Brother Waters. You will have to try again.

Moving Assemblies Together

Then to the two classes six blocks apart. He said, "Porter makes his classes parallel to public assemblies." Well, I referred to the two groups you said could meet in separate places. You admitted, in answer to my question, that *two groups could go to separate places* if they didn't first have an assembly, and be taught at the same time, if they were not taught like my groups. And I specifically mentioned the two groups like you say can go to separate places. If that's parallel with public assemblies, as he calls it, then Brother Waters admits that two groups can assemble in public assemblies in public places and be taught, provided the public assemblies are not like mine. If it's sauce for the goose, it's sauce for the gander, Brother Waters.

Public Teaching By Women

And he then says in that connection that women may teach, but women may not teach publicly. He declares that Porter is coming out with the idea of women teaching *publicly.* But women may not teach publicly, he says, and Porter has a female ministry. Why, I thought you said last night, Brother Waters, in answer to those questions, that a woman can *sing.* Do you sing *publicly?* When you have your singing, when the church comes together for the purpose of teaching, you said a woman *can sing in that assembly.* I want to know if that is a *public assembly.* When she *sings* in your *public meetings,* right at the hour of worship on Sunday morning at eleven o'clock, for the communion service, does she *sing publicly?* Brother Waters says that a woman *cannot teach publicly,* but he says she can sing *in their public meetings.* Well, Paul said in Eph. 5:19 and Col. 3:16, when she "sings" she "teaches." *"Teaching* one another is psalms and hymns and spiritual songs"—"singing and making melody in your heart unto the Lord." Paul says *singing is teaching.* Brother Waters says that a woman can *sing publicly.* All right, if Brother Waters told the truth and Paul told the truth, then in Brother Waters' meetings the woman that sings *teaches publicly,* because she sings publicly, and Paul said that's teaching. So there's no difference between us on that principle. We are *both agreed* that a woman *may teach in a public assembly.* Brother Waters agrees that that's so because he says that she can sing in the public assembly. Absolutely so. Don't you, Ervin? You say she can sings publicly, and Paul said that's teaching. So there's no difference. And so we both agree that a woman can actually teach in a public assembly. *She does when she sings.*

Authority Over The Man

Now then, I Tim. 2:12, which I will get to again presently, Paul said, "I suffer not a woman to teach, nor to usurp authority over the man." Now here is a statement that says, "I suffer not a woman to teach." Well, over in Titus 2:2, Paul commanded women to teach. Did he contradict himself? No. For the simple reason that it's modified. "I suffer not a woman to teach nor to usurp authority," or "have authority," as the Revised Standard Version reads, "over the man." The prepositional phrase "over the man" modifies the compound infinitive phrases. And, consequently, she must not be placed in the place of a teacher "over men." That doesn't mean that she cannot teach a man informally if she meets him on the road somewhere, but she must not be set up as a teacher as she would before a public assembly over men. If not, then she could teach the whole congregation. She could become a public preacher, if that were not so, and that very thing keeps her out.

The Examples Of Jesus

Matt. 13:1-9. Verse 36. "He sent them away and went into the house." He said there was no *segregation* about that. Well, there was *separation*. There was division there; he took one part away. He said that Porter makes these things parallel with his classes. So Porter says women may teach in classes—or may teach in *such classes*—and such classes are public assemblies, and that the women may teach in these. Therefore, the women may teach in all of his classes. No, my proposition says she may teach in some of them. A class made up of men is not exactly the same as a class made up of women. There is some difference between the two classes. If not, then since Brother Waters says she may teach a group in her home, if they are not like mine, and even call them for that, then she could call a group of men there and teach them exactly the same way. I am asking him, Is that so? And if so, then doesn't he have a little female ministry?

Mark 7:14—where Jesus called the people together. And then, verse 17, they entered the house. He wanted to know, Could the women answer a question in this? Would merely answering questions be *teaching over men?* If so, what about it when your sisters call out the song numbers sung in the assembly of the saints? Are they speaking in that case? Would that be parallel with asking a question? Just what about it anyway? And now, the fact is, he didn't *even notice the argument* I made on it. Mark 7:14 shows that Jesus called the assembly, and that He taught the assembly that He called together. So there's a "called group." And if a "called group" constitutes an assembly, there was an assembly. Jesus called them. And then in verse 17, He left them and went aside into another place and taught His disciples there. So He took a group away from this and *divided the assembly.* He didn't even pay any attention to that at all.

Mark 9:2. Peter, James and John went up into the high mountain. He said, "Porter can see classes everywhere." But when he saw all those assemblies he had on the board last night, he saw *in everyone of them* the statement made that *you must remain in one assembly* to be taught. Saw it everywhere. It wasn't in any of them, but he saw it every time he read about an assembly. He saw that statement, he read that statement, that they must be taught in an undivided assembly. They must be—he saw it everywhere.

Walkie-Talkie Classes

Now, then, he said they were just talking along the way. Porter makes everything in a class, and the women teach in them. So he said they walked down the mountain, and that's the walkie-talkie class. That's all right. Yes, women can have a part in that, he says, if you take a group like Jesus did. Jesus took a group away. He said it wasn't a class. I wonder what a class is. He took the group composed of three away from the other disciples. If that didn't constitute a class, *what is a class?* Took them away for the purpose of teaching them the lesson on the Mount of Transfiguration. And then He came down with that *same group* that He *had taken away,* and *the group that He had left behind* was engaged in a religious discussion at the same time—simultaneous teaching. Brother Waters says you can do simultaneous teaching, if you do it while you are walking. Yes, sir. If you will just walk while you are doing it, it will be all right. If you will do it while you are walking—if you will just make a walkie-talkie out of it—you can do it all right. If you sit down, it becomes sinful and will send you to hell. Don't you see?

Simultaneous Teaching By Judges In Israel

Then Exodus 18. I was really amused at Brother Waters on that. Here I showed that in the choosing of the judges to help Moses in the great responsibilities that he had, his father-in-law suggested that they be divided into groups of thousands, hundreds, fifties, and tens; and place these judges over them to help him out, because the people sat there from morning till evening waiting their turn to get some matters settled and adjusted for them and some teaching to be done. I read from the Book of God there, Exodus 18, where the Book says they were *"teaching them the law of God,"* and "making known unto them the way in which they should walk and the work which they should do." It was absolutely teaching done by those judges. Brother Waters said now we will just look at that. And he said now you have a group of ten, a group of fifty, a group of a hundred, and a group of a thousand. You have one teacher over the ten, and another over the fifty, and another teacher over a hundred, and another teacher over the thousand, and Moses over the whole bunch. So you have five teachers teaching one man at the same time. And he said, "That's confusion."

Moderator: "Four minutes."

Four minutes? All right. "That's confusion." Then Brother Waters, you have, according to your idea then, confusion there among the judges, because you have a judge over ten, a judge over fifty, and a judge over a hundred and a judge over a thousand, and then Moses over all of them. And if they were all judging at the same time (and Moses said that judging was making known unto them the law of God), you would have Moses engaged in confusion. It wasn't all at the same time. But, if each one took his turn until sixty thousand of them took their turn, I wonder how long it would take them to get through. Would they be any better off and any more nearly not worn out than they would if they were just waiting for Moses?

Miscellaneous Matters

Now, then, regarding his "Boys' Meetings," he said, Porter didn't know what it was about."

He proved by all his brethren here that they didn't teach that their churches do not engage in teaching, a Singing School. He read a lot from John O'Dowd. Did John O'Dowd say that he signed an agreement that he wouldn't oppose anything like that? Brother Hawley, did you ever sign an agreement that you wouldn't oppose anything like what Brother O'Dowd said? (Brother Hawley shakes head "No.") Brother Adams, did you ever sign an agreement that you wouldn't oppose anything like that? (Brother Adams shakes head "No.") Did you, Brother Newell? (Brother Newell shakes head "No.") Brother Watson, did you ever sign an agreement like that, that you wouldn't oppose anything like that? (Brother Watson shakes head "No.") Well, then, the cases are not parallel at all. The case is not parallel at all. We have never signed such an agreement. You said the agreement which Brother King and Brother Gay signed was not elaborate enough to explain. Then they ought to make an explanation through the paper and let people know about it.

CHART NO. 3 On Teaching

By Waters

Porter Has Not Found The Elements of His Proposition

- (1.) Church Come Together
- (2.) To Teach The Bible
- (3.) Divided Into Classes
- (4.) Both Men And Women
  Teaching These Classes

Then to his charts. And we have here these different charts that he gave.

Elements Of The Proposition

"Porter has not found the elements of his proposition: The church came together to teach the Bible; divided into classes; both men and women." And Brother Waters hasn't found his "Boys' Meeting." Now, he hasn't found his song books, and he hasn't found his Singing Schools; and he hasn't found his plate; and he hasn't found his blackboard and his chart, or anything of that kind anywhere in the Book of God—either example or anything of the kind. And so we stand parallel on that thing.

CHART NO. 4   On Teaching
By Waters

Porter Has Not Found In Bible

(1.)   Name of Sunday School
(2.)   Practice of Sunday School
(3.)   Idea of Sunday School
(4.)   Regulation For Sunday School

Not Found In The Bible

"Porter has not found in the Bible the name of the Sunday School." He hasn't found in the Bible the name of his Singing School; he hasn't found in the Bible the name of his chart or his blackboard. He hasn't found in the Bible the name of his Boys' Meeting—"The Annual Boys' Meeting of the Faithful Brotherhood of Oklahoma." He hasn't found that either. All right. And then over on this side, he gives chart No. 6.

CHART NO. 6 On Teaching

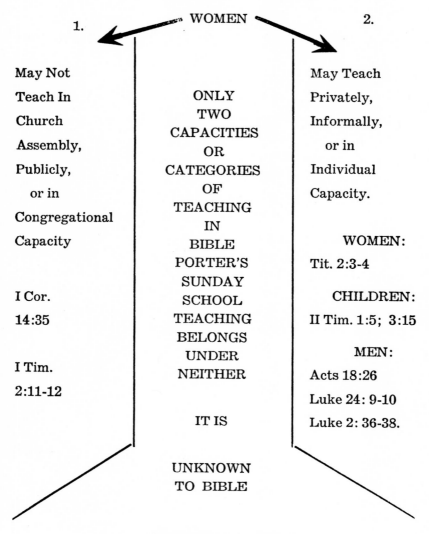

WOMEN

1.   2.

May Not	ONLY	May Teach
Teach In	TWO	Privately,
Church	CAPACITIES	Informally,
Assembly,	OR	or in
Publicly,	CATEGORIES	Individual
or in	OF	Capacity.
Congregational	TEACHING	
Capacity	IN	WOMEN:
	BIBLE	Tit. 2:3-4
	PORTER'S	
	SUNDAY	CHILDREN:
I Cor.	SCHOOL	II Tim. 1:5; 3:15
14:35	TEACHING	
	BELONGS	MEN:
I Tim.	UNDER	Acts 18:26
2:11-12	NEITHER	Luke 24: 9-10
		Luke 2: 36-38.
	IT IS	

UNKNOWN
TO BIBLE

Categories Of Teaching

"Only two categories or capacities in which teaching can be done." Women may not teach in the church in the public assembly, as in I Cor. 14:35, I Tim. 2:11, 12; and then he turns right around and says she can *sing* in the *congregational capacity*. She can *sing* there, and *singing* is *teaching*. So he admits that she can teach in the church in the public assembly, because there's where she sings. And over on the other side (of the chart), "She may teach privately, informally, or in an individual capacity." (Titus 2:3, 4); and she may teach children (II Tim. 1:5; 3:15); and she may teach men (Acts 18:26), etc., on down the line. And he says now, "She can teach all of them anywhere except in the public assembly." But *in the public assembly she can sing.* And when she sings, she teaches, because Paul says so. If she doesn't teach when she sings, she is not doing what Paul said to do. If she doesn't speak when she sings, she is not doing what Paul said to do.

Now when Brother Waters comes before you and begins to talk about the idea that Porter hasn't found the name of his Sunday School, he hasn't found this in the Bible and he hasn't found that in the Bible, and he hasn't found this in the Bible and he hasn't found that in the Bible, remember and ask yourself the question: Where did he find his blackboard? And where did he find his Boys' Meetings? And where did he find his Singing School? Where did he find his chart? Where did he find his radio preaching? And where did he find his plate? He gets his blackboard, his chart, his Boys' Meetings, and his Singing Schools from the generic command to "teach." God did not specifically name every method of teaching. From the same generic command we get the class teaching. They all stand or fall together. Let Brother Waters face the issue and meet the arguments.

Thank you, Ladies and Gentlemen.

Fourth Session
Waters' Second Negative

Sunday School Question

Brethren Moderators, Brother Porter, Brethren and Friends:

Porter Refuses To Answer Questions

Do you remember how Brother Porter treated some of my questions? He left several of the questions entirely unanswered. Last evening he handed me twelve questions, and I answered those twelve questions in the speeches I made on the floor last night. Tonight I asked him twelve questions and he did not give me as many answers as I gave him last night. Here's the list of questions he handed me last night—twelve questions on that sheet of paper—and I answered them. I handed him twelve tonight. I gave him back just as good as he sent out, and he hasn't answered all of them, And he said, "If I answered some of them, what would that prove about the classes? You, Brother Waters, are the man that promised to stay on the question."

I'll Stay On The Issue If You Will

But, Brother Porter, I just simply made you the proposition, that I would stay on the issue just any time you did. And you said you wouldn't do it. You said you absolutely would not agree to stay with the issue. You said so last night. I said, "If you'll agree not to mention plates, song books and chairs, etc., I'll agree not to say anything about instrumental music and missionary societies, and will just stay with the issue." But you said, "I'll not compromise. I won't do that. I won't agree not to mention anything." Well, when I just hand him packages like he hands me, he says, "What has that got to do with the question?" In other words, Brother Porter just can't take it like he dishes it out. He just can't take it. There are several questions there that you absolutely have not answered, Brother Porter. Then he has the nerve to ask of some of my questions, "What has that got to do with the issue?"

Last night he asked, "Does the command to sing ever involve the playing of a musical instrument?" What has the playing of a musical instrument got to do with teaching in classes? Not a thing. But I answered, "No." Tonight when I asked him something, he said, "What has that got to do with the proposition?" He can dish it out but he just can't take it.

Any time that you agree to stay with the issue, Brother Porter, I'll stay with the issue. I just want you to see tonight how it is for me to get off the issue—See, you don't like it, do you? You don't like it. You see? Now you answer that question about carnal warfare.

Answer, Brother Porter, May a Christian Kill?

Do you believe that a Christian may go into the armed services of the nation and with carnal weapons shed the blood of his fellow man on the battlefield? He didn't answer. He said, "Well, you answer it." *I'll answer it. I don't believe they can,* Brother Porter. Now will you answer?

Porter speaks up from seat: "Do you believe they're murderers?"

Waters: Will you answer it? *Are you going to keep asking me questions without answering the ones I gave you? What's the matter with you?* You want to keep stacking questions up and not even answer the ones I give you. I just gave you the same number that you gave me. I answered my own question. Now, will you answer it? Will you? *Are you afraid to stand up for the Lord?* Are you afraid to stand up for the truth? Do you have any convictions on it? I have and I'm not afraid to preach it. *What do you believe about it?* Do you believe they can go out and kill their fellow man? Is it murder, or not? What do you believe about it? Now I ask you the question. Will you be fair? Will you answer the question? I've answered it. It'll just be easy to say, "Yes", or, "No", Brother Porter. You won't have to comment on it at all. Do you believe it, or don't you? Do you? Will you just nod your head? Or shake it? Will you do it? Nah, he won't do it. *I told you he can't take it like he can dish it out.* He just can't do it.

Sundry Differences

All right, I asked him if he endorsed or opposed the missionary combinations among his brethren. "I do not endorse centralized control or oversight," he replied. I just wanted to show that these brethren have differences among them. They differ on the war question. Differ on the missionary question. They differ on the colleges. They differ on orphan's homes. And they have a multitudinous number of things over which they differ. Yet last night he brought up the fact that we had differences on the marriage question. He brought up an agreement which I hadn't signed nor which a brother who is here tonight had signed. And furthermore, Brother Porter brought up something that had nothing to do with the issue. What has the marriage question to do with the class question, Brother Porter? Oh, you can hand it out, but you can't take it. That's right. You can't take it. I just wanted you to feel how it is for me to get off the issue, Brother Porter. I have tried to get you to stay with the issue every since this debate started.

Exodus 18 Is Still Too Much For Porter

Oh, he went back to Exodus, the 18th chapter, and you know if you just listen to him try to explain that Exodus 18, it's just pretty hard, I'll tell you right now, to understand what he means by it. It's pretty hard to understand. He has a man over a thousand, and he has ten within that thousand over hundreds. He has twenty within that thousand over fifties, and a hundred within that thousand over tens; and he says that's equivalent to classes. If it is, he has a student being taught by a teacher of tens, a teacher of fifties, a teacher of hundreds and a teacher of thousands, *all simultaneously*. And then Moses was given charge over all Israel. He tries to make that parallel with his classes. *One student being taught by five teachers at the same time! Talk about confusion! Why, the man can't even explain what he believes about Exodus 18 and do it coherently and intelligently. He can't do it.* It doesn't fit the class system at all; doesn't look like it in any way at all. It absolutely doesn't resemble it.

Mount Of Transfiguration Again

He went back to Matt. 17. What do we have? Jesus took Peter, James and John up on the mountain and was transfigured before them. The next day they came down the mountain, and while they were coming down the mountain, they carried on a conversation. He said, "There's a class." And I said, "If it is, then you brethren need a 'catwalk' and not a Sunday School room." I said, "If it is, you had a 'walkie-talkie' class." And I just simply said this: that a woman might talk to the same three men, or three other men, under the same circumstances while they're walking down a mountain. If that parallels a Sunday School class, a woman can teach men in the Sunday School class. But he says, "No, she can't do that." Can a woman teach three men walking down a mountain, Brother Porter? Will you answer? Can a woman teach three men while they're walking down a mountainside? Could she talk to them and teach them? Now you've tried to make a class out of such circumstances. I told you that he thought he could see a class just everywhere he looked. That's the way these brethren are.

Moderator Watson rises to his feet and says: "Brother Waters, now Brother Porter has no opportunity to reply to this speech. I'm not complaining, but when you ask him a pointed question, do you want him to answer?"

Waters: Brother Porter may answer any question I ask with a minimum number of words. If it's just a plain question, with a "yes" or "no." Yes, I expect that.

Moderator Watson: "Well, if it takes no more words to answer it than it did to ask it, how about that? That's fair, isn't it?"

Waters: Yes, that's fair.

Moderator Watson: "All right."

Waters: *But I'll not have him asking me questions in my last speech. I want you to understand that.* (Audience laughs)

Moderator Watson: "You mean you'll not answer them if he does."

Waters: Now you can understand that. We are not going to get involved in all that kind of confusion.

Porter Admits Aged Women May Obey Tit. 2:3-5 Without A Class

All right, now let's notice again he brings up Tit. 2:3-5 and the question of the "aged women" teaching the "young women" at home. And do you know what Brother Porter did with that? Why he said, "Brother Waters, according to you, if that teaching is to be done at home and not to be done in an assembly somewhere, why when it said for them to be 'chaste,' that just means for them to be chaste at home, and they don't have to be chaste at church. And if they are to love their husbands at home, why they don't have to love them at church. And if they are to love their children at home, why they don't have to love them at church." You just think about an intelligent man like Brother Porter making an argument like that. Think about it.

Let us apply his logic to his position on Tit. 2:3-5.

Where does he say the teaching applies? He says it applies in the class. He says that's where the aged women are supposed to teach the young women. In a class. When I asked him if every aged woman was supposed to teach, here is what he said, "Is every man supposed to preach?" I couldn't make out this argument. He implied that not every one was—just some of them. All right, if it applies in the class, they must be chaste; but they may be unchaste at home and they may be unchaste in the general assembly. They must love their husbands in the class, but their husbands are not there. So they must love their husbands when they are not with them; but when they get with them in the assembly or at home, they are not supposed to love them. See?

And they are supposed to love their children there in the class, but they do not have their children there. They have them off over there somewhere in another class. But when they get home, they are not supposed to love them there. And when they get in the general assembly with their husbands and their children, they don't have to love them there; because he says that teaching is supposed to be done in a class.

Porter: "I didn't say it had to be done in a class, Brother Waters."

Waters: You didn't.

Porter: "I said it was not limited to a class."

Waters: It's not limited to a class? It can be done at home then. Well thank you, Brother Porter. I want you to get that. In other words, it doesn't have to be be done in a Sunday School class. That's what I have been trying to find out. And I had to press him into it. He has given up Titus 2:3, 4, for it does not necessarily apply to a Sunday School class. He says, "I don't limit it to a class." In other words, aged women can do their teaching outside that class. She can do it somewhere else. I thank you, Brother Porter. I tell you, you're pretty generous tonight, aren't you?

Porter Places Sunday School On Par With Singing School

Oh, but now let's notice. He says teaching music in a singing school is on par with teaching the Bible in a Sunday School. Porter says so. But teaching music in a singing school is public teaching. It's public teaching. Brother Clovis Cook, you are a singing school teacher. Is the teaching done there public teaching?

Brother Cook: "Yes, sir."

Waters: It's public. Brother Tommy Shaw, you teaching singing schools. Is the teaching done in singing schools public?

Brother Shaw: "Yes."

Waters: It's public. The public is invited. The public is *present. We all admit that it is public. Therefore the teaching of the Bible in the Sunday School is public teaching. You have put it on par.* Thank you, Brother Porter. Teaching the Bible in a Sunday School is public teaching. Listen to what I can prove: Women may teach the Bible in the Sunday Schools. Therefore, women may teach the Bible publicly. But he won't accept that conclusion. There's the inexorable law of logic. Porter won't accept it.

(1) Teaching music in a singing school is on par with teaching the Bible in a Sunday School. So Porter says.

(2) But women may teach the science of music publicly in a singing school to both men and women. She may teach the science of music in a singing school. She may teach it in high school. She may teach it in the colleges operated by anyone to both men and women. We have never denied that.

(3) Therefore, women may teach the Bible publicly in Sunday Schools to both men and women. But he won't accept that conclusion.

Some Syllogisms

All right, let's try again now.

(1) "God is not the author of confusion" (I Cor. 14:33).

(2) The three simultaneous classes in one room here in Quincy, Ill., is confusion.

(3) *Therefore, God is not the author of the three simultaneous classes in one room here in Quincy, Illinois.*

Notice now, a woman may teach where she may sing. (Looks at Porter) Isn't that what you said? Isn't that what you said?

Porter: "I said she teaches when she sings."

Waters: All right now: (1) A woman may teach when she sings,—Porter.

(2) But women may sing in the general assembly,—Porter.

(3) Therefore, women may teach the general assembly.

Thank you, Brother Porter. You are very generous tonight. Awfully generous. I'll tell you right now, a man is hard pressed when he brings up the women singing, because he gets himself in a fix every time.

(1) Women may sing in the general assembly,—Brother Porter.

(2) But women may not teach in the general assembly. He has already taken the position that she cannot teach in the general assembly.

(3) Therefore, singing is not on par with the teaching under consideration in this debate.

But he says, "Let's stay with the issue, Brother Waters." You see?

Notice. (1) Waters is inconsistent when he permits a woman to sing and confess faults in the general assembly but will not permit her to teach there. Porter says so.

(2) But Porter will permit her to sing and confess in the general assembly, and yet will not permit her to occupy the office of a teacher there.

(3) Therefore, Porter is inconsistent. Thank you, Brother Porter.

(1) If Brother Porter is consistent in permitting a woman to sing and confess faults where he will not permit her to teach.

(2) Then when Waters permits her to sing and confess faults where he will not permit her to teach.

(3) Waters is also consistent.

What Is The Matter With The Man?

Do you think that I am going to let Brother Porter get away with stuff like that? *What's the matter with the man* that cannot make an argument any stronger in the discussion of the class question than a woman singing? He will permit that woman to sing in the assemblies, and he will absolutely refuse to let her get up and teach, or occupy the office of a teacher there. And yet he will say, "Brother Waters, when you do that, you are inconsistent; but when I do it, I'm consistent." I'll tell you, the man is hard pressed, and is hard up for real arguments. I thought better of you, Brother Porter.

Where May A Woman Teach?

Notice that I asked him this question: "May a woman in a private, informal, and individual way teach a man, or men, the word of God?" He said, "Yes." There you are. I want you to notice this chart.

CHART NO. 6 On Teaching

WOMEN

1.   2.

May Not	ONLY	May Teach
Teach In	TWO	Privately,
Church	CAPACITIES	Informally,
Assembly,	OR	or in
Publicly,	CATEGORIES	Individual
or in	OF	Capacity.
Congregational	TEACHING	
Capacity.	IN	
	BIBLE	WOMEN:
	PORTER'S	Tit. 2:3-4
	SUNDAY	
I Cor.	SCHOOL	CHILDREN:
14:35	TEACHING	II Tim. 1:5; 3:15
	BELONGS	
	UNDER	MEN:
I Tim.	NEITHER	Acts 18:26
2:11-12		Luke 24: 9-10
	IT IS	Luke 2: 36-38.

UNKNOWN
TO BIBLE

Women may teach children, women or men. *Where she may teach a child or woman she may teach a man the word of God.* He says, "She may teach women and children in the Sunday Schools, but she may not teach men there." He has manufactured a category which he cannot find in the Bible. All right, notice.

(1) A woman may teach men, or a man, privately. Porter said so.

(2) A woman may not teach a man, or men, in a Sunday School class. Porter said so.

(3) Therefore, the teaching in a Sunday School class is not private teaching.

Will you accept the conclusion, Brother Porter? There's logic. There's a major premise, a minor premise and a conclusion you can't deny. That's the conclusion you must reach when you say a woman may teach a man privately but a woman may not teach a man in a Sunday School. Therefore, the teaching in **a Sunday School is not private teaching.** Now you get that.

In reality he has manufactured him a third category which he cannot find in the word of God. There are certain circumstances, places, and conditions under which a woman may not teach." Notice them on the Chart No. 6. There are other circumstances under which she may teach. And get this, Brother Porter. If I understand your position with reference to a woman teaching a man, as to where she may or may not teach the man, *I believe that she may teach anyone where you believe that she may teach a man.* But he thinks, "I'm not involved in any kind of difficulty when I say she can't teach men in the Sunday School, but she may teach them out of the Sunday School. But Brother Waters is involved in inconsistencies." Now if he can see that a woman can teach a man somewhere, if he can understand the circumstance under which she may teach that man, then he can understand the circumstances under which I believe she may teach or she may not teach. Can you see that, Brother Porter. Can you? Or do I have to draw it on tissue paper so you can see through it? Can you see it? If you can understand your own position about where a woman may teach a man and may not, then you can understand my position about where she may teach and where she may not teach. The fact is, where a woman may teach a child or another woman, she may teach a man. That's a fact of the matter. I have always believed that. *But where she may not teach the man, she may not teach anyone.*

I Tim. 2:12 Says "Be In Silence"

Let's see. I Tim. 2:12, "I suffer not a woman to teach, nor to usurp authority over the man, but to be in silence." All right, may she teach the man in a Sunday School class? Brother Porter says, "No." Paul, what do you say? "But to be in silence." Under whatever circumstances that woman cannot teach that man, brother, there's something wrong with it, and she had better not do any teaching at all. Under whatever circumstances that woman may not teach that man, watch out! *She is teaching in the wrong place.* Brethren and sisters, you better be careful. That's right! You better be careful. *Wherever it is that you won't let that woman teach that man, you had better not let that woman teach.* You've got her in the wrong place. *She is teaching in the wrong place. There's something wrong,* because all the teaching you find in the word of God falls in one of two categories. *That first category where she may not teach at all, and then that one where she may teach any one.* It all falls under one of these two categories. But Brother Porter has manufactured him a third one. He had better manufacture a fourth one for he cannot find any Scriptures in the word of God to describe it and he cannot find any rules whatsoever laid down in the word of God to regulate it. It just is not there. He cannot find it.

Women Teaching Church Assemblies

I asked him what per cent of the church must come together before it becomes a church assembly, and he said, "Well I'll just endorse Matt. 18:20." He said that's all it takes. Well, then, that's a church assembly. Thank you, Brother Porter. *Then your women are teaching in church assemblies, aren't they?* You have to have at least two, don't you? *And so those classes are church assemblies. That much of the congregation.* Now they have to come together and you have got women teaching in church assemblies. Thank you, Brother Porter.

Porter Admits Announcement Affects Nature of Teaching

But I want you to notice now, question 9, "What would make it right for a woman to privately, informally, and without announcement, teach men in her home, but wrong for her to call a group of men into her home and teach them?" He said I Tim. 2:12 was what was wrong. Now he is that man who said, Waters is inconsistent when he said you could teach or have a class if it's not announced, but you can't have it if it's announced." He said, Brother Waters is inconsistent when he says that. But Porter says a woman can teach a class of men as long as she didn't call them into her home. *If they just happened to drop in, she could teach them; but if she calls them to her home, he says she couldn't teach them.* Well, I want you to listen to that! Oh, he can understand himself when he takes such a position; but he can't understand Brother Waters. Isn't that strange? What's the matter with a man that will do that? What's the matter with a man that will resort to such tactics in honorable controversy?

How Classify

Say, what about that question that I asked him about last night and just begged him to tell us about? *It was left completely unanswered,* either last night or tonight. And that is about *how to classify; whether to classify according to physical age,. spiritual age, according to knowledge, or according to I. Q.?* What has he had to say about it? I asked him word by word, and tonight I just wrote it out so he could see it. And he hasn't had a word to say about it.

CHART No. 5—On Teaching

By Waters

HOW CLASSIFY?

(1.) According to Physical Age?

(2.) According to Spiritual Age?

(3.) According To Knowledge?

(4.) According To I. Q.?

How to classify? He hasn't told us. In fact, these brethren just don't know how to classify. They don't know how. I'm going to show you that they don't.

Physical Age

Suppose you try to classify according to physical age? Suppose they send the aged people, the senior adults, all to one class? In here, you may have a man who has been a member of the church for fifty years; and he is a veteran. He has acquired a great amount of knowledge of the Bible. In this same class, you may have an eighty year old man who has just obeyed the Gospel. He's almost twenty years older than this man who has been a member of the church fifty years, and yet he's a babe in Christ. You would put him in that aged adult class, wouldn't you, if you classified according to age? There's an eighty year old man physically, and a babe in Christ spiritually. Put him in the adult class? *What have you gained?* A man in the church forty-five years placed in there with a babe in Christ. What have you gained? That's what you had out in the assembly to begin with. Did you gain anything there?

All right, suppose you have two men sixty years old who have been members of the church the same length of time, forty-five years. One of those men has far out-progressed the other man. He knows far more about the Bible than the other man. He has acquired more knowledge than the other man. He has a greater receptivity and capacity for the teaching, but you have them in the same class. *Did you gain anything by doing this?* That's what you had to begin with out in the general assembly. Some had greater receptivity, and some had greater knowledge. There you are.

Well, suppose you have a young peoples' class. You might have one boy that's eighteen years old, been a member of the church five years, and has made remarkable progress. And another one who has just obeyed the Gospel, and doesn't know much. Don't you see? *What have you gained?* That's what you had out there in the general assembly to begin with. You might have a thirteen year old who is a babe in Christ, and an eighty year old who is a babe in Christ.

Spiritual Age

Well, somebody might say, "Let's divide them according to spiritual age then. Let's divide them according to the length of time they have been members of the church." All right, divide them according to spiritual age, and if you do that, it will have no reference to physical age. It will be according to the length of time they have been members of the church and will have nothing to do with how young or old they are physically. But if you do that, you will find that some who have been members of the church the same length of time, or relatively so, have not acquired the same amount of knowledge, and who do not even have the same I. Q., and who don't even have the same amount of receptivity for the receiving of instruction. You put all of them together. Now what have you gained? Now you have got them divided according to spiritual age. They don't have the same amount of knowledge. They don't have the amount of receptivity. *Did you gain anything? No. That's all you had out in the general assembly to begin with.* That won't work, unless you just try to make it work like you brethren do.

Knowledge?

What if you try to divide them according to knowledge? Look at one man, judge acccording to the outward appearance and say, *"Well, I don't think you know very much. You go down yonder into that class."* Then to another one, "I believe you know a whole lot. You go up yonder." *How are you going to know just precisely how much they know?* Going to give *graded exams,* I guess. *Is that what you brethren are coming to.* If you divide according to knowledge, it could not have any reference to physical and spiritual age.

I.Q.?

Suppose you divided according to I. Q.? That could have nothing to do with the physical age, spiritual age and even according to the amount of knowledge actually possessed. I asked him how divide into classes? *And he has utterly failed to tell us and explain to us how it is.* He has not done it.

And, then, tonight, with reference to these questions which I asked that didn't have anything to do with the issue, he said, "What good would it do if I answered those?" *He talked about song books, alto, bass singing, schools, planes, automobiles, chariots, plates, baptistry, boys' meetings, adultery, walking, riding, radios, printing presses, etc., all through the debate.* And then when I bring up one or two matters that are not on the issue, he complains about it.

We Are Growing

I want to mention this. That those of us who have opposed the classes,—and his proposition has remained utterly unproved—, *believe in teaching the word of God; but we believe in teaching the word of God Scripturally.* We believe in doing what the word of God tells us to do and we are growing. *We have more than doubled the number of congregations that stand with us in the United States in the past ten years. We are growing.*

Some of Our Young Preachers

We have, tonight, several young preachers present who have remarkable ability. *Those young preachers have never in their lives sat in a Sunday School class.* I call your attention to Brother Larry Robertson, a young man nineteen years old. Stand up, Brother Larry from Lebanon, Missouri. He is one of the most fluent young preachers that I have ever heard in my life and he has never been in a Sunday School class.

I call your attention to Brother Billy Orten, twenty years old, from Lawrenceburg, Tennessee, and he has never sat in a Sunday School class. He is a fluent and eloquent speaker. *It does not take Sunday Schools to train young men and young women as my respondent seems to think.*

I call your attention to Brother Tommy Shaw, Commodore, Pa., twenty-two years old. He has been preaching for a couple of years. He, too, has remarkable ability for his age, and he has never been in a Sunday School class in his life.

Brother Johnny Elmore is over here, eighteen years old of Ardmore, Oklahoma, who is beginning to preach the Gospel and has never been in a Sunday School class in his life.

Brother Lynwood Smith over here, twenty-six years old, who is recording this discussion for printing and publication, has never been in a Sunday School, and has been preaching for at least eight years.

Brother Nelson Nichols, twenty-two years old from Hollywood, California, has been preaching for four or five years, and has never been in a Sunday School class in his life.

I call your attention to these young men that you might know that we can progress without such. (To Moderator: How much time do I have?)

Moderator Cook: "One minute."

Conclusion

Brethren, in this discussion I have tried to manifest the spirit of Christ. I regret that divison has come into the ranks of the disciples over the individual cups and the Sunday School; but they are modern inventions of men. They are innovations of which our forefathers knew nothing. They have been the cause of division and a bone of contention. Some fifteen years ago, when I began to preach the Gospel, I knew that:

> Men would frown on me, and brethren would despise;
> Yet in the hope of seeing God, I made the sacrifice.
> And now, O God, if we are right, Thy grace impart
> Still in the right to stay.
> If we are wrong, Lord, teach our hearts
> To find the better way.

I thank you.

End of Debate

Moderator Sterl A. Watson:

Now, in just a few moments, we are going to close this service, and this debate will be history. You have all the arguments on both sides. I trust you will keep them in your hearts and will study them carefully and prayerfully and compare them with the New Testament, and that they will do you good. It's been a genuine pleasure for me to have been here and to have served as Brother Porter's timekeeper. I am glad to be associated with these men again. I had met most of them, and I am glad to meet them and to be here for these fine discussions. Before we have the closing prayer, I believe my fellow moderator has an announcement that he would like to make.

Moderator Clovis T. Cook:

I concur heartily with Brother Watson who has aided me in keeping time. That's about all we have had to do considering the good spirit and fine order that has prevailed throughout the discussion. At times it heated up like we were going to have a little controversy on the side lines, but it didn't amount to a great lot. I want to compliment the debaters. I believe they are representative men. And I thank you.

Audience was dismissed by Brother Pierce Adams.

Printed in the United States
22530LVS00006B/103-105

9 781584 270751